Sailing Down:
THE LONG WAY HOME

GREGG A. GRANGER

"You're going to a lot of places where they don't value human life like we do." That was the reaction Gregg A. Granger received when sharing with other friends and relatives, his plans to sail around the world with his wife, two teenage daughters, and five-year-old son.

Prior to their departure, the Grangers' sailing experience was limited to one week aboard a charter in Florida, and a sixteen-foot Hobie Cat at their Gun Lake, Michigan, home.

The journey was about travel and culture, but more about relationships. Relationships with their creator, with each other, with people on similar journeys, and with others in the thirty-eight countries the Grangers visited during their four and a half years abroad.

Learning to sail was the least of the obstacles they faced as they traveled headlong into places where they struggled through preconceptions and prejudices to discover how strong and how wrong their preconceptions were.

Time abroad also afforded the Grangers a view of America from a different and not always popular perspective.

The impact of malaria, broken bones, storms and other struggles was a small price to pay for the personal and family growth they experienced; that same impact was dwarfed by the Created world and goodness the Granger family witnessed.

Cover Photo: Anzac Bridge, Sydney, Australia

Gregg A. Granger

Sailing Faith: The Long Way Home

Published in Middleville, Michigan, by Gregg A. Granger

This publication may be purchased in bulk for educational, business, or sales promotional use. For information, please email gregg@faithofholland.com.

Scripture quotations taken from the Holy Bible, New International Version, Copyright © 1973, 1978, 1984 by International Bible Society. Used by permission of Zondervan Publishing House.

Photographs, unless otherwise noted, are by author's immediate family. Maps Copyright © 2010 Digital Vector Maps often altered or traced by author for clarity.

Library of Congress Control Number: 2010902530

ISBN - 978-0-9843482-1-3

Printed in the United States of America by:

Color House Graphics
http://www.colorhousegraphics.com

Acknowledgements

The greatest portion of my gratitude, admiration, and love for another person in this story and in life goes to my wife, Lorrie, without whom none of this account could have been possible.

Two groups deserve mention in bringing this story to print: those who enabled the adventure to occur, and those who held me accountable in telling the story.

Of the first group, I wish to thank Alton and Jan Granger, my parents, for their role in the values I hold, and for their support, especially in prayer along our journey. I wish to thank Joseph and Sally Lorenc for no less a role in shaping Lorrie, and for their support.

I wish to thank the crew of *Faith*: Emily, Amanda, and Gregg II, both for their role onboard *Faith,* and for their subsequent input into this book, often in the form: "That's not what happened, Dad!" Thanks to Emily for the editorial input.

Of the second group, I wish to thank Neal Petersen, Ed Gillespie, Jon Styf, and Lisa Granger, for their encouragement and input.

I especially want to thank Marlys Admiraal, Professor of English at Calvin College for challenging me to think through difficult passages, and for her huge editorial input.

Above all, thank you God for the people in each of these groups, and for your creation in which we found ourselves.

Introduction

Just because you're a great nobleman, you think you're a great genius! Nobility, riches, a title, high positions, that all makes a man so proud! What have you done for such fortune? You went to the trouble of being born, and nothing else.

Pierre Beaumarchais

A Question of Values

The feeling grows in intensity over a period of six months, a sensation between a dull ache and numbness. When I grab a knife in the kitchen or a steering wheel just so, the pain hones itself, radiating toward and diminishing, as it nears the crook of my elbow.

Of the discomforts I experience, of course my wrist is the easier operation; it's only carpal-tunnel. Given the choice, I'll carry physical discomfort over emotional baggage any day.

The doctor cautions I might, because of some obstacle, need full anesthesia; or I can skip the local altogether and start with the full. Reaching this point in life with not unpleasant memories of recreational anesthesia, I choose the full approach. I wake—sore, groggy, and refreshingly stoned—and my wife, Lorrie, drives me home to lounge guilt-free on doctor's orders until we both realize I'm taking advantage of the situation.

Drugs, cut, sort out the problem, stitch, and heal—that's the process. What I would give to have it so simple for the discomfort and numbness in my sense of direction, my sense of fit, and in those barely audible questions of my adequacy, worthiness, and value as a human being. I progress enough only to experiment with an assortment of the available drugs of the day before settling comfortably into the legal side—alcohol and cigarettes.

What *was* I thinking? My solution could never work without cutting into the mix of emotions, sorting out the problems there, closing the wound and taking the time to heal. How could I deceive myself into believing anesthesia alone possessed healing powers? They told me during my relatively successful rehabilitation for alcoholism that deception was the drugs talking.

The loafing of recovery gives me time to reflect. It isn't as if the surgery and the time off are costing money. I struck-out on that years earlier and have known long enough that I'm no financial wizard. Time away from a job making no money costs nothing, and my self-employment, building seawalls and waterfront improvements, isn't making money.

I never proved *successful*. Sure, I graduated from college. Never mind that was after several failed attempts and I was 35 years old. I found college good, and two years later, received my master's degree. The eighteen years between high school and college graduations saw my success limited to taking a 1970 Triumph Trident motorcycle around the country, marrying the best girl in the world, and starting our family with Emily's birth in 1987. Following college, my success was in growing our family with Amanda and Gregg II and accepting Christ's promise.

My successes hinge on youth to manage a motorcycle tour, an introduction to the girl I would marry, an ability to shoot something more than blanks on three known occasions, and openness to Christ. None has much to do with me, and none fit the American definition of value.

I am gifted with my hands in a world where such giftedness is devalued. I know what works and what doesn't, and which changes enhance waterfront property, and which don't. But I'm cursed with the honesty to tell customers in the hardware store I once owned that this or that product is junk—contrary to what might have been "seen on TV!", and I refuse to build stupid things just because people think such things might work—"You do realize, don't you, that if everybody had me build a seawall ten feet out from their beach, to support a larger lawn, this lake that you love so much would be significantly smaller." To survive in business you must sell stupid stuff, an act I found sufficiently distasteful to affect my performance.

My life has witnessed a transformation in America from a place where production of real goods and real services and real value are esteemed to a world where perceived value and brand are more important. My perceived value and brand are similar lies; my bubble suffers the fate of Wall Street bubbles on sad days when only real value matters. Producing real value requires an attachment to the work. How can the wholesale transfer of value from those who offer such attachment to brokers, financiers, marketers, advertisers—those engaged in creating *perceptions* of value—not result in the destruction of moral values, family values, and community values? It's a dream to believe devaluing productive man doesn't devalue man.

The idea of sailing around the world is the result of a confluence of ideas, but even then, a catalyst is required.

Summer, 2002 brings graduations, Father's Day, Emily's fifteenth birthday, Amanda's eleventh, and my wrist surgery. Somewhere in the mix comes the wedding. My niece is getting married. The ceremony is a grand wedding and an expensive wedding, as we've been told by people in the wedding-perception industry that weddings are supposed to be.

The catalyst is the wedding, not that there's anything wrong with the celebration. My whole life to this point is unearned pomp and perhaps that's why this wedding affects me so much—either that or the lingering effects of the anesthesia earlier in the week.

As a parent, I think about my children and their own weddings in the future. God reveals an inability in me to provide that sort of matrimonial spectacle for my own kids; He's given me other gifts to share with them and uses my discomfort to get His message through.

I think of Jesus' parable of the servants entrusted with talents, and thoughts ring louder and louder that the talents entrusted to me have the names Emily, Amanda, and Gregg II (hereafter Greggii).

On my way home from the big event and in the company of my three-year-old son, who stays awake for the first few minutes, I ponder the contradictions. I beat myself up and take myself away from my children to build a business that provides for us, and to one day give them. Considering my business history, this qualifies as my grandest self-deception.

In the hour it takes me to drive home—Lorrie and the girls are driving separately because of their special wedding jobs—I have two inspirations from God. The first is to stop taking myself away from my family, pretending to provide for them. I am not good at it and am not getting ahead. The second is that it isn't socially acceptable to drop out to take care of my family, so why not buy a boat and sail around the world? That isn't socially acceptable either, but the reminders won't be so constant.

Arriving home, I carry Greggii to bed—parents know the debate—do you wake him or carry him? Sleeping babies are easy, sleeping toddlers are manageable, but sleeping preschoolers are like a big bag of water. Depending on how long they've been sleeping, chances are good that they *are* a big bag of water so the trip detours to the bathroom, and with a sleeping little boy, I'm just glad he hit the room; putting the seat up isn't going to make a difference.

Having spent the past thirty minutes on this life-dream, I can't wait to tell Lorrie. When she gets home, we stand in the kitchen, and I say, "I had a revelation. I think we should sell everything and sail around the world." She gently strokes my forehead for fever, maybe from the drugs or surgery earlier in the week. I share everything I feel with Lorrie, *except* the excitement which she seems reluctant to grasp. She thinks we should sleep on it.

Good strategy! We pray about it, and soon, she starts believing that what was first attributed to drugs is God's plan for this point in our lives.

We now have direction. It's no longer a maybe. Within weeks, we watch people's eyes roll when we tell them our plan. The drugs and self-pity and frustration and rolling eyes need to take a seat on the sidelines, as God reveals what we are about.

I don't need to know too much about sailing because God blows the winds, creates the currents, and makes the seas behave. He's brought us this far, and He won't abandon us now.

But, I don't have a clue when it comes to buying a boat. I need help, and one day I walk into Anchorage Yacht Sales in Holland, Michigan. I hear a warm baritone voice, "Hi there. What can I do for you?" while soaking in my first yacht brokerage: two nautical charts hanging on the wall, two desks, two windows, a door, and the smell of burning coffee. The only difference from any other kind of brokerage is the listings taped on the windows and the magazines on the desks.

My eyes find the source of the voice, Tom Rodenhouse, and I say, "Hi. My wife and I want a boat to take our family sailing—around the world."

"Ho, ho, ho, ho, ho." He turns into jolly old Saint Nick, "Who put you up to this?"

"N-n-nobody. What are you talking about?"

"You're serious? Nobody told you to come in here and say you're going to go sailing around the world?"

"No. What's so funny?"

"Oh man, I'm sorry! I just got back from circumnavigating two years ago, and thought you, that someone told you to come in here and, come on now, tell the truth—are you sure nobody told you to come talk to me?"

"I just saw your sign, and here I am."

"So, you're going to sail around the world. How many of you are there?"

"Five."

In Tom, I find someone to help locate the right boat, and someone with knowledge of what we're getting into.

The few boats we view in Michigan grow in me an awareness of my ignorance, but I do learn a few things. From the magazines, I see the lines and looks, but now I hear the creaks and groans, feel the joinery, and realize that every boat has a smell. The smell of new boats is chemical—paint, fiberglass, woodshop, or cleaning solutions. The smell of other boats can be anything: sewage, rotting wood, mildew, cooking grease, or just the stale smell of old air in a closed space.

I also learn that the Great Lakes don't have the boat we need.

Tom lines up an agent in Annapolis, Maryland, to show a boat there. This agent first shows me one at the dock, *Antipodes of Sydney*, before driving to the specific boat I came to see. Once I see the layout, I know *Antipodes* is perfect. I look at a number of others, but now have *Antipodes* from which to draw less than favorable comparisons.

Later, I learn the interior paneling isn't teak, but nyatoh, another rich Asian wood. The floor creaks, but less than the others. The smell, not unpleasant, is of stale cooking grease, especially in the galley that serves as the corridor to the aft stateroom with its own head and a separate, stand-up shower. A bow cabin with a single bunk is accessed through the starboard cabin that holds two bunks, one above the other; a private port cabin has a double bunk; a large salon wraps around the companionway, with a navigation desk and bunk on the port side, opposite the galley (page ix).

I return the next weekend with Lorrie and Greggii. While we make the decision to purchase *Antipodes*, a pep rally across the river for the opening home football game of the United States Naval Academy sends a fireworks show overhead.

As a family, we need to choose a name so she can be documented. Though *Antipodes* is a good name, it's not ours. We don't hash around too many before settling on *Faith*. *Faith* satisfies several criteria: it's one syllable, easily pronounced and phonetically spelled for radio transmissions—Foxtrot-Alpha-India-Tango-Hotel—easy on the eyes, and we don't know any other boats by that name. Most of all, it reveals how God brought us to this point and is a constant reminder of our approach to this adventure. *Faith* says it all.

We have a plan to depart in about a year and to sail around the world in two. All we must do now is prepare ourselves and *Faith* for the trip.

There aren't many people saying, "Wow, that's really something, go for it!" There aren't many people who think we'll be going too far at all.

The most telling story comes five years later, while sitting at anchor in St. Lucia after our Atlantic crossing, the final passage that marks our circumnavigation. Rich and Samantha approach in their dinghy and ask, "Did *Faith* used to be *Antipodes*? Do you recognize us?"

"Hi. Yeah, you were the captain and mate on *Antipodes* when we bought her."

"People asked us what ever became of her. What have you been doing with her?"

"Our stop here marks the completion of our circumnavigation of the world, just like we said we were going to do when we bought her."

Sam says, "Nobody ever believes that. People always say they're going to sail around the world, but nobody ever does."

While preparing for our voyage in Hampton, Virginia, we find a number of folks planning voyages of their own and a few who have actually left the dock. The planners are dreamers, conjuring obstacles to maintain the dream: As soon as the boat is all ready (boats are boats, and will never be *all* ready). As soon as they have accumulated enough money (there will *never* be enough). As soon as the kids are older, or the kids have moved out, or ...

I recall a man I worked with years earlier who refused a sizeable Christmas bonus. "I always wanted a Cadillac," he said, "but as soon as I get my Cadillac, the dream is gone. I just think the car can't be as good as the dream."

People know when they leave the dock, the dream is gone.

Regarding our lack of experience, even we admit it's a valid concern. Not many people upgrade from a sixteen-foot Hobie Cat on Gun Lake, Michigan, to a fifty-six-foot monohull on the blue waters of three oceans. For us, though, the prize is making this journey as a family, and precludes any *normal* progression toward that level of competence.

I always ask, "So, how do you think we should go about getting experience?"

"You've got to sail," comes the reply, and I shrug that off the list of concerns. If nothing else happens, we *are* going to sail.

The other concern that people express is about our itinerary. A recurring theme surfaces:

"You're going to a lot of places where they don't value human life like we do."

Nobody, least of all me, with my conservative Republican roots, my Reformed religion, and my resistance to change, could foresee the unintended truth of that statement.

We will learn that, where joy is concerned, less is more. The farther we travel into worlds where less stuff drives people's lives, the more joy there is.

We will also learn that fear of the world makes us prisoners of our borders, and we will grow a healthy suspicion of the proponents of that fear.

This is our story.

Note: photo references are provided as (*nn*).

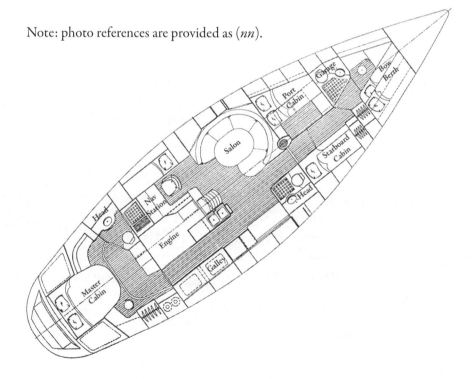

Notes on navigation and measurements:

Navigation: Airplanes and boats measure distance in nautical miles. A knot is a measurement of speed equal to a single nautical mile per hour. A nautical mile is 6090 feet, approximately 1.15 statute (highway) miles. The nautical significance is that the distance between minutes of latitude equals one nautical mile. There are sixty minutes in one degree of latitude.

Nautical charts are maps, nearly always oriented with north at the top. The guide lines on the map that go up and down are in some increments of degrees and minutes of longitude, measured as degrees east or degrees west of the Prime Meridian, or zero degrees, which passes through the Royal Observatory at Greenwich, England. (Early navigators required accurate timepieces to determine their longitudinal positions, a lasting result of which is Greenwich Mean Time.) The International Date Line (with the exception noted later in this book) is where degrees east and degrees west meet at 180°.

Those lines on the chart that run from left to right are in some increments of degrees and minutes of latitude, measured as degrees north or degrees south of the Equator.

With a few measurements on the chart, the coordinates of latitude and longitude for any place can be determined.

Most navigation happens with the aid of GPS—Global Positioning System. A destination's coordinates are determined from the chart and entered into the GPS, which then provides a target to sail toward. Or, the GPS will provide the vessel's current coordinates, which in turn, can be plotted on the chart.

The Metric System: The meter is the basic unit of length in the metric system. The meter is about three feet, three inches long. A kilometer is a thousand meters, or about six-tenths of a mile. A cubic-meter filled with water is the weight of a metric tonne, which is the same volume as 1,000 liters of water. A liter is a little more than a quart of water, and weighs a kilogram, about 2.2 pounds.

A liter of water will freeze at 0 degrees Celsius. That same liter of water will boil at 100 degrees Celsius.

A three-meter shark is about ten-feet long.

Part I. Leaving the Dock

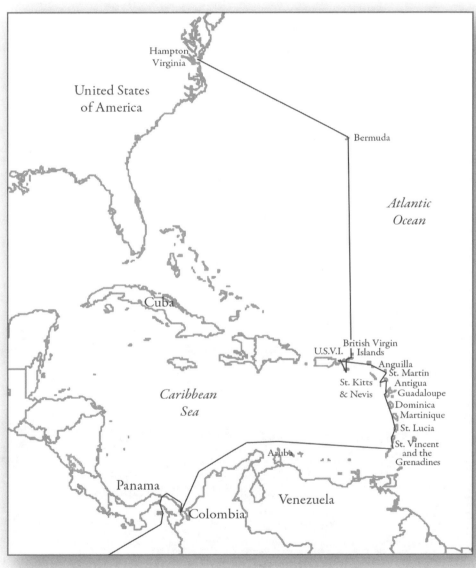

Hampton, Virginia to Colon, Panama
2 September 2003 to 13 March 2004

Dodging Doubts and Dodging Isabel

The deal's done; it's time to move. With cheaper berthing in Baltimore on account of next week's pomp and pitch at the Annapolis Boat Show, I move *Faith*. Some suggest sailing her to Baltimore alone, given my level of experience, relates to the magnitude of a certain couple parts of my private anatomy; I miss the connection. October reds and yellows frame a crisp blue sky and the reflecting mud of water as I pretend seamanship.

Through the Michigan winter, we read what we can to learn what to expect, focusing an inordinate amount of energy on stuff and technicalities, and not enough on who we are and how our family can work together to make this journey happen. Sailing publications help maintain our misdirected focus.

Heeding the wisdom of these seasoned journaltisers, we replace the obsolete radar system with a new radar system, a functional charging system with a new functional charging system, and a good SSB radio—single sideband, for long range communications—with a new one of questionable merit. In early April, a marine-electronics guy from Michigan accompanies me to Baltimore to install the equipment. He mopes mostly, having discovered a few days before that his wife isn't coming home. Apparently, she decided, now that the kids are grown, it's her turn to live, and her living doesn't include him. All he has left is his work, our work, being stripped of that part of his life that holds meaning. It's a sad two days, but *Faith* appreciates the attention; she doesn't care that most of the work is unnecessary. If *Faith* spoke, she'd tell us nobody spends much time at the helm,

3

relying instead on the autopilot to do the work, and that our installation of the new radar screen in that direction isn't very clever. I can't know today that for the next five years I'll live with it there, silently kicking myself for four of them, or that I'll reinstall the older radio after our first passage to a foreign port and not kick myself nearly as long.

I also use Mr. Mopey's sailing experience—a year in the Caribbean on his boat—to help sail *Faith* to Hampton, Virginia. Icy rain on our cheeks turns icier and drips down our necks as grey fades to a darkness that fans the forty-knot breeze. He mumbles more than once about the inadequacy of the charts on board for the task at hand, and I make a mental note to correct that. The trip teaches me that *we sailed* carries a measure of humility not found in *we're going to sail*.

The move to *Faith*, on Sept. 2, 2003, follows a period blurred by fantasies conjured in anticipation of our new life. Months pass before reality returns. Home-schooling for the kids begins with trips to the historic landmarks of Jamestown and Yorktown, while we wait for the hurricane season to expire before sailing south. Then, to demonstrate that we're already too far south, Isabel, the season's last hurricane, targets the Chesapeake Bay. Our options are to either move upriver in the James, York, or Rappahannock and ride the storm or move beyond Isabel's reach to somewhere like New York.

The miserable ride to New York scares me. Lorrie and the kids don't know any better than to have confidence in me, but I'm in charge now, and I don't have anyone to project confidence in except God. I have some serious conversations with Him.

My nerves for this experience are new and turning raw and I assume everybody else's nerves are too. I'm scared, but as captain, it's my job to assure the others that things are fine, that this unnatural sensation is normal. *Faith* is now our home, and our home is rocking like a hobby-horse, riding up one wave and landing on the next with a jarring crash. I go below to offer comfort and talk first to Lorrie, who's showing an annoying susceptibility, more than the rest of us, to sea-sickness. She finds sleep to be the best treatment. My comfort is received with the same gratitude I recall in the delivery room when Emily arrived so many years ago.

In addition to her seasickness, she's developing a keen fear of the unknown and a broad vocabulary of expletive description.

She instructs me to comfort the kids because they're all shook up. I check in on Greggii and Emily, whose anxieties are masked by a deep sleep, then on Amanda, lying on the top bunk of the starboard cabin, where I can put my arm on her shoulder.

"You're still awake?" I ask.

"Yeah, I'm sorry, I can't sleep."

"Are you OK?"

With 12-year-old innocence, she responds, "Yeah. Why?"

"The boat is going all over the place, and the crashing waves, does that bother you?"

"No. Why would it? It's a boat, Dad!"

There exists in man an attraction to otherness that seems to drive the human spirit, and manifests itself in many marriages. In the same manner that gravity and centrifugal force hold the planets in orbit with the sun, the moon in orbit with the earth, so too are Lorrie and I bonded as opposing forces providing balance to each other. A team emerges from my search for opportunity and Lorrie's assessment of the risks such opportunity might pose to our family.

Lorrie's convictions are marble, painstakingly chiseled to an immutable reality, that suffer little weathering from the patterns of my own fluid convictions. There is no room for *maybe* in her world, where all phenomena are explained by yes or no, black or white. Her life mission is to provide form to the unfired clay of my inventory of beliefs.

Our personalities and positions among each other—that we're taking possession of or that are taking possession of us—are gaining definition.

My burden is to keep *Faith* and our family on an even keel. *Faith* is the easier task. She takes her share of attention, but her emotions are straight-forward, without the cyclical component of the other girls onboard. I'm gifted with the ability to figure out how things work, so it falls on me to sail and fix, and as captain, father, and husband, to comfort, teach, and guide.

Lorrie, as admiral and mother, enthusiastically takes responsibility for keeping me in check. With an iron-will borne of a mother's love, she proclaims herself *Faith*'s "Prevention Specialist," a proclamation that undoubtedly keeps us all alive and healthy during our voyage and relieves me of the fatherly burden of saying *no*. The kids realize soon enough that *just ask your mother* means *no*.

I happen to be the second child of five, while Lorrie is the first of three. The reason I say this is that somewhere in my mental archives of college psychology, certain characteristics can be traced to birth order.

The kids are cast in roles and identities on top of their first, middle, and baby-of-the-family traits. All of them must continue as students and as children. That they

5

can sleep soundly and aren't nervous about the discomfort of getting to New York affirms the innocence of childhood.

Emily is first, with a well-ordered sense of the world and of herself, and when this sense is not supported by reality, she's frustrated. She's sensitive to others, as first children tend to be, when the occasion suggests she must be. She's able to create and follow an ordered recipe for any situation, whether changing the oil of *Faith,* or baking cookies or comforting somebody in a time of need. She's pragmatic in everything.

Amanda is full of the dreams, creativity, and sensitivity of the second child. She needs a logical pattern only to aid this creativity. She needs a recipe only so the cookies she gives away serve to build a solid relationship, while Emily's focus is on the cookies. The drawback of her sensitivity is the tendency to take possession of others' feelings. This I know as a second child myself.

Greggii is the baby. Normal is a construct developed from experience, and his five years have not yet provided him sufficient experience. He adapts better than the rest of us to our new surroundings, perhaps because he hasn't a normal from which to base expectations.

Anyway, all of my worrying, my fears, and my stress don't help. What matters is that we're going to New York, and God hasn't chosen this moment to bring us home.

We often take more credit for our circumstances than we are due. It's no different with me in the calm of the early morning Hudson River. "Wow, I managed to get us here, isn't that special?" But God uses our lack of experience to show that He will get us to our destination.

We make it past Sandy Hook by midnight and enter the Hudson River at one. It's now three, and the security guard is helping us tie off. "Wow, it's really peaceful here," I say.

"Just wait until six, when the ferries start running," is his reply.

He's right. The dock, floating so peacefully on our arrival, turns into the Caribbean Steel Drum band that doesn't get to play the good gigs, but makes up for it by playing loud.

We're less than fresh in the morning as we motor downstream, past the Statue of Liberty, get fuel, and talk to people about going somewhere comfortable for the sloppy weather that Isabel will send our way. Everybody suggests we take the East River to Long Island Sound and find someplace secure there. "Just watch the currents at Hell Gate!"

That sounds menacing enough, so I ask, "What's Hell Gate?"

"Oh, you sure don't want to be there when the tide is wrong!" says the fuel attendant.

"So, when's a good time?"

"You should be all right, if you go now. You have two hours before the tide comes in."

The East River flows both ways, strong at times, depending on the tides. Hell Gate is an elbow in a narrow run of the river where strong, changing currents create dangerous eddies. I'm new at this, and hold the cheeks of my rump together to pass Hell Gate without incident.

It's a beautiful, bright, morning when we enter the southwest end of Long Island Sound. Sails dance and the atmosphere breathes a festive mood.

We're on a mission of avoidance and don't join the festivities. We know now that Isabel is no longer a threat, but we're tired and want quiet shelter. We radio a marina that tells us *Faith* is too deep and suggests we continue to Oyster Bay, where we can grab a mooring ball.

Our entry into Oyster Bay witnesses the eeriness of changing weather. The graceful flight of the birds becomes erratic, the bright color of sky and water and land fades, and the breeze imitates the birds. We sup and go to bed, all of us with enough fatigue to sleep in our new home that dances awake on the water.

We're safe.

By morning, it's chilly, grey, and windy. The change came and a new rhythm settles in: the waves on the hull, the halyards on the mast, the intermittent rain on the deck, and life—cooking, eating, napping, and school.

The next day, the rhythm stills, the colors return, and the birds soar gracefully again.

Returning to Hampton sees us sailing in a steady breeze to an anchorage for the night in the mouth of the Delaware Bay. By morning, it's calm again, and we enjoy a beautiful day's motor, as motoring goes, down the Atlantic coast of Maryland. The opportunity to practice our radio skills presents itself with the approach of a Coast Guard cutter to about thirty meters off our port quarter to practice their own radio skills. They ask about the passengers, the boat, the last port of call, the next port of call, any ports of call outside of the United States, and we have a generally decent chat on this pleasant afternoon.

Just as they bear off at the end of the conversation, we lose contact. Emily is sitting in the cockpit and asks, "Why is land on the other side of the boat now?"

Our radio doesn't work nor do any other electronics, including the autopilot that was doing a good job of keeping the shoreline to starboard until now. We're in the middle of cutting a large circle of sea on our maiden voyage for the Coast Guard to see.

Emily takes the helm while I investigate to find Greggii and Amanda playing down below in the salon. The master power switch just below them was kicked.

The Caribbean 1500

Motoring into Hampton, we sense two things. The first is that Isabel pounded the Chesapeake Bay. The bay is full of leaves and limbs and mud and lumber, and that's only the stuff that floats. The people on boats anchored in the rivers tell of tense times, and say our move to New York was smart. The second is that it's time to get busy on last-minute preparations.

Partially to ease the fears of those close to us, but mostly to mask my misgivings, I project a confidence in our plans and abilities that is easily perceived as arrogance; it's funny how much easier this trait is perceived in others.

John and Linda, whom we met at a nearby slip, recently completed the Bluewater Rally, a twenty-two-month circumnavigation along a route not too different from what we have planned. Their British tongue is genuine, and the Union Jack on *Magic Dragon* gives the marina its link to the world beyond America. Her singsong lilt and his dry wit make their friendship especially enjoyable.

My confidence doesn't wane when John asks about our route to Panama. We've been telling everybody that we're leaving Hampton, sailing to Florida, then Cuba, then Panama.

A rally leaves Hampton, Virginia, for the Caribbean every year—The Caribbean 1500 Rally for Cruisers—and follows a route through the Gulfstream to the Virgin Islands. We're invited to participate and feel the seminars, safety checks, weather services, and nifty pink *Caribbean 1500* flag they provide are a bargain.

When we tell John our new plans to join the rally, he looks up from his laptop and over his reading glasses to say, "You sounded so set on getting to Florida that we didn't want to say anything, but we think the rally is a better way for you to start." Linda chimes in, "Florida is a tough passage from here, and there's nowhere to go when you get there."

Sometimes *Faith*, by being such a nice boat, projects confidence for us. People assume we know what we're doing. One neighbor, standing outside the pilothouse of the trawler that he and his wife call home, sees me prepare to strip the varnish from our toe-rail as I carry scrapers, stripper, brushes, and a drop cloth out of the companionway. He, almost afraid, says, "So—you don't use a heat gun—but you've probably gotten accustomed to the way you're doing it."

Curiosity grips me, "What do you mean?"

He turns toward his wife, who's making sandwiches in the open pilothouse. "My heat gun is in that locker, would you hand it to me?"

She does, and he extends it over his rail to me. "Here, try this on a small area."

I give it a try, "Wow, this is a whole lot easier than what I was doing!"

"Why don't you finish your job with it? I don't need it right away."

Many people around us hold keys to valuable insights, and the only path to those keys is to minimize my arrogance and hope they can overcome their fear of condescending.

The rally organizer doesn't mind condescending, and urges us to take crew for the passage to teach us about offshore sailing. The prospect of strangers on board doesn't garner much excitement, but since it holds certain logic, plans are laid for two experienced crewmembers to join us for the trip to the British Virgin Islands.

We wake on the morning of the rally, Sunday, Nov. 2, 2003, and putt-putt to the fuel dock before opening this chapter in our lives.

The thrill of departure overwhelms us as the Chesapeake Bay Bridge Tunnel shrinks in our wake. *Faith* is enveloped by the freshness of ocean. Until now, our experience has been in waters of varying colors of bluish-grey to coffee, sometimes with cream when the runoff was heavy. Our trip to New York saw a grey and black sky reflected in the water. Now, with distance from land and depth of the water, we experience colors that cannot be captured on canvas or film—colors that appear by day to be illuminated from within and at night, *are* illuminated from within by an eerie green glow from the bow wave, along the hull, and trailing in *Faith's* wake to the horizon. The term *phosphorescence*—as millions of organisms emit this glow when disturbed—enhances the romance of this phenomenon.

During daylight, we swim and fish. Swimming is a treat when all that's inside the horizon is sky and water and when the depth is measured in miles. Fish go from hook to pan, except for tuna, where we skip the pan and eat it raw.

A marker trespasses our horizon, a marker I think might be a life raft because of too many such tales in sailing magazines. We're compelled to rescue it. When we discover it to be a fishing marker, we lose our sense of heroism and allow it to perish.

Midway through the Gulfstream, hundreds of small dolphins swim past us with purpose to reach an unknown destination beyond *Faith*'s bow (49). A few linger to show off before resuming their journey.

Faith is in water conservation mode, and we take showers not as we *think* we need them to greet each new day, but when we *know* we need them in a social sense. Even with our water-maker—a high-maintenance, high-pressure-pump-and-membrane gizmo that desalinates sea-water—we treat water as finite while on passage. Greggii and I have fun on deck, dumping seawater on ourselves, with a brief lather between buckets; his five-year-old laugh and the water against the hull are the only important sounds.

We learn to ignore the hum of the engine and the trip grows peaceful. The hum necessitates a fuel stop in Bermuda, where we pay $400 to Bermuda's immigration (to account for our presence) and Customs (to account for *Faith*) to legally stay for the twelve hours we're here. We fuel, celebrate my forty-seventh birthday, and on my insistence, depart for Tortola amid reports of less-than-ideal weather.

Although the decision to keep moving isn't very bright, I stubbornly refuse to wait in Bermuda for better weather, fearing discouragement at our lack of progress. I know that every one of us has a stew of emotions boiling over from our departure and I believe that distance from home will lessen our imaginations of turning back; I insist we move on.

The remaining passage to Tortola is more comfortable than our trip to New York was, only because experienced crew are on board. They provide no knowledge that couldn't be learned by books. They cause the additional dynamic of strangers in our home for the duration of the passage. But knowledge is only a fraction of sailing, and witnessing their experience provides us far greater benefit than their presence costs. I sleep with knowledge that there are skilled hands and eyes at the helm, and learn to appreciate their company.

The seas quit pummeling us as we round the east side of Tortola. We anticipate a festive welcome from the rally organizers and boats that arrived before us, but it's either too late or too early, and our welcoming party is asleep. We tie up at the marina in silence.

Critters in St. Croix

The other boat in the Caribbean 1500 Rally with a family on board is a catamaran crewed by John, Po, Jaimie, and Skyler Martin, who reunite in Roadtown, Tortola, after John sails from Virginia with other crew to help.

One of the first goals of both our families is to leave the marina. I'm sure it could be a beautiful place, but Roadtown witnessed record rainfalls just before our arrival, and the harbor is a blond mud color from the runoff.

When we leave, we sail to the Baths—batholiths are massive rocks—on Virgin Gorda, then to the Virgin Gorda Yacht Harbor, where Greggii and Jaimie decide to get married when they grow up. We explore the Virgin Islands together for two weeks. Hearing of a Thanksgiving Buffet at a resort in Francis Bay, St. John, we celebrate our first of many holidays abroad.

After Thanksgiving, the crew of *Faith* explores St. Croix (map, page 15). We test our sailing skills by sailing through the first couple of channel markers at Christiansted, but I get nervous, so we drop the sails and motor the rest of the way. While we circle the anchorage, and run *Faith* aground more than once, a guy on a boat leaving hollers, "You can use this mooring if you like. Just run into Stixx and tell Woody that Ingo told you it's okay to use his mooring."

We shop in one of the few stores open on Sunday, where Emily finds some sandals she's been looking for. We ask the woman who sells sandals what we should see in St. Croix, and she tells us not to miss the beer-drinking pigs at the Domino Club. She and everybody else we meet at Stixx—a waterfront restaurant—are friends of Ingo and all promise to relay our message to Woody.

To tour the island, we rent a Jeep Wrangler convertible. Lorrie knows we could have something comfortable, but we four kids think the Jeep is cooler.

Arriving at the Domino Club, we're told we need to get there earlier in the day. The pigs get a lot of beer and go to bed around 3:30 in the afternoon.

Lorrie has been reading in a guidebook some good reviews of the Lobster Reef Restaurant, just east of Cane Bay. With us looking like tourists, a couple pulls alongside to tell us we look lost and to ask if they can help. I ask, "Where's Cane Bay?"

"You turn right at this light, and you'll come straight to it."

Then I ask, "Where are you heading?" because I have a hunch where they're heading is more interesting than where we think we want to go.

"There's a dam that's been dry for years. It's flowing from the recent rains and we want to see it!"

I've never been able to shake that kind of curiosity, so we follow to where a bunch of cars are parked in the road. Many people are washing cars, doing laundry, and bathing. In Michigan, we never concern ourselves much with where our water comes from. Here in this corner of America, we learn a different look.

Continuing, we arrive at the west end of St. Croix and see that the sun has already set.

The map in the Jeep shows another road back to Christiansted. On the map, it's a solid line, depicted as no less a road than the one we came on. Since this route looks shorter, we take it. We're soon surrounded with lush greenery and doubts about being on the right road. The vegetation, recently watered to a heightened vitality, encroaches on parts of the road that I consider traffic zones; two-lane highway, then two-lane country, then maybe a lane, then a bike path, then we barrel through and hope we don't hit anything. Occasionally it widens to give us hope, but narrows again and again.

We regret not stopping to put the top up earlier. Deepening dusk brings critters we aren't used to seeing, and things rain on us from the vegetation we plow through. A lizard lands on our windshield-wiper, wondering how he could one minute be peacefully snagging bugs from a comfortable limb of new life, and the next having a chaotic vision of a bunch of laughing kids, one hysterical woman, and a crazy man looking at him on the motion picture screen that just abducted him. The hysterical woman thinks we should turn around, but the crazy man resists. Then, the crazy man feels a feeling he's not accustomed to, as if somebody's finger is wiggling around between the arch of his foot and his sandal. Since everybody's sitting upright, and nobody can reach his sandal to put their finger in it, he decides the issue needs to be addressed. *Soon.*

We break out of the underbrush and overbrush and end up on a real road. In a well-lit gas station, the critter is released, a four-inch-long, hard-shelled worm with a bunch of legs. He went from sniffing around in my sandal to the rigorous wilds of the pavement in a heartbeat, my heartbeat. The sensation I felt wasn't nearly as uncomfortable as the one he's going to feel if he doesn't move those legs to get off the parking lot. We don't wait to see. The girls think it's gross. Greggii interrupts the hysterical woman's "I told you so," with "That's cool!"

We eat at the Lobster Reef Restaurant where Frankie, the island's best chef, prepares our dinner. Life is good, and we're back on *Faith* by 9:00.

In the morning, we arrive early at the Domino Club.

Norma, big, black, and pleasantly brusque, charges ten dollars for three beers, escorts us out, and beats on the side of a shed, bellowing, "Time to get up—JJ— GET UP!!" and the biggest, ugliest creature I've ever heard called a pig puts his front legs up on the gate to his stall. Norma tells Greggii, "He won't hurt you," and instructs him to put his whole, unopened can of beer in the monster's mouth. JJ pops the can with his teeth to an explosion of foam, guzzles the beer and spits out the empty in the dirt near Greggii's feet (56). Emily and Amanda follow with the same dramatic results. I have doubts about yesterday's bedtime; today's beer is non-alcoholic.

We spend our last evening in St. Croix at *Tito and Sue's Crab Races.* Tito is em-cee, Sue is scorekeeper. They're busy selling rights to a hundred or so hermit crabs, and Greggii, in a fit of five-year-old creativity, names his crab *Gregg.* Gregg can't be coaxed out of his shell and winds up losing. Greggii reaches into a consolation grab-bag for something forgettable.

As we leave Christiansted, we catch a three-foot *wahoo*—a pretty silver fish with charcoal-colored tiger-stripes (50). We learn that five miles away is Buck Island Reef National Monument, where plaques are laid on the seabed next to the more prominent corals, telling what each is. This underwater park is supervised by my favorite US government agency, The National Park Service. Our family road trips before *Faith* saw us in many US Parks. Public space, dwindling as it is and socialist by definition, is a true asset of America.

We return to St. John in the afternoon and hang around with John and Po, planning to sail to Sint Maarten together when the weather allows. Early one morning, John bangs on our hull and tells us the outlook is good, get ready, and let's get going. In a crisp breeze and the comfort of following seas—as opposed to having the waves coming at our bow—we make Simpson Bay by 10:00 at night and into the lagoon during the 9:00 AM drawbridge opening (57).

After several days, John and Po want to go to Marigot, on the French side of the island, then to St. Barths for Christmas (Sint Maarten is Dutch, Saint Martin is French). We go to Anguilla. Without knowing it when we depart, we won't see each other again. Their plans are to cruise the Caribbean for six months; ours are to go through Panama and take the long way home.

Island Hopping

—

In Road Bay, Anguilla, Customs and Immigration is in a classroom-sized building with the penetrating, almost-echo, of an empty room. The only two desks are to my right, one in front of the other with two women and a man at the second. One of the women asks, "Checking in?"

"Yes."

She gives me two identical crew lists to fill out, one with *arrival* crossed out and *departure* penned in its place. Leaving me to my task, she returns to the other desk and takes interest there. The woman sitting there appears to be going over some documents for the man amid quiet chatter. I complete the forms and say so. She comes back, stamps our passports, and motions me to the next desk. Thinking it impolite to interrupt, I wait. I don't know if it's the look in her eyes, or her voice that says, "Now!" but at the next desk I see the papers they're consumed with are playing cards. I excuse my interruption and we complete our work.

Claudell Richardson is a lanky sixteen years, outgoing and bored, when we meet him on the beach outside the Customs classroom. He's on winter break from school and works for his brother's fishing boats when the charter activity warrants it; this week no charters are booked. Since Claudell enjoys school more than break, he is killing time until it starts again. He accepts when I ask him to join us as a guide.

We motor and sail around several areas close to Road Bay: Prickly Pear Cay, Sandy Island, and Little Bay, where at this last site, we climb a cliff by rope and jump off a rock that stands twenty feet out of the water. Greggii and Claudell hit it off well, and Claudell holds him while they jump off the rock together from a lower point. We return to Road Bay in the afternoon and sit on the beach talking with Claudell. We leave Anguilla in the morning (60).

Saba, our next island to visit, provides a unique experience in our voyage. It's the only country where we clear into Customs and Immigration that we don't go on shore. The officials are in an office trailer on the south side of the island, and to complete the formalities I leave *Faith* and her crew uncomfortably anchored in four-foot waves. After checking in, we move to the west side of the island, where several moorings are placed in the 160-foot deep water. The earth falls at the same slope below the water as it does above, and we see tall cliffs above. There are stairs, called *The Ladder*, where all goods shipped to and from Saba were brought until recently.

We snooze through some early afternoon showers. When the rain subsides, I take Amanda to climb *The Ladder*. We dinghy to shore. I have the camera around my neck after telling Lorrie there's no need for the waterproof bag. Our approach shows that the beach is actually smooth, softball-sized rocks. The breakers are three feet; I get nervous and ponder our landing for a moment. Then, we race in and cut the engine in time to turn sideways to the surf and have it roll us over.

Standing in three feet of water, I lift one side of the dinghy to let Amanda, who's trapped under it, out. Then we right it, get back in, and point toward *Faith*, without climbing *The Ladder*. Amazingly, the engine starts. Amanda is shivering, crying, and bleeding from her thumb.

Lorrie's input helps us decide not to try that again, so we eat dinner, sleep for the night, and leave for friendlier shores in the morning. The friendlier shores are those of St. Kitts, where we berth at the municipal marina in Basseterre to celebrate Christmas.

Since Hampton, Virginia, Greggii has been the door to our social life. There, he formed a friendship with a boy at the library. While they were in a reading program, this boy's mom and Lorrie talked. We shared dinner on *Faith* one night and again at their house on another. At the Caribbean 1500's awards dinner, it was Greggii who danced the night away with the nanny of the family on the catamaran, leading to our friendship with them. Now, Greggii introduces us to the parents of his latest playmates. After presents on Christmas morning, we join this family for a traditional Norwegian Christmas dinner in the Caribbean, reflecting the father's Norwegian roots.

In Antigua, we have some maintenance done on *Faith*: the water-maker, the generator, and the refrigeration system are fixed, and each of the guys coming aboard does a good job. I note that what they do isn't all that tricky. Because it takes longer to find and organize their coming on board than to fix anything, I decide to fix what I can myself from now on. This is a good decision because some places we visit over the next four years are ill-equipped for repairs.

We can't find officials for clearance into Guadeloupe and are still nervous about these sorts of things. After anchoring overnight, we sail on.

Dominica is generally and wrongly accepted by many cruisers as a place to avoid. The Caribbean Sea in general has suffered from the winds of trade and economics, and Dominica has suffered more than most. When the Caribbean slave trade ended, and sugar production moved to the beet farmers of the mid-latitudes, poverty struck. A number of islands sought independence from colonial rule, Dominica gaining such independence only months before being devastated by hurricanes David and Allen in 1978-79.

Dominica possesses a lawless mystique, with marijuana farms in the mountains, no regularly scheduled cruise ships, and an impoverished population. Our visit allows us a different interpretation: Dominicans enforce their own security outside of contractual obligations to cruise operators. They haven't learned the ease of standing on the dock to wait as thousands of tourists disembark a cruise ship to hand out dollars. The Dominicans we meet own a hard-earned integrity based on work and service, and exchange value accordingly. They look at us as a means of fulfilling this exchange, never assuming anything more.

Lorrie heard of a tour-operator in Rosseau, Dominica, named Sea-Cat. While we are motoring toward Sea-Cat's house, a speedboat carrying Roots approaches. He's Sea-Cat's partner, and shows us where and how to anchor. We put the anchor down forty meters from the beach and then use reverse to back toward shore, where Roots takes a line from *Faith*'s stern and ties it to a palm tree. He and Sea-Cat then board *Faith* to greet us.

Roots has the smooth, self-assured voice and presence of Snoop Dogg, just plain cool. Greggii asks him for a boat ride and soon our little boy is driving Roots around the anchorage (9).

The tour with Sea-Cat is our highlight in the Caribbean. We visit the usual sights: the botanical gardens, centered on a massive Banyan tree, Trafalgar Falls, where you climb the rocks and dive into the pool (58), the sulfur springs, the Emerald Pool, and then the Atlantic coast. Sea-Cat takes us to a restaurant on our way to Trafalgar Falls, where we can order ahead of time and pick up our dinners when we leave the falls. The price is between US $15 and $20 per person. When we decline, our tour changes for the better. If we don't eat, Sea-Cat doesn't eat. For the rest of the day, he stops along the road to pick bananas here, oranges there, a sweetsop or sour-sop or papaya at the next place.

Sea-Cat realizes we're more interested in the day-to-day life of the island and takes us to a home with a large garden. The older couple there is working in the shed, she, roasting cocoa beans on an open fire, and he, grinding them into a paste with a large mortar and pestle. Sea-Cat has each of us taste a roasted bean with a pinch of raw cane sugar. The result is chocolate.

He then takes us to a souvenir shop in Carib Indian Territory where Lorrie, Emily, and Amanda buy postcards. Greggii and I stay outside and watch a small girl with long braids play while her grandfather stands erect next to the fire he's tending, using a stick to move around three volleyball-sized, green fruits in the coals. When I ask him what the man is doing, Sea-Cat takes two dollars from me. As we climb back into the van, Sea-Cat returns with a roasted breadfruit. About the texture of the meat of an apple with all of the juice removed, the only part of this breadfruit with any flavor is near the charred rind, where it tastes like campfire.

Dominica holds a special place in all of us, but not without Sea-Cat and Roots—in the same way that Anguilla can't be the same without Claudell. This becomes a recurring theme: places are special because of the people. We're meeting many people in different places, but are yet to find one of the *places where they don't value human life like we do.*

Amanda is keenly aware of the comfort she derives from her friends. Her best friend is Jacob. Before we left Hampton, Virginia, Jacob and Amanda were plotting his visit. Early in the Caribbean, Jacob and his mother, Loraine, asked to join us in St. Lucia for a week, and there becomes our first destination with a fixed schedule.

We enter St. Lucia at Rodney Bay, an area defined by the cruising sailors passing through on their way to someplace else. We then sail south to Vieux Fort, where the airport is located. While we walk to the airport, giggling school girls touch us and place their arms next to ours to contrast the colors. White is exotic, and Greggii, blond and cute, is a special attraction.

The streets are lined with fruit markets under lean-to shelters or no shelter at all, selling gum, knickknacks, rolling papers, fish, and jewelry. Everybody nods acknowledgement, maybe because we're from somewhere else, or maybe that's how they do things here.

Once Jacob and Loraine join us, we try to show them our lives on their brief timetable.

We return to Rodney Bay, then go to Castries to show them the contrast between the true life of Vieux Fort, the meshing of cultures in Rodney Bay, and the departure from reality of places that host cruise ships. We hire a day trip from Marigot that disappoints most of us who toured with Sea-Cat (nothing will disappoint Amanda this week) but is enjoyed by Jacob and Loraine. The botanical park, built around a waterfall, has the handrails and barricades one expects at Disney, meant to keep you in the right place. The waterfall appears reinforced with concrete, because nature doesn't need the same definition where tourism is involved. At the end of the tour, our guide takes us to his wife's restaurant, where the prices reflect the captive market.

When we return to *Faith*, a man waits to collect his fee for watching our dinghy, which is locked around a palm tree next to the guard's booth of the restaurant we're anchored in front of.

We enjoy island hopping less and less as we move among them, staying only long enough in each place to become slightly amazed or annoyed based on our sentiments that day. We experience growing irritation with many islanders' approach to us, as if we approach and they see big ATM signs on our foreheads. My sensibilities challenge me to look at myself, to look at a racism I never previously acknowledged, and to wonder what other surprises—surprises I've kept hidden in my life—will surface as our journey continues.

We're new to this life, and we share apprehension and even fear of the worlds we will come into contact with over the course of our voyage, much of it bred in our American perspective that the world *is* a scary place.

Greggii wakes early while I'm listening to the Caribbean 1500 chat—a discussion, with a prearranged time on the single sideband radio, SSB. He asks if he can call *Magic Dragon*.

"*Magic Dragon, Magic Dragon*, this is *Faith*."

"Faith, this is Magic Dragon. How wonderful to hear you," sings Linda.

"Um, yes...where are you?"

"We just got to Tortola last week. Where are you now?"

"Um," he looks at me, "Where are we, Dad?"

"St. Lucia."

He keys the microphone and says, "Magic Dragon, this is Faith, We're in St Lucia."

Linda says, "Faith stand by," then a moment later, "John and I will be there in three or four days. We want to see you again. We'll come to Rodney Bay and call when we get close."

"Um, OK, Faith out."

"Magic Dragon, out."

After dropping off Jacob and Loraine at the airport in Vieux Fort, we return to Rodney Bay to visit John and Linda. Their arrival is the best thing possible for Lorrie at this time, and they tell her what we're doing is great. John, sensing I'm too close to be a good teacher, schools the three girls in sailing basics for two hours on each of the two days we're with them. My insecurity creeps out, and I ask what they're learning and what John does different than I do. John instead uses this time to build Lorrie's confidence in my abilities and in our plans.

The Caribbean is a difficult place to start, but by necessity, it's our place. Maybe it's not the Caribbean at all, but the start of our journey that's difficult. We're fortunate for the friends we *are* meeting, but they're fleeting because of the paths chosen.

The Dangling Goober

After we flounder around in the Caribbean for a couple months and continue south to St. Vincent, Bequia, Tobago Cays, and Union Island, it's time to move.

We're finally free of Caribbean tourism. Though we think about breaking up the passage to Panama with a stop, the honeymoon memories Lorrie and I have of Aruba, nineteen years ago, don't offer compelling reasons. I recall the green space on Aruba being in low-lying areas, especially the drainage ditches along the roads where Heineken bottles proliferate.

There's no warning until we're downwind of Aruba enough to not turn back. Then the wind starts blowing. A lot of life comes without warning and that's a good thing. Too much warning might mean not moving at all. Maybe that's why some boats never leave the dock.

As the sun sets, the wind builds to forty knots and holds all night and through the day.

The seas are big. I have no way of telling how big a wave is, except that my eyes, when I stand in the cockpit, are eight feet above the water line. If a wave goes above the horizon, I know it's over eight feet. On this passage, I can only guess we're in waves around thirty feet. They *are* over eight feet.

I can't shake the word *knockdown* from my head. From the little knowledge I have, a knockdown can occur when a boat is parallel to the waves. *Faith* isn't. The breeze and the seas are following. It doesn't help that this weather develops as dusk deepens. Sleep blankets those who are able to with security; my own sleep, when I take the opportunity, is like that of a nervous cat.

Before dawn on the second morning, the wind tapers to ten knots, eliminating the pressure against our sails that held us in balance. Now the high seas toss us like a cork. *Faith's* radar displays an echo in the distance. Later, the ship is in a different position. I finally make a visual sighting on the ship in yet another position in the colorless light before the sun rises. I go to the mast to fiddle with the sails. When I return to the cockpit, Lorrie tells me that a ship is hailing us. I contact the calm voice of someone who hasn't been thrown around as we have for the past thirty-six hours. "This is the aircraft carrier *USS Enterprise*, and we cannot determine your intentions. We changed our course three times, and request that you now change yours to maintain a five-mile separation."

He is correct; we are sailing all over the place. I agree to maintain our separation as best I can. I think it's pretty cool, though, that our little boat can make an aircraft carrier work around us as much as it did. (It would be fun to see that in a movie sometime.)

Following six days at sea, we arrive in the north-facing bay of Puerto Obaldia, Panama, and anchor in four-foot swells. While we prepare to go to Customs, six men pointing to official patches on their shoulders paddle a canoe out to us. They board *Faith* to look around. We use few words of each other's language, but determine four things: 1) the transom will be fumigated for something, 2) the police will board us soon, 3) after the police visit, we are to go to immigration, and 4) after that, we must go to another office.

We use papers and pencils and pictures and gestures to communicate.

The police, thirteen men and one dog, board *Faith*. Their covered launch scratches through *Faith's* finish while they board us, and Duke scratches through the varnish on Emily's floor while he sniffs it. Both Customs and the police are interested in where we came from. They ask several times, "Did you go to Colombia?" whose border is less than a mile away.

We say, "No," every time.

The scratches aside, they're all friendly in a professional manner and appreciate the chance in this sleepy village to conduct official business. We enjoy the experience too.

We take two trips in the dinghy to get to shore in the rough water, with Emily and Amanda greeted on our first trip by a man wearing a machine gun. When I return with Lorrie and Greggii, one Customs officer escorts us past other soldiers in the streets to the police station, where a young woman completes some paperwork. While we sit in silence, she occasionally, without moving her head, aims her eyes at us in a blank look that betrays nothing. After a five-minute hour, she hands us a piece of paper. We're then escorted to the immigration office.

Lorrie, Emily, Amanda, and Greggii abandon me to walk to a lonely playground.

The immigration official clears us in and points me to another office for our cruising permit. On the way back to *Faith*, a man waves us over to sign a document that I believe has something to do with the fumigating, or turtles, or our first born. Language is a slight barrier.

Everyone says, "Welcome to Panama!" Asking about the soldiers, I learn we're in a war zone. I don't know what war it is, but they take it seriously. One soldier suggests, not because of the war zone stuff, but for a calm anchorage, that we move an hour away, to Puerto Perme. That anchorage is in a lagoon near the *Kuna Yali*—an indigenous population—village of Anachucuna.

At Puerto Perme, two ten-year-old boys bring us bananas, lemons, and a sugar cane. They speak as much English as we do Kuna. We show them our atlas—where we started, where we've been, and how we got here. They ask how to say things in English, and we learn a little Spanish and Kuna.

Beaching the dinghy in the village, we're greeted by a hundred children under ten years old. After several misspoken or misunderstood requests, we're taken to the *Sila*—village principal—for permission to anchor and visit.

The dwellings have thatched roofs, cane or bamboo walls, and dirt floors. The store is stocked with rice, soaps, fabrics, and other necessities, most in bulk without the packaging we've learned to pay extra for in America.

The children show us to a house where the Sila lies in a hammock. He doesn't get up, but asks, through an interpreter, our names, how we got here, and about our boat. He motions us to sit, and we sit and look at each other uncomfortably until he rises and motions us to follow.

It's quite a parade—the Sila, the interpreter, the hundred children, and us—as we wind our way through the pedestrian streets and between the houses.

We arrive at the Sila's house to enter a large porch with dirt for the floor. The Sila's age commands respect. The interpreter, almost as old, spits a big rolling goober into the dust as he settles into his seat. Moments later, while the Sila pontificates for the benefit of the assembled children, the interpreter tries to let go of another one, but it hangs up on his lower lip, does a cartwheel off his chin, and lands half-on and half-off the seat of his chair between his legs. He uses the straw of grass he is chewing on to try to flick it away, without success. It just dangles. Being the only non-white guy who speaks any English in the room, he knows all of the English-speaking white folks are looking at him, and he knows we're distracted by his dangling goober, so he moves his legs around on the chair to make the problem disappear.

While he struggles to regain his composure, several of the children who can't fit inside the porch or get a spot outside of the screenless windows are climbing on the roof to look in from the ventilation holes. Generally, roofs are not designed for humans, and this is especially true for thatched roofs. One kid makes a rapid entry into the room from above along with several palm fronds that give way. He isn't hurt, but redirects the interpreter's embarrassment to himself.

Now we can get down to business.

The Sila grumbles a few things, and then looks to the interpreter who holds up his hand, fingers and thumb spread and says, "Dollar." I give him a $5.00 bill, and then he says what I think is, "No, All." Leading me to believe it is $5.00 for each of the five of us.

I give him another $20.00, and he gives me my $5.00 back and leaves. Now I *am* getting confused. We sit for a minor eternity with children pressing on our backs because they're being pushed against us by the children behind them who also want to see the action.

We sit and stare at each other: the Sila, the children, and us. It's hot, it's crowded, it's sweaty, and we don't know what we're waiting for. I know for a fact that at least one of the white guys in the room is growing uncomfortable.

After twenty minutes, the interpreter returns and hands me a $5.00 bill and a receipt for $15.00. My guess is it took that long to find somebody to make change. I don't know what that transaction is for, but we have a receipt.

The Sila then waves his arms around in a broad gesture to indicate that the village is ours to roam, which we do with children following us at every point.

Five minutes later, Greggii falls down and comes to me with a small cut on his finger. He's crying and says that when he fell down, all the children laughed. We learn much later that in many cultures, laughter is meant to offer comfort to somebody in an embarrassing or painful situation. That knowledge came too late; it nearly killed me to not laugh at that dangling goober.

Women approach Lorrie, Emily, and Amanda to offer *molas*—beautifully colored blouses, or fabrics.

In the morning, we wake late. Puerto Perme is full of *uhus*—dugout canoes—each with a father and his children fishing. Vergilio de Leon Diaz, the most inquisitive of the boys that welcomed us yesterday, brings two of his three sisters, Bertalicia and Fidelecia, two and five years old; Vergilio De Leon is ten (10 & 36).

We invite them in for a movie and popcorn. *Scooby Doo*. After that, a man with six granddaughters comes, then three boys. Amanda suggests we give them pictures of themselves. We take and print photographs and cut them out for them, to their great excitement.

After Anachakuna, we want to see more of the San Blas, but the weather doesn't let us. Our confidence has not yet developed sufficiently to enter the reefs in the eight-foot seas we're encountering. It's one thing to bump into something slowly in calm water, but quite another to be thrown onto rocks or reefs by waves. We sail overnight to Portobelo, twenty miles from the entrance to the Panama Canal.

Portobelo is an old Spanish port where men would carry Peruvian gold over the isthmus to ship to Spain. We try to get information on the canal here, as it seems a nice place to wait, but are told only to bring *Faith* to Limon Bay or to the Panama Canal Yacht Club for assignment of a transit date.

Faith's lines suggest movement. The marina in Hampton gave us waves and tides, but keeping *Faith* at the dock felt like trying to hold a thoroughbred in the gate. *Faith* possesses sufficient adrenaline to keep us all doped up, waiting for the start. Waiting becomes a recurring frustration. In Hampton, it was for the end of hurricane season; in Panama, it's to transit the canal, then on the Pacific side to obtain visas for French Polynesia; in the Galapagos, it's the wait for fuel; in Malaysia, it's the ten months' wait to complete the forty-five day contract for work; and in Gran Canaria, it's a wait for the end of hurricane season again, to make the Atlantic crossing.

Panama is special to us because of the people congregated here with plans similar to our own—plans to sail to the western horizons of the Pacific.

On arrival in Panama we know we managed to leave the dock.

Part II. The Point of No Return

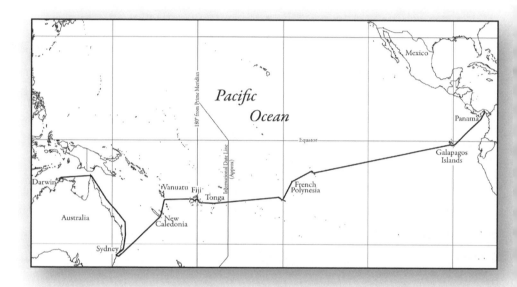

Pacific Crossing
Las Perlas, Panama to Coffs Harbor, Australia
13 March to 10 November 2004

Friends

Two types of events mark the emotional highs of our voyage: the departures, holding anticipation of broad horizons at sea, and the landfalls, marred slightly by unfounded apprehension of a new round of officialdom, but filled with anticipation of developing relationships and seeing friends on similar journeys whom we may not have seen for six months or a year, sometimes longer.

Each of us approaches these events in our own way. I enjoy the water most and look forward to departures. The water is Lorrie's least favorite, and she breathes relief on arrivals. Emily and Amanda enjoy both, the exception being when relationships cast shadows of sadness on our leaving. Greggii always has difficulty with goodbyes. He never lets on until later, but he yearns for a relationship outside of our family with a measure of permanence.

Smilla and Ardi are the worst goodbyes, those goodbyes that reach into our chest and give our heart a quarter-turn and hold it that way for days, weeks, or longer. *Smilla* travels with us through most of the Pacific Ocean. We meet Ardi later.

Our time since leaving Hampton, and through the Caribbean, especially after we moved south and away from the boats in the rally, was lonely. We didn't know anybody, and it wasn't easy to meet anybody in this charter-boat Mecca: thousands of boats, many with families, but few with plans to live aboard more than a week.

In Panama, it's different. Yachts here hold cruisers destined for somewhere else. In the tropics, that somewhere else is generally west because of favorable winds and currents. It becomes not uncommon to see many of the same people again and again.

We meet one family of which the father carries whiffle balls, a bat, and enough enthusiasm to get a makeshift game of baseball going on the lawn of the Panama Canal Yacht Club, where we wait two weeks for our canal transit date. I don't know many players, but there's a Swedish family—two girls, a boy, and their parents—beginning a voyage like ours. The name of their boat is *Smilla*.

The difference between Thomas and Helén and their family on *Smilla*, and Lorrie and me and our family on *Faith*, is that they know what they're doing. Thomas and Helén did this earlier, as kids fresh out of school, before many people sailed around the world. They married shortly after their first voyage, built a family, grew a business, and felt it important enough to give their kids—Nicóle, Lucas, and Nadine—the same experience by doing it again.

I like to pretend my loneliness is a way of gaining solitude and rationalize it into a positive. It's not, but I have the optimism to make it so. While I'm driven to get ourselves so far into our adventure that we can't turn around, I'm also aware of how our crew is holding out; none of them possess the same optimism.

Their loneliness consumes them, and here at this baseball game on the shaded grass of the Yacht Club is a nice family heading our way. Between innings, my girls are around me and Thomas's girls are around him; I forever brand myself *Dork* in my loving daughters' eyes when I blurt out to Nicóle and Nadine, "Do you girls like to shop? Emily and Amanda *love* shopping!" in a forced and clumsy remark that doesn't have anything to do with our crossing the Pacific with them. We experience the start of friendship.

We also meet Carl and Maggie and their daughter, Maddie, in Colón. Their boat is *Geneva*. Many people learn the canal as line handlers on somebody else's boat, and I join *Geneva* for their transit. Carl and Maggie are Australians who worked for several years in the United Kingdom and are now returning to Australia on a boat. In the worst sense of the word, they are the *luckiest* people we meet. As they were leaving the UK, a drawbridge crunched their mast, forcing repairs at the expense of the drawbridge operator, and causing *Geneva* to be the first boat in history to be shipped overland to Gibraltar for the start of the Bluewater Rally they joined for their trip home.

Faith's transit of the canal occurs three days later on Shrove Tuesday. The sun rises for us over the Atlantic and rests in the Pacific as we cross the American Continents in the engineering marvel of the rerouted rivers, locks, and excavations that comprise the Panama Canal (61).

Then we join Carl, Maggie, and Maddie for Panama City's family-oriented Carnival parade. We agree to meet in the Pacific Islands but don't see them again until nine months later, when we arrive at a marina in Newcastle, Australia. There, I notice a little girl bolt the other way down the dock as we tie *Faith* up. The next thing I see is Maggie and Maddie running to greet us. Their engine failed after departing Panama, and they sailed non-stop for forty-five days to Norfolk Island, about 6,800 miles, because they didn't have confidence to enter anchorages under sail only. As they approached Norfolk, they had just eaten the last of the rice hidden somewhere on *Geneva*.

We learn a couple years after our time with them in Australia that they're moving to Tasmania on *Geneva*. They time their departure to be in the Bass Straits during the Sydney-to-Hobart Race as a safety measure with the additional traffic in the straits, racing and watching. They're disabled, and the thirty-foot-long, steel-hulled *Geneva* is towed to Hobart by the Coast Guard, "not for their own safety, but because of the hazard they posed for the boats in the race."

Carl and Maggie are truly special people who probably make it to Hobart and shrug their shoulders while Carl wryly remarks, "Well, that worked out nicely."

One afternoon, during our stay in Panama City, I hear Greggii running through *Faith* and then, *thump*. I look from my perch in the aft head to see him on the floor of our cabin. When he turns toward me, there's blood over his eye.

Lorrie calmly grabs a Kotex for him to hold on his forehead. Some friends take us to shore, and we hire a taxi to the Children's Hospital with Greggii holding his Kotex all the way. He gets eleven stitches. It costs $2.00 to fill out the registration forms and $1.00 for the stitches.

The stitches slow us down. *Smilla* encourages us to slow down even more, saying we won't see much if we're locked into two years. That idea deserves another think.

The Point of No Return

We leave Panama City for Las Perlas, a group of islands in Panama Bay. Late on a new moon, I pee over the lifeline. Phosphorescence glows green in disturbed water, and pee disturbs the water. The inkiness of the new moon makes it more pronounced and ... *whoompsh*, and a glow of brilliance in the water first a couple feet in diameter, then radiating outward 20 feet, like an underwater special effect of a satellite video of an atomic mushroom cloud. Silence ... silence ... then *whoompsh* in a different location. And again. As my eyes acclimate to the darkness, I give the name *Pelican* to the unidentified flying and diving objects.

Morning marks *Faith's* point of no return, into the Pacific Ocean, where weather and currents push us away from the American Continents, and west toward the Galapagos Islands.

I know we aren't turning back, but I also know we have *Smilla* to share our apprehension with. This morning, over coffee, Thomas and I spend a couple minutes talking about radio frequencies and grunting a couple of guy-type grunts while Lorrie and Helén spend the same time talking about moods and foods and candles, relating on a feminine level about their men being interested in things like peeing over lifelines and radio frequencies.

It's foolish to pretend that friendship just happens, just as to pretend an abundant harvest needs only someone to drop the seeds. Take one of the simplest crops, the tomato. No, not the tomato that mysteriously ends up on the shelf at the supermarket after being picked green, refrigerated, gassed to a glossy ripeness, and bland as a bottle of water. I'm talking about real tomatoes, the ones you grow in your own garden or get from the neighbor, or at least grow to be red on the vine of the grower you purchase them from.

It's a mix of work, time, and care to grow a tomato. It's no different to grow a friend.

Passage-making this time is much calmer and more enjoyable than our previous passages. We have less seasickness, less busy-ness at the helm, and fewer flying objects in the cabin—I never knew how durable a small TV can be—to occupy ourselves. The moon doesn't appear until two hours before sunrise; the crispness of the stars pierces the black, and phosphorescence trails *Faith's* wake to the eastern horizon. Reading and stargazing, passing the time. I show Greggii the kite lying on its side—the Southern Cross—that amazing constellation that lies on the horizon at its dawn and its dusk, but stands vertical at its noon elevation. Then he wants to see "that guy's belt," and while I point to Orion, the sky lights with brilliance as a meteor tears open the inky canvas.

"Did you see that, Gregg?"

"Wow dad. That was cool!"

I know a treasure I'll miss most after our voyage is the night sky as it was created, without the haloes of lights packaged as protection and marketed as a measure of security.

Emily and Amanda pass time playing Uno. Occasionally, the silence of the passage and stargazing is pierced by one's squeal of glee and the other's squeal of frustration.

At night, we imagine shadows and hear peeps. We see them during the day. Most are seafaring birds, but there is the occasional one lost. One joins *Faith* for days at a time, waiting for morsels, no less captive on *Faith* than we are, knowing to leave is death.

We maintain our twice a day contact with *Smilla*.

Our home in Michigan lies 42°30' north of the equator—forty-two degrees, thirty minutes north. One degree is divided into 60 minutes, and the distance between adjacent minutes of latitude is one nautical mile, 6,090 feet. Thus, our home is 2,550 nautical miles from the equator. Hampton, Virginia lies 37°00' north, Panama City, 8°56' north, and San Cristobal, the easternmost of the Galapagos Islands lies 00°46' *south*. This passage marks the first time in each of our lives that we cross the equator, an event marked with a party and general silliness by the crew of *Faith*. Maritime tradition dictates an offering to King Neptune at this juncture of our voyage.

For the party, we dress in our tackiest outfits, pop some champagne to pour overboard for the good king's pleasure, and pop some fake champagne for our own.

The first few times I plot our course in the southern hemisphere, it doesn't look right. According to my plots, we're off course. The world is now upside down and calls for new thinking; an increase in latitude means *down* now. With land in sight, Greggii hollers, "Land Ho." We round San Cristobal, and a large eagle ray leaps six feet out of the water to do a flip. Before the anchor is down, we see several turtles and are visited by the first of many sea lions.

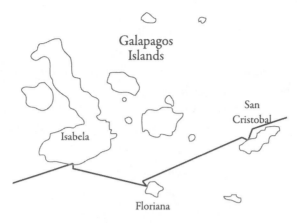

Galapagos Islands

San Cristobal

Isabela

Floriana

Ecotourism

The Galapagos Islands find us groping like a second date with those folks on *Smilla*. In a budding friendship with little form, a relationship takes root.

San Cristobal welcomes us warmly. The Galapagos don't live up to the expectations built on the nature shows we watched in past lives, but this speaks more to the expectations than to the place. Again, we discover that people are the variable that makes a place special. Not all people, mind you, but there's nowhere that all the people make a place special.

Greggii and I visit the port captain, Customs, and Immigration for our clearance, and one of the officers there turns on the TV and changes the channel to let my brand new six-year old watch cartoons while we men do important men stuff.

While walking to a place to copy our passports for the officials, we meet Placido. He provides fuel delivery and island tours. Placido is reserved and serious and, we soon find out, owns the responsibility of parenthood.

When Greggii and I return to *Faith*, Placido, accompanied by his eight-year old son, Joseph, is there talking to Lorrie. Joseph, like Greggii, is big for his age and searching for friends. When they discover that today is Greggii's birthday, they leave for a half-hour and return with a piñata as a gift (11). We schedule fuel delivery and an island tour with Placido.

We celebrate Greggii's birthday with Joseph, *Smilla*'s family, and another family we met in Panama; everybody swings at the piñata.

When you're in the Galapagos, you will see marina iguanas, tortoises, turtles, boobies, sea lions, and tropical penguins (62). All that stuff is scenic and it's an important part of creation. But what's special about our island tour is when Placido takes us to his property and hacks off a bunch of bananas for us; it's the afternoon we share with him and Joseph. A flat tire in the middle of nowhere reminds us of a month ago, in Panama, where Emily and I pushed the taxi we were riding in the last fifty meters to the fuel pump. We begin to learn that much of the world isn't as professional or sterile as home, and that's fine.

Our diet changes as we travel farther from home, but nothing can account for the disgusting noises and awful smell coming from Lorrie's side of our bed one morning. As foulness forces consciousness, Lorrie isn't there, but a sea lion has its head inside of the port light over where her head normally is (54).

Joseph continues to befriend us. He takes us to church and escorts us through the Darwin Interpretation Center. Returning to *Faith*, we find two sea lions on our transom and a small one sunning itself on deck. I feel guilty prodding the small one off with the blunt handle of our boathook, but recalling the breath and burps of the one in the port light, I believe sea lion poop on deck would be a bad thing.

Lorrie's birthday falls three days after Greggii's. I remember Fernando, who greeted Greggii and me at the beach on our initial landing to offer fuel delivery. He mentioned as part of his pitch that he could even have his mother prepare a home-cooked meal for us. Fernando's eyes sparkle when I talk to him about having his mother host a party. We plan a dinner for ourselves and *Smilla*'s family, and are treated to lobster, steak, and sweet corn in the garage Fernando has decorated with balloons, banners, crepe-paper, and candles. Fernando's dancing through the party like the ultimate host makes the evening great.

Nicóle, Lucas, Emily, and Amanda go to the beach. Greggii and Nadine want to go, but they're too little—too little for us to want them at the beach without us, but more painful for them, too little for the big kids to want them around. To ease their pain, we take them for a walk through the navy base and past an old cemetery to a place where blue-footed boobies nest. Lorrie, Helén, Thomas, and I find it fascinating. Even Greggii and Nadine are surprised that we don't see birds in cages but up-close in the wild. After the instant that surprise takes to settle in, they think looking at stupid birds is a stupid way to spend our stupid time. When we do get to the beach, Greggii and Nadine swim and play for fifteen minutes before we leave. Greggii had his heart set on the beach. All day long, that's what he wanted.

He didn't want to see boobies, iguanas, cemeteries, or restaurants; he wanted to go to the beach. Poor guy—we no sooner get there than we tell him it's time to leave.

We waste a lot of time talking to other cruisers about things that no one has a clue about. Floriana receives an abundance of words, but nobody in our circle knows much about it. For this reason, it seems, everybody wants to go there. All who have asked the port captain to go have been refused permission.

Two traits cloud my judgment about Floriana: first, I like forbidden fruit, and second, I believe it's less a sin to just do a thing than to do a thing after someone has said *don't do it*. I request *Faith*'s clearance to Isabela.

On our way, having not been denied permission, we stop at Floriana. Miguel, Floriana's lanky port captain, imparts important information like, counting us, Floriana's population is ninety-eight, the island's taxi is in for repairs and the parts are due in a couple of weeks, and Miguel would like to join us when his friend, Alejandra, takes us for a tour in his boat.

We want to see Post Office Bay, where whaleboat crews, explorers, and traders would dump their mail to be taken by the next boat going in the addressed direction. For some reason—perhaps the mating of some rare and exotic creature—it's closed. We go instead to Flamingo Lagoon, where hundreds of flamingos are wading, then past Cormorant Point to a long stretch of sugar-sand beach with what look like giant tire tracks from the water to the base of the dune, where turtles lay their eggs. Then, we go to Devil's Crown, a mostly submerged and eroded hollow cone of a volcano, and snorkel inside it. Often, snorkelers are visited by sharks of various threatening and non-threatening species, but today we're joined only by colorful reef fish and a friendly sea lion.

When we leave Floriana for Isabela, we're becalmed and motor through the night. I'm on watch, admiring the beauty of the Southern Cross, when slowly, brightly, for seconds instead of the usual split second, a shooting star appears. Rather than dying before meeting the horizon, it explodes with the effect of a single, silent firework.

We look forward to seeing *Smilla* at Isabela. They're waiting to discuss with us a horseback trip to the volcano, and we sign on with a tour guide named Joseph.

This Joseph is twenty-four years old, but looks like fourteen. He's a decent guide, taking us on horses well past their prime, to a black, rock-covered part of the island. It takes only a few minutes to remember why horseback riding is not on my list of passions. My horse develops lather and makes an odd noise that causes me to contemplate how far I must walk if he dies. In a line lifted from John Stein-beck: "I was heartbroken for him, but not sufficiently to get off and walk. We both suffered up the trail, he with pain and I with sorrow for him." (*The Log from the Sea of Cortez.*)

As the catalyst behind this tour, Nadine gets her own horse; her passion list does include horses. Greggii shares a horse with Joseph.

I gingerly nudge my horse over this hot, black rock, where we're treated to rare shapes of beautiful, hot, black rock. The whole time I hope we're looking at the last hot, black rock, only to discover that Joseph wants us to get our money's worth.

We find a tree that provides enough shade for a third of us to eat our sack lunch-es under it in comfort. We tie our horses to a post, which is silly because they're too tired to contemplate escape, and we're surrounded by hot, black rock.

To celebrate our survival, we go to a lodge-type resort and eat dinner at tables set on the grassy lawn in the shade of a mango grove. There are several large, three-sided hammocks tied to the trees that the serious adults try to relax on while we kids pretend they're trampolines.

Thomas asks Joseph about fresh fruit, and we make plans to go to an orange grove tomorrow where we can pick our own.

With time, we have developed a reliance on our water-maker, but it's showing signs of fatigue. I *thunk* the casing of the motor every now and then to get it going. While running it in Isabela, I smell the sweet stickyness of hot electricity. I let it cool for a couple of hours, and try again. Looking at the casing, I see blue flames dancing inside the vent holes. It's cooked.

The Galapagos Islands don't breed high expectations for getting things done, and Isabela is on the other-world side of the Galapagos. I ask Joseph if somebody here can fix it.

On our way to the orange grove, we stop at the guy's house whom nobody in the States wants for a neighbor. Luis (40). His inventory, prominently displayed in his yard, includes cook-tops and ovens, televisions and refrigerators, all several generations from today's models. He tells us to leave *Faith*'s water-maker motor with him and check on our way back from picking oranges.

I learn three things at the orange grove. Thomas, smarter than I, probably al-ready knows these things. First, oranges in many places are green; second, orange trees bear fruit far from the trunk and farther from the ground; and third, orange trees have thorns.

Thomas and I climb the trees and throw the fruit to (at) our waiting children. Here we are, providing for our families by climbing trees, bloodying ourselves, and throwing semi-solid objects at our kids, while our lovely wives are at the harbor, discussing Thomas's and my flaws.

Friendship is blossoming.

Returning to the harbor, we check on the water-maker motor. Luis says a diode burned up and the motor's winding needs re-winding. The diode is easy, but the copper for winding isn't on Isabela. If it's available on Santa Cruz—another Galapagos Island—he'll finish Tuesday. If it has to ship from Quito, on the mainland, it will be Thursday. I ask the cost and he says US$200.00. A new motor would cost more than twice that, plus shipping. In the United States, it's easy to throw away a good motor that needs fixing and get a new one. Nobody fixes stuff there, where parts-changers masquerade as craftsmen, and the economy is built on the speed products move from the import house to the landfill. Here, value is different.

I go to the jetty on Tuesday to check. Luis is waiting and helps load the motor into the dinghy. When he puts his tools in, I ask, "What are you doing?"

"I go. Make test on generator. Make good amperage," he says, showing me an ammeter from his tool pouch. "My work no good if generator not right."

We install the motor, he checks it, I pay him for his work, and we complete our circumnavigation with his fix.

We are exotic in Isabela. My daughters are exotic. Joseph, our tour guide, invites our twelve-year-old Amanda to a small gathering on a neighboring yacht. We let her go, telling her to radio when she wants to be picked up. An hour later, a man from a neighboring yacht comes to our boat to say that Amanda is trying to hail us. I don't know why, but all of our radios are turned off. When I get Amanda, she struggles to keep her tears from showing themselves to the people on this neighboring boat.

"What's so wrong with just being friends?" she asks when we get to *Faith*. Apparently Joseph told her that he has feelings for her more than just friends. He never touched her, but it scares Amanda into the knowledge that what looks like one thing is sometimes different.

Sure, Joseph is a worm. There are many worms in the world. But we still haven't found one of the *places where they don't value human life like we do.*

Faith needs fuel for the longest passage of our circumnavigation, but the fuel station has run out. The small tanker motors through high seas to make Friday's delivery. The sloshing fuel polishes the inside of the tanker to a brilliance unseen since it was launched. All the crud is pumped out with the fuel. We wait until Monday, hoping the crud settles somewhere else before taking the fuel on *Faith*. That isn't long enough, and we change our primary fuel filter four times during our passage.

While waiting for fuel, the night after *Smilla* departs, we cook on the barbeque on *Faith*'s aft deck. After dinner, I go to cover the grill. The sail locker—a big hatch in the deck—is open and I step into it, falling feet first about three feet. My forearm gets hung on a sharp, ¼" by 1½", end of a cotter pin that points upward on the backstay. I must lift my arm 1½" to get it off. Blood flies everywhere, just like in the movies. The boat looks like a crime scene or how it looks after cleaning a big fish, which I suppose is the same thing to the fish.

A neighbor takes me to the village where a Colombian-trained (good) doctor stitches me up. She's still in training, and before long I discover an area she needs more training is in knot-tying. The stitches come out two days after we leave, so I fix the wound with duct tape and gauze. However, the price is right, US$5.00 for the stitches and $3.00 for the antibiotic I must take for a week. To be fair, I probably should add a quarter for the duct tape.

The Big Passage

I'm one who reads the article in the Travel Section, usually in the paper in mid-June, which offers tips on how to survive the family road trip. The object is to provide kids enough distractions from the experience. Everybody knows the drill: games, snacks, license plates from different states contests. The list goes on, sometimes even mentioning personal electronics capable of disengaging the child from life altogether. These articles always amuse me in that they offer parents the tools to disengage from their children during these special times of family bonding.

The key on our road trips was to talk. I enjoyed driving slow on two-lane highways with barns, hand-painted signs, and livestock in a time when livestock lived and grazed in fields. Passing another barn, I'd remark, "Say, there's an interesting barn that would look nice if that one side was straightened and it had a new coat of paint." This gave the rest of my family an opportunity to roll their eyes, snicker among themselves, and mumble something under their breaths about, "... dad ... another dumb barn." It provided a rallying point from which a closer bond was forged.

We're now on *The Big One*, the longest passage we will make in our journey, three thousand miles as the frigate flies, more the way we go. We have a guessing game, the number of days we think this passage will take. In my losing optimism, I have 17 days; Lorrie, 18; Greggii, 19; Emily, 20; and Amanda guesses 21 days.

41

Now, with the crew showing snippets of boredom, I wish I wasn't so cynical about those great tips in the travel section; there are no barns, or hand-painted signs, or anything else to look at save a few dolphins, some birds, a night sky, a day sky, and a lot of water.

After several days of easy sailing in easy seas, the wind grows tired. The water calms. We sit. We swim a couple times, which is an experience a thousand miles from land, in water where depth is also measured in miles. We motor several days until concerns of needing the motor in the future overtake the frustration of so little progress in the present. We have food on board, and the water-maker works. The food I mentally inventory doesn't include the fish caught since leaving Isabela. It's not that I forget to count them, but of the five fish we hook, we land zero. We know some of the fish we don't catch are big from the song the reel sings.

We have three lures from Hampton, cedar plugs—hollow, cigar-shaped pieces of cedar with a lead weight on one end. The line runs through the hollow to a hook. After school in the first day of Greggii's boredom, I tell him to paint whatever he wants on them using his sisters' nail polish. He paints one of them red chrome, silver chrome, and blue chrome, in the manner you'd expect of six-year-old hands on a rocking boat. This is our all-time best fishing lure.

A good way to occupy Greggii's hands and mind is cleaning the tackle box. He likes doo-hickeys and gadgets more than most six-year-olds, and other than the sharp pointed objects in a tackle box that our Prevention Specialist, Lorrie, makes note of, a better collection of doo-hickeys and gadgets doesn't exist on *Faith*.

No wind and short on fuel. *Faith* drifts as fast as any coconut bobbing in the same water. Lorrie notes our heading—the direction the bow points—sometimes to Antarctica, sometimes to Alaska, occasionally to the Galapagos Islands we just left. The autopilot is turned off because it takes motion *through* the water for the rudder to work. We move *with* it, not through it and the heading doesn't matter. The water is going to the Marquesas, and we're stuck to the water.

Every day, the kids study until 2:00. Then Lorrie hosts a game of bingo for prizes, which for some odd reason, are souvenirs available only in the Galapagos.

I knew I lost the arrival bet the minute the wind died, and the longer it doesn't blow, the more Lorrie and Greggii see their hopes dashed. Then, after our forced period of patience in the Pacific, we register three, then five, then seven, then eight knots of wind. The boat again moves fast enough, three knots, to get steerage. The autopilot again keeps the bow pointed at the sunsets and our time to the Marquesas is halved.

Finally, a fish on board. Tuna. Big tuna. Not fish market big, but big for us. Maybe it's a forty-pound fish, but judging the weight of a fish without a scale is called guessing, or lying, like judging wave heights.

Black beans and rice with tuna.

The light breeze is ideal for our asymmetrical spinnaker, or gennaker, or cruising chute, or whatever real sailors call it this week. The only problem is that ours tears from top to bottom the first day we set it. I spend the next twenty-four hours of *Faith*'s drift sewing the seventy-foot seam back together by hand. When we raise it again, we discover my new-found talent doesn't exist. Within a half hour, it tears again, this time to be stowed to wait for professional repair.

Black beans and rice with tuna again; it's surprising how far a fish can feed a family.

After seventeen days at sea, Emily looks at her legs and says, "Aren't they disgusting?"

"No, not really," I reply, "Why?"

"Because I haven't shaved since we started this passage."

"Emily, there are a lot of interests that will keep you disgusted with yourself your whole life if you let them."

"What do you mean?"

"You know all of those commercials and magazine ads that look so nice with all those good looking people? The companies behind those ads will never sell anything that really makes you feel good about yourself. They want you to believe your legs are hairy, your breath stinks, your scalp is scaling off, your teeth are yellow, your eyes are the wrong color, and your hair is too grey. These are flaws they need you to believe about your personhood because their business is built on maintaining ugliness. If they ever provide a solution to God's creative mistakes, it'll put 'em out of business. They must disgust us with ourselves."

"You think funny, dad."

"Yeah, that's a problem I have."

While I make some adjustments to our mainsail, I hear something snap and see the cover of our mast mounted EPIRB—Electronic-Position-Indicating-Radio-Beacon—land on deck. The device itself is nowhere to be found. An EPIRB is a safety device that emits a signal to GPS satellites and back to a number of coast guard or rescue stations around the world. It's triggered when immersed in water. It transmits our position and a code referencing our ship, our crew, and an emergency phone number to call. After a couple of hours, wondering what to do, I use our satellite phone—one of our more ridiculous investments—to call the US Coast Guard.

"Yeah, uh, I was fiddling around with our sails a little while ago, and my EPIRB ended up falling overboard. I just didn't want you getting a signal and wondering what to do, and especially, I don't want you calling my brother." My brother Gary is the emergency contact on our EPIRB registration, and I don't want our loved ones at home thinking about what great people we all used to be when we aren't even having a problem.

"I understand. Can you give me your position?"

"Yeah, our position is nine degrees, sixteen point five-three minutes south, one hundred seven degrees, thirty-eight point two minutes west. Do you have a signal near here?"

"We're not currently receiving anything in the Pacific Ocean, but I'll make a note of it."

Reefing is a term applied to reducing the amount of sail area. We sail most of the passage with one reef, meaning that the lower five feet of the mainsail is tied to the boom. Two days before our landfall in the Marquesas, a squall dumps a bunch of rain on us. We don't see lightning as the squall approaches, but after several minutes of rain we see a flash. There aren't many things to fear at sea, but lightning is one of them. Then, another flash. And another. This is one odd electrical storm. The lightning is of uniform brightness and timing, and not accompanied by any of that annoying thunder to set your nerves further on edge. I look into the baggy, reefed part of the mainsail and there, in a puddle of rainwater, is the missing EPIRB with its strobe emitting the strange lightning.

Other items do fall overboard or break during our passage. The whisker pole, used to pole out the staysail, comes unhooked and disappears. One of our lifeline stanchions cracks, and one lifeline breaks at the terminal, requiring repair when we arrive in the Marquesas.

Our frustration turns to anticipation as we approach Ua Pou, then to excitement when we see *Smilla's* dinghy coming to greet us. Thomas is steering with one hand and waving a bottle of wine with the other; Helén is in the bow with both arms outstretched in a long-distance hug (14). We're practically in tears of joy and exhaustion when we set the anchor and are joined by their family and the family from *Willy Flippet* in celebration.

Amanda's twenty-one days wins our passage bet, and the *I Love Boobies* tee-shirt prize—another Galapagos souvenir.

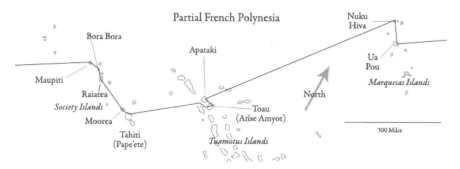

Partial French Polynesia

Nuku Hiva

Bora Bora

Apataki

Ua Pou

Maupiti

Marquesas Islands

Raiatea

North

Society Islands

Moorea

Toau
(Anse Amyot)

Tahiti
(Pape'ete)

Tuamotus Islands

300 Miles

Landfall in the Marquesas

Ua Pou is a postcard (64). Massive rock spires splashed with tropical green jut heavenward.

It's good to be on land at Hakahou, the village where we're anchored.

We have a guide scheduled with *Smilla* and *Willy Flippet*'s families, but he cancels because of the mud on the trail from recent rains. We hike without him.

Willy Flippet is home to a wonderful family from Seattle. Scott's a builder, Stacy a teacher. Their kids, Lauren and Clay, are great, with one exception. Every time we get to an anchorage where *Smilla* and *Willy Flippet* are, poor Greggii gets left out, as the girls, Lauren and Nadine find girl things to do without him. For today's hike, there are fourteen of us. We walk out of town and everybody soon tires of hearing the kids and me asking, "How much farther?" One of the responsible adults suggests we hitchhike. The first two vehicles stop and take us to the next village, Hakahetou.

There's a waterfall and we want to find it. I'm not sure *who* wants to find it, but that's the way with people not confident of their standing in a group of new friends, no dissenters.

All the Ua Pouans we meet assist in our quest, and tell us the waterfall is just down the road, never the five or six kilometers it actually is. Every time we know we've walked too far, someone walking the other direction tells us it's just down the road. One more person approaches to say it's that trail there, and presently we find the muddy trail to the waterfall.

Often, the return trip is shorter because expectations are more tuned to reality. Because we're tired, today's return is not shorter. When I try to remember the waterfall, I fail. The waterfall doesn't matter, but the time with these two families—that's important. Beginning in the Caribbean with Claudell, Sea-Cat, and the family on the catamaran, through Panama, to Joseph and his father in San Cristobal, and now with *Smilla* and *Willy Flippet,* we are learning that all the postcards of sunsets and landforms and waterfalls pale next to a fine relationship with other people. God's splendor is revealed in postcards; human beings reveal His image.

We devour sack lunches at a park on Hakahetou's waterfront. A woman about sixty years old approaches and asks if we want anything. We ask only for drinking water. She returns with three *pampelmousse*—giant grapefruits—banana sausages, and a tall bottle of ice water. Banana sausage is six or eight smushed bananas, dried together with sugar paste, and cased in plastic wrap, the consistency of a giant raisin.

The guide that cancelled earlier resides in Hakahetou and finds us here. He explains that this woman is the mayor.

He tells us the story of Ua Pou's spectacular rock spires. It happens that the champion rock spire, the largest on Ua Pou, was on neighboring Hiva Oa. The ruggedness of these spires comes from the battles, of course. After one of the spires on Ua Pou lost his brother, he got into a canoe and went to Hiva Oa to seek revenge. He cut down the largest spire on Hiva Oa and laid it in the water, and that's why a narrow point of land juts out of Hiva Oa. Then he cut off the head of one of the other spires, and it sits in a bay of Ua Pou as a little island.

Our almost-guide then says we should start back because there isn't much traffic to Hakahou, and the walk is long. After convincing him to call taxis and friends for a ride, we finally get the taxi to come from Hakahou. One group hitches a ride in the bed of a pickup-truck belonging to some Jehovah's Witnesses on their way to the Kingdom Hall, and the rest follow in the taxi.

Taiohae, on the island of Nuku Hiva, is our port of entry to French Polynesia. Not wishing to begin too soon on our ninety-day visas, we wait through the weekend and into the week thinking about clearing in. We walk past the Gendarmerie a couple of times so we'll know where it is when we do get around to it. Once we're officially in French Polynesia, duty-free fuel becomes available at half the cost otherwise.

After a week, we sail to Anaho Bay to sit surrounded by another postcard.

Amanda and Emily say something about manta rays as big as the dinghy.

Lorrie snorkels with Helén and Stacy to see these manta rays. While snorkeling, Helén starts shouting something in Swedish, "Haj, h-h-haj!" Neither Lorrie nor Stacy understand what she's saying so they keep snorkeling.

Later in the afternoon, Helén tells them she was hollering to warn them, but was too shaken to remember the English word for shark; it was three meters long.

We return to Taiohae Bay to get fuel and for Lorrie and I to celebrate our twentieth wedding anniversary at the Hotel Keikahaniue Nuku Hiva Pearl Lodge, a five-star resort on the mountainside overlooking Taiohae Bay. Lush, landscaped paths lead to bungalows. It's our first night on land in over eight months.

In the morning, we move to Daniel's Bay, the site of one of television's *Survivor* series. Daniel tells us how the show's producers purchased his house from him to move it to its present location so they could fabricate the perception of the show's wilderness where his house used to be. Within two hundred meters is a telephone booth, and less than three miles away is the resort where we spent our anniversary.

We depart in the morning for some of the best sailing we've had since leaving the dock in Hampton, Virginia. Some squalls miss us early, but offer a nice lift in the added breeze. Our passage takes us past the north shore of Takaroa, where the iron skeleton of *The County of Roxburgh* and several smaller shipwrecks litter the beach. Before GPS and auxiliary power, these atolls weren't even charted, except a note as something to watch for on the way to Tahiti—low, sandy rings of coral that can't be seen unless you're within six miles of them.

We have three fish on, but lose them all, and I retire Greggii's gnarly old hand-painted lure before we lose it. You can still see some paint, but it's a chewed up mess that I want as a memento. No fewer than twelve fish hit that plug; we landed three.

I radio Thomas on our approach to Apataki, and he tells me there are three boats in the anchorage: *Pacific Pearl*, Swedish; *Acapella*, Swedish; and *Smilla*, again Swedish. I think we should go somewhere else and let them claim Apataki for Sweden, but they invite us to join them, either because they like us, or because of the ice-cream in our freezer, a rare luxury on a yacht.

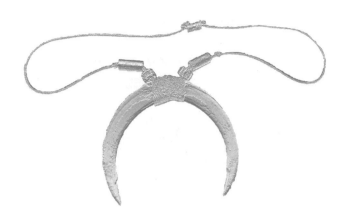

The Tuamotus Tango

Ciguatera is fish poisoning common to certain species of reef fish. The toxin is local enough to where the fish carrying it here aren't the same as the fish carrying it over there. The only way to know which fish are safe is to ask local fishermen.

Thomas speared a fish yesterday and asked three nearby fishermen—Coco, Raimaina, and Taihana—about it. They said not to eat it, but invited *Smilla*'s family to the beach for a fish barbecue. On our arrival, we join *Smilla*'s family and these fishermen for two types of turtle stew: one spicy and one mild, both good. The irony is our proximity in time to our *save the turtles* experiences of the Caribbean and the Galapagos. We now get a different taste of turtles, which, like most exotic foods, tastes like chicken.

The fishermen must take today's catch to the village, but will return tomorrow.

In the middle of the night, the wind shifts, and an uncomfortable anchorage ushers in the morning. We move, and hope our fishermen friends find us. Late in the day, we see a boat barreling toward us in two-foot waves with Raimana standing on the bow playing the ukulele. We join them on *Smilla,* where they teach Lucas, Thomas, and me Tahitian dance, and Helén and Amanda to play a few notes on the ukulele (12). Coco tells us of the famous Billabong Surf Competition on the beach of his village this Saturday, and invites us to watch him surf. After we return to *Faith,* our new friends find comfortable sleep in *Smilla*'s cockpit.

Thomas looks frazzled in the morning as we pile into Coco's runabout to go fishing. He woke up several times during the night, not used to people other than his own family sleeping in his cockpit.

While we are fishing, they let me carry a spear gun. I swim around trying to find something to shoot, but my heart isn't in it. When Coco's gun breaks, he takes mine and I sit on the bow of their boat to watch. A half hour later, when Thomas and Taihana are still in the water, a three-meter shark joins the hunt. Coco and Raimana urge Thomas back into the boat, and Taihana stands on top of the shallow coral-head to untie us.

With a mere fifty pounds of fish in the icebox, barely enough to cover the bottom, we go into the palm forest in search of the elusive coconut crab—a large-bodied land crab that dwells in the sandy floor beneath the palms. Coco catches one and we take it to *Smilla* for cooking. We each try a tiny bite. It's delicious and firm, and I wouldn't mind having a whole kettle of them if they weren't so tricky to catch.

Then, Coco and his brothers return to the village. We interfered with their livelihood; I'm sure they wish their ice box was full but this morning's catch is all they have. If the village relies solely on these guys, they'll be hungry.

We motor in the lagoon of Apataki. Eje—after several tries at his name he says to try saying *a-a* quickly—and Marita from the Swedish boat *Acapella* join us to tour the pearl farm, the most interesting part being the nurse sharks that live here and are fed by the pearl farmers. Two of the sharks come to the beach for petting in the ankle-deep water. Since the farm isn't seeding or harvesting pearls now, we don't see the operation, but they are carving shells for souvenirs. We purchase fish-hooks and other things carved out of oyster shells.

Oysters create pearls around an irritant, a piece of sand or a hunk of calcium. Seeding is when a farmer manually adds an irritant to the oyster so it will develop a pearl.

A lot of good things in life—indeed our current voyage—start with an irritant.

On Saturday, we move to make Coco's grand surf competition. The village of Niutahi is home to the big event, and our approach hints that Coco might have hyped it beyond reality. When we tie up, many children check us out. Then an old, dust-caked, beat-up, little white car with a loud radio screeches to a stop on the sandy road. Out jump Coco, Raimaina, and Taihana.

"Wow! You made it. It's good to see you."

Thomas says, "Yes, it is good to be here. What time is the surfing competition?"

Coco looks at Thomas and then at me, and says, "Oh, ha ha ha, that was yesterday. Did I tell you Saturday?"

"Yes. Oh well. The cleanup crew has done a nice job. Really. It looks like nothing happened. How did you surf?" says Thomas.

"Yes they did a good cleanup," says Coco. "I was second place. Since everybody is here, I want you to come to my house for a party."

We ride, some inside of and some on the hood and others on top of the car, to Coco's place, and visit his and every other family in the neighborhood. We eat and drink and dance well into the evening, bathed in loud music until the generator runs out of petrol.

We leave Apataki for our best experience of the Pacific. Planning to stay in Anse Amyot two days before continuing to Tahiti, we're charmed into two weeks.

Valentine is the matriarch of Anse Amyot; her husband, Gaston, is the only Frenchman—half French at that. The houses are painted white or not at all, constructed of wood, with tin roofs that *are* painted as protection from the salt air. Valentine's nephews, Jean-Paul and Mana, live next door near the boat house. Grandpa and Valentine's ex-in-laws live on the other side of Valentine's house, toward the lagoon. Behind is the copra shed, and between Valentine's house and the boat house is a solar-powered telephone booth that was installed just last month. The smells of fresh and less-than-fresh fish blend with the copra and the sea air, which become more pleasing when Valentine bakes coconut bread in the coconut-husk-fired oven.

During dinner at Valentine's, she tells us we *just can't* leave until her daughter, Davina, has a chance to meet Emily, Amanda, and Nicóle. A number of cruisers call on Anse Amyot, rarely with families and rarer still with girls near Davina's age. Davina studies on Fakarava, thirty-five miles away and comes home on weekends. In waiting, our daughters are richly rewarded with a friendship for life. Davina teaches them how to do Tamurri dance and how to weave roof panels, headbands, skirts, and smaller trinkets from palm fronds. Valentine shows us a poster she has of the French nuclear testing in the Tuamotus—a poster of a mushroom cloud framed by ocean and atolls. She poorly masks her anger and tears as she displays the photo. All powers need an over-there to test stuff on. Washington has New Mexico, and just as folks in New Mexico don't much care for being Washington's over-there, folks in the Tuamotus don't like being France's over-there.

One day, a dozen cruisers come to dinner. Amanda and Emily feel almost like family when they're asked to help Davina and Valentine prepare for it. Twelve is too many people for such short notice, but cruisers do everything on short notice.

Gaston shows us his copra shed (63). *Copra*—the dried white flesh of coconuts—is a mainstay of rural Polynesia. The roof rolls on rails to cover the copra when rain threatens. As an incentive to maintain rural populations, the government pays higher than the world price of copra. Pape'ete, on Tahiti is a big city with big-city problems. Inflated copra prices are presumed to slow Pape'ete's population growth and troubles.

After *Smilla* leaves for Tahiti, Valentine and Gaston invite us to their *motu*—island—in the lagoon of the atoll. We clear dead palm fronds and build a large fire. Some of us snorkel and spear-fish the perimeter of the motu for the protein of our lunch. We see the two-meter reef sharks, generally harmless but... Amanda, Greggii, and I watch from shore. Emily joins the hunters and they see a tiger shark, in addition to the less threatening reef sharks.

Greggii plays with a pet wild bird Davina rescued (15). Napoleon is a large grouper that Valentine calls to the surface by slapping her sandal on the water so we can pet him. Davina's pet chicken, Leonardo, also made the trip from Anse Amyot to here. This family lives in oneness with the creatures and creation around them.

After fishing, Gaston cooks the fish on a piece of chicken wire he lays over the fire. We feast on grilled fish, fish salad or *poisson cru*—Tahiti's national dish—coconut bread from Valentine's special oven, rice, and potatoes all served on big leaves from a nearby shrub.

Our return to Anse Amyot is a wet ride through three-foot waves that kicked up during dinner. I have the honor of holding Leonardo for the trip.

Valentine asks us to dinner again at Anse Amyot. We're treated to fish, chicken (not Leonardo), salads, wine, and a coconut birthday cake for Emily. I search *Faith* for a gift for Gaston and Valentine, and find some stainless nails and other stainless hardware Gaston can use to maintain his docks and traps. He leaves for a half-hour after receiving the hardware and even Valentine begins to wonder where he went. When he returns, he ties a boar's tooth necklace on my neck that he just now made from game he killed. We acquire some souvenirs on our trip but for me, this is the best (page 48).

Valentine gives Emily and Amanda each a single-black-pearl necklace. We give them *Faith*'s small Christmas tree with lights and decorations. They earlier asked about our holiday celebrations on *Faith* and told us they never had a Christmas tree. Dinner masks melancholy as we prepare to depart for Tahiti in the morning.

Pape'ete: South Pacific City

Depending on where the city limits are when you ask, Pape'ete has between 100,000 and 120,000 people, more than half of the island of Tahiti's population. Pape'ete is the capital of French Polynesia, with the amenities and headaches of city life. We stop for the amenities.

Several things need to be addressed while we're here. Sail repair heads the list. We must also finalize our entry to French Polynesia by posting bonds.

Once we feel sufficiently tardy with the formalities, Greggii and I go to the bank and ask for two bonds for the adults on our boat. The paperwork fee is 2,300 Polynesian francs, and the bonds cost 89,000 francs, roughly US$890.00, each. I put it on our credit card to be refunded when we leave. The purpose of the bond is if we create too much of a nuisance of ourselves, they can buy a plane ticket for us to go bother someone else.

Another boat later tells us they were required to put a bond on four of the five people on their boat when they, just like *Faith,* had only two adults. We were lucky.

Then we go to immigration, where a laid-back official has me fill out some forms. When I get to *date of arrival,* I tell him we arrived two weeks ago and ask him what I should put down. He tells me to use last Friday's date, 2 July.

The sail maker comes to the fuel dock to take *Faith's* sails for repair. He needs them in his shop before he can give us a price. Having never done this, I'm not sure what fair is, but his price is in line with everywhere we subsequently have repairs made.

After a week in Pape'ete, without warning, the anchorage turns into bumper boats. The wind starts blowing from the only direction that offers no protection: the southwest.

Emily wakes first, looks out her port light, and in the blur of almost-awake, thinks a dinghy is bumping us. The rest of us feel the bumping while still pretending sleep. Our comfortable slumber turns to a wide-awake nightmare; *Faith* is tangled with *Faiz III*, who's on our port bow, sliding aft and trying to maneuver under power. The wind screams through the rigging of both boats and foamy brine mixes with the rain, cutting our visibility to near-zero. Briefly, our dinghy acts as a fender, protecting our aft port side. *Faiz III* slides past our stern and ends up with its bow crashing into our starboard toe rail. I feel its anchor chain on our rudder. They cut it to free us from each other.

Once we are free, our anchor fails, and we slide sideways, as does a catamaran that anchored next to us yesterday. The catamaran ends up on a reef where a red channel marker stands, and we ground hard on the reef next to it with *Faith*'s starboard rail hitting them. They let out more anchor rope to clear us. We take a queasy ride over the reef, bouncing and moving slightly as each wave lifts *Faith* enough to move a couple of inches, at what one observer later says, is a thirty-degree heel. Once free of the reef, we end up bow to the wind with our stern again approaching the catamaran. Both of our anchors hook on the far side of the reef. I power *Faith* to stay away from them, and cut their rope instead. They blow in to a nearby marina and tie off.

The wind started at 2:30 AM. We're still hooked to the reef eight hours later, as the wind diminishes from recorded seventy-four knot gusts to thirty-five knots and shifts enough for protection from the waves. The skies still menace. Greggii's Walker Bay, a nice sailing dinghy, is gone.

Thomas comes with his dive gear, unshackles our chain from the anchor, and guides our chain through the coral as we bring it in. Then we motor around the reef, and drop our chain so he can reattach the anchor.

The skipper of *Faiz III* says we can discuss the situation later, indicating he thinks we should pay for their damage. Feeling enough worries, I set that one aside for now.

The red concrete channel marker is visible on the bottom. I look for red paint on *Faith* and find none. Someone else must have knocked it over.

Thomas helps us reanchor away from other boats. He again dives to look at our hull and reports no structural damage, only deep scratches forward of and on the keel itself.

During the morning radio chat, I ask about Greggii's missing Walker Bay. One of the mega-yachts at the marina says it's on their swim platform. Greggii and I retrieve it.

I stay on *Faith* for the next couple of days. I'd like to go to shore, but with the wind still gusting, I don't feel good about leaving.

Worried about *Faith's* hull, I ask a yacht builder about our damage. He tells me *osmosis*—damage to fiberglass from exposure to salt water—is a slow process and we can haul out and repair it at our convenience instead of rushing it—one less worry for now.

Nobody's hurt, but we all feel the nausea of an adrenaline hangover. Lorrie says she can't go on like this. We have only two options: to continue or quit. I try to be supportive of her, and after devotions, I tell the kids we've failed. Somehow, either God let us down, or we didn't quite hear right about this being His plan for our lives.

This makes Lorrie mad. "You need to talk to me first."

"I thought we did talk, and you said you can't go on like this."

This ushers in another unhealthy bout of venting on each other, causing us to feel like crap. The time it takes for the bad feeling to go away is directly related to the pride we possess at the moment.

The kids don't like it when we argue. I'm not convinced we argue any more than we ever did, but our arguments are now fueled by stresses of a new life on a small island named *Faith,* where we can't hide them as well. Lorrie and I love each other and always have; we tell the kids the time to worry is when we quit arguing.

As seems the case when bad things happen, worries diminish with time. Although the discomforts continue, we have a better feel for tomorrow. Lorrie and I again work together to forge ahead.

Greggii and I meet a man at the marina who's welding some parts for *Faith:* the brass rub rail, the grill top (which is smashed), and a couple stanchions. As we come out of the marina in the dinghy, we see *Faiz III* retrieving their anchor. I know we must face them sooner or later, and they look as if they can use an extra set of hands, so we stop. After we help them reanchor, *Faiz III's* skipper takes off his hat, wipes his brow and says, "How about you just fix yours and I fix mine." That, to me, always was the best solution.

During the week, the weather and our attitude grow better. Thirteen miles away, the peak of Moorea beckons. The sun rises over Tahiti and burns off more and more stress.

The more I dwell on *Faith's* repairs, the smaller the problem grows.

We go to church in Pape'ete. The women are clad in white dresses, wearing broad-brimmed, white straw hats decorated with big flowers, peacock feathers, stars, foil-paper, and pipe cleaners (65). Church lasts two hours and a half, with five baptisms, a half-hour of announcements, and Communion. It's in French, so we don't follow too well, but the singing makes it all worthwhile. A song starts with an old woman sitting somewhere in the congregation, wailing a sound like fingernails on a chalkboard before being joined by other men and women scattered throughout the congregation in beautiful harmony. Then, a wail from a different location and another song begins.

There's another depression coming—meteorologically speaking—and I don't want to go too far in case conditions change. Our plan for the morning is to go to the fuel dock to receive our sails. It rains all night. We raise all three anchors and head toward the fuel dock. The sail maker arrives with two of the five sails. The man working on them missed two items on the work order and the spinnaker sewing machine broke last night.

The wind builds, so we berth at the marina. I spend the afternoon installing the mainsail in thirty knots of wind. At noon, the *yankee* and *genoa*—both headsails of different cuts—are delivered, and in the evening, the spinnaker arrives. It's good to have the sails on board, the welding done, and the tanks full. When the weather breaks, we can leave.

The wind eases through the night. I sleep light and wake at 5:30, then again at 6:30, and finally by 7:30, it's calm in the marina. Calm enough to finish installing the sails.

After tending to most of the stuff on the predeparture checklist, I go to immigration, Customs, and the port captain for departure clearance.

Polynésie française, au revoir

Moorea (66), again a postcard, is a break after Tahiti, where from the time we landed until we departed, we worked. The storm cast more work on us. The cost of nearly everything was understandably high, given Tahiti's location, but everything *was* available from spare parts for *Faith* to fresh produce and meats.

Arriving in Moorea, we talk to other cruisers to find out what to do here. The consensus is: not much. We're in the dinghy, making the rounds of friends, and learn we can dinghy to the beach of the Club Med and swim with stingrays. We call them *rays*.

Bastille season continues, and in celebration, there's a popular race of traditional canoes with outriggers that started in Pape'ete at 6:00 this morning to paddle around Moorea and back, thirty-some miles in all. We see the race passing about a mile outside the reef. The kids and I dinghy past the last of the channel markers and out to sea to watch the race.

Greggii gets scared and upset and moves near me. I ask, "Why are you so upset?"

"This isn't where the rays are; they're over there," he replies, pointing to the Club Med. Emily, Amanda, and I came to see the race; Greggii, the rays.

We board another boat to motor to the oldest Christian church in French Polynesia. The singing is fantastic with the whole congregation, smaller than in Pape'ete, building on the lead in perfect harmony. There's no keyboard, and when they are not singing a cappella, the accompaniment is ukuleles and guitars.

Later, Emily, Greggii, and Lorrie swim with the rays while Amanda and Nicóle spend the afternoon wakeboarding. We unwind and enjoy ourselves again.

In friendships, I have an irrational ability to turn minor misunderstandings into doubts and paranoia about the friendship. One perceived insult occurs when Greggii radios *Smilla* and gets Nicóle. In midsentence, Greggii is cut off and hears nothing more. Thomas calls later and says that Nadine can't play until after breakfast. He shut off the radio in the middle of their conversation because he was busy on something else. That's it, and with no rhyme or reason, I take it badly. We know that sometime we must say goodbye to *Smilla's* gang, but it hurts to think that time might come sooner than necessary.

Later, Lorrie and I join Thomas and Helén for dinner, and I realize I am wrong about these perceptions of a crumbling friendship.

Thomas says this anchorage had six boats in it last week. It now has twenty with more on the way. We contemplate moving and plan on Raiatea. When Emily and Amanda hear Lorrie and I discuss hauling out to repair our keel, they get excited. "Nicóle's hauling out, and they're going to a motel, and we can have slumber parties and..."

I say, "Don't get too excited yet. We're only tossing the idea around."

Raiatea is a hundred miles away, meaning there aren't enough daylight hours in one day to get there. The object is to get *Faith* out of Moorea's reef before sunset, and through the reefs surrounding Raiatea after dawn.

Once we have a better look at the old tractor and trailer with which the small shipyard uses to haul boats, the urgency of *Faith's* repairs diminishes.

Scott and Stacy do haul *Willy Flippet* to paint *antifoul*—hull paint required periodically to minimize the attachment of critters and algae below the waterline. During their first night out of the water, Helén, Thomas, Lorrie, and I put on our masks, snorkels, and fins, and bang on the hull, just below Scott and Stacy's cabin, and holler that their anchor's dragging and they're on the reef and we're in the water to take their anchor for them to make sure it's set good. They tell us they have things under control, and we should go back to our own boats.

"I would need to stick my head in the mouth of a crocodile to get on US TV now," says Antoine of *Banana Split*, who is docked next to us in Raiatea. Antoine was a seventy's pop icon in France. He quit that life and has since been sailing and making films. He tells me he just completed his fifteenth travel documentary, this time on Madagascar. These documentaries used to be aired in the US when travel programming was about places and the people in those places rather than on the thrill-seeking lifestyles of the travellers.

Willy *Flippet* is stuck in the shipyard until the marina's tractor is fixed. A part broke and must be shipped to Pape'ete for repairs. The marina says it will be working later in the week, confirming our hunch about hauling here.

We spend the day before leaving for Bora-Bora tied to the city dock on the northeast side of Raiatea. We're here because of the 14 July Parade in the main streets of Village Atitautu. It's an event for locals, like a festival parade on any small town street in America, with floats towed by tractors and trucks, children in costume, dancing, and candy.

Smilla and *Faith* sail to Bora-Bora together; it's almost a race, and *Faith* is ahead as we pass the first marker into Bora-Bora's lagoon. When I look back, I see *Smilla* turning away. I get them on the radio, and they say they saw a whale near their boat and want to get another look. Then, they follow us into the pass. We grab the last two moorings in front of Bloody Mary's Restaurant.

We celebrate Amanda's thirteenth birthday with *Smilla*'s family at Bloody Mary's, a fixture on Bora-Bora for the sand floors, the bamboo interior, the raw fish laid out on the display table, and the chef manning the grill to cook your selection to order. If this isn't enough, there's also a list of famous names prominently displayed on the sign suggesting *if it's good enough for them…*

After exploring Bora Bora for a day, we move to Maupiti.

A physician looks at some sores on Amanda and Greggii. In the Pacific, probably in all tropical oceans, sores don't heal well. The doctor gives us some non-stinging stuff that looks like the stinging Merthiolate my mom tortured us with when we sprung a leak, neon-pink skin stains and all. This stuff works wonders through the rest of our voyage. The best part is we're in not-America, where access to health care is a human right rather than a protected industry and status symbol. We're given the stuff free.

Maupiti has a road around the perimeter, and we rent bikes with *Smilla* to travel it (13). We bid French Polynesia *au revoir* in the morning by crashing into the oncoming surf in the shallow pass. We aim our boats toward that point on the horizon where the sun sets, and trim the sails.

Sailing into Tomorrow

Aside from the blahs of the first few days, the passage starts well. The sun shines for added bonus. We lose a fish, a lure, and all of the line on the reel to something that splashes only once. I almost lose the rod when the rod holder breaks while I'm fiddling with the reel. It about yanks me over the top of the dinghy we keep suspended on *Faith's* transom during passage.

We go to Tonga instead of stopping at any of the atolls along the way. Feeling crummy for the first days of every passage makes us rethink how many passages we want to start.

After we pass Palmerston Atoll, Emily takes a call on the radio and hands the microphone to me. "Hello, this is the sailing vessel two miles northwest of Palmerston. Who's calling please?"

"My name is Simon. I live on the atoll, and want to know if you are to stop here."

"We are going to Tonga. It looks very rough with many breakers in your anchorage."

"Ok, I just want to say hi. If you like, I will help you anchor. I'm just checking."

Lorrie is touched. She just finished reading about Palmerston, and wonders if we made the right choice. Looking at the breakers in the anchorage, I know we did.

During the comfortable numbness of a late-night watch, the weather turns. The wind rapidly shifts from eight knots out of the north to thirty knots out of the south. The world acquires clarity when this happens. After trimming the sails for the new breeze, we sail at nine knots for the next seven hours, with *Faith* pointing toward Vava'u.

Several hours after sunrise, land emerges, and I look forward to the lee of the island, where the seas lie down.

Once in the lee, we use the motor and headsail to calmly motor toward the village of Neiafu. There's something in the water, a change in the wave pattern or an eddying wind a quarter-mile away. Then they surface. I holler, "Whales! Come up here and look at this!" Three humpback whales, nearly the size of *Faith*, cross our bow and surface within a boat length, then wave their tails and disappear.

A look at any map or globe with lines of longitude will show the International Date Line with an odd characteristic: the line jogs to put Tonga's time zone first in the day rather than last, where the islands' physical location would have them otherwise. By sailing into Tonga, we've sailed into tomorrow.

We try more than once to tame *Faith* at the Customs dock in Neiafu. A swell is entering the bay, and the government dock is taking the brunt of it. We manage, though, and the officials board *Faith* for a look.

The Moorings charter boat company has operations in Tonga, and theirs are the best moorings for us. We radio for an assignment after clearing Customs and Immigration. As soon as we tie ourselves to the mooring ball, before getting comfortable, Chris kayaks over for a visit. He and his brother Nick sailed to Tonga with their parents, who are filming a documentary about the whales. They've been in Tonga for over a year. Another Chris and his sister Amanda, who also sailed here, come to visit. They've been here for several months with their parents.

There are many cruising kids in Neiafu. Among them are teenage boys, a new experience for Emily and Amanda and their mother and me since moving onto *Faith*.

We go to a charity beauty pageant one night. We don't go out of charity, that's just how it's billed. *The Miss Cosmos Pageant*. I wouldn't normally go to a beauty pageant, but this pageant is different, too otherworldly to turn down. It's a beauty pageant for fakaleiti.

Fakaleiti is part of Polynesian culture. The last child, especially in families of all boys, may be raised a girl. Sometimes fakaleiti are considered a *third gender*, often, but not always, homosexual. All I know is that *The Miss Cosmos Pageant* is first rate entertainment that we wouldn't find ourselves watching in the United States—you just don't take your family to something like this there. Here, it's good entertainment for Thomas and Helén and their children, and Lorrie and me and ours, and a number of families from Nieafu.

Intermittent showers occur every day during our first two weeks in Vava'u. It finally clears enough to cruise the Vava'u group of islands. We tour the islands for six days before returning to Nieafu.

The Neiafu Agriculture and Industry Show is hosting the king of Tonga. He hasn't visited Vava'u in several years. It isn't much different from a county fair at home, except there isn't a midway and a bunch of rides—just produce, livestock, marine products and several booths loaded with crafts and carvings, and the King. The locals are entertained when I ask a vendor about the urchins on display. "Just break it open and eat the eggs," is what I understand them to say. Judging by the amusement of those nearby, I misunderstand. It tastes like the swampy salty smell of low tide at a concrete pier when all the creatures are exposed. Maybe it's an acquired taste and I haven't eaten enough.

The king has a flashy motorcade led by a police car with the lights blinking, then a new SUV followed by a great big Ford van that he rides in. Nobody looks us over on our way into the fairgrounds, which is the soccer field of the high school. Nobody looks us over as we wander toward the tent where the king is sitting, or when we find seats in the grass less than a hundred feet away from him. Next to us is a policeman who does nothing except watch the King and the other speakers. I think about security at home, and how unnatural it is when the more security there is around, the more we fear what will happen without it, so we demand more security to protect us from our imagined fears in an emotional spiral.

Faith sits at The Moorings' mooring with her crew waiting for the right time to go swimming with the whales. Emily and Amanda spend a lot of time with Nicóle at Ana's Cafe, a little restaurant on the water. They make friends with the staff and spend afternoons there, cutting potatoes for French fries. They go for Karaoke nights and entertain themselves as best they can.

Thomas and Helén stop over to discuss plans for Fiji, and we agree to sail together to Savusavu on the island of Vanua Levu.

Before swimming with the whales, we check out of Tonga Customs and immigration, only to be told we must leave the kingdom immediately—most places allow up to twenty-four hours afterward. We anchor out of sight of the government offices and arrange for a whale-watch boat to pick us up here. Thomas and Helén can't go because, an hour before we embark on the watch, Thomas hears from *Pacific Pearl*, another boat from Sweden, that they're twenty miles out of Vava'u and have lost steering. Thomas and Helén offer to tow them into the anchorage and want to be available to help if they need it.

When we board the whale-watch boat, there's a man who's the pilot, a young Tongan woman who's the guide, and a young American woman with a video camera to document the experience on DVD in the event we want to purchase one at the end of the trip. Also onboard is a group of three Americans for their own whale-watching experience: a mother, her thirty-something son, and a friend of theirs. They're from San Diego.

Nicóle, Lucas, and Nadine go with us. The pilot takes us into open water where we see five adult whales lazing about, surfacing, then diving for several minutes, then surfacing again. While we're all ready to pee our pants with adrenaline, the guide runs through the safety precautions: if they breach, get out of the water, don't go any closer than the guide, and do not swim over the top of them. She then takes three of us at a time, in masks, snorkels, and fins, into the water to swim to a comfortable observation point.

Greggii, Lucas, and I go first. I hold Greggii as we swim to these twenty-meter animals lying motionless in the depths, shadows of greyer blue against an aqua background flickering with bolts of sunlight honed by the gentle roll above. Then slowly, almost imperceptibly at first, one whale builds effortless momentum to float to the surface and spout like Old Faithful to drink the air in a loud, hollow sucking noise, then peacefully descends after the violence of breathing, while another one or two follow the same ritual in a well-choreographed dance of life (53).

We rotate quickly through our first turns to make sure everybody gets to swim with them. Once everybody has had a chance, Lorrie, Greggii, and I swim out. Lorrie and Greggii tire and return to the boat to let Nicóle, Emily, and Amanda join me. We watch as one descends while a more distant whale rises; our vantage is such that they form a huge X as they pass each other.

Few events cause my world to freeze, but the underwater silence broken only by my breathing, while watching these magnificent shadows dance, is one such event.

Soon and suddenly, while the San Diego folks are in the water, one whale breaches. He comes out of the water at least half his length. That ends our swimming because the guides get nervous about one landing on a customer. Maybe that's why they make us prepay.

The young man from San Diego was the closest of anyone when that whale breached, and once he is back on the whale-watch boat, he sums up the feelings of all of us: "Ma! Did you see that? Did you see that, Ma? Wow! I've never seen anything like that in my life! Did you see that, Ma?" This is about all he is good for until our drop-off at *Faith*.

We leave Tonga with *Smilla* and sail within sight of each other for this five-hundred mile passage. Our departure witnesses another pod of whales, including calves, breaching. All we think about is the moments we shared their space.

On Passage with Friends

A major factor of boat speed is the length of the hull at the waterline. *Faith* is longer than *Smilla*, so we are the faster boat. That means we must slow *Faith* down to stay together. On passage, we do many things, but trimming the sails to slow down is new.

For entertainment, we perform a radio show for *Smilla*. Real sailors talk about proper radio protocol; to hail another boat, you say that boat's name three times, and then give your own as the hailing vessel—something like, "*Smilla, Smilla, Smilla,* [this is] *Faith,*" rarely saying *this is*. At some anchorages where there are many boats, conversations happen, and a lot of airwave molecules are killed with such issues as whether everybody can hear each other or not. Call it a silly ritual of bored boats at anchor. Another curious element of these conversations is that they are gender specific; just think of who dominates the phone in most households. A relay is a third boat that connects two boats out of range of each other.

During our passage, when no other boats are within range, we perform on channel sixteen, normally reserved for hailing and emergency use. The cast is five different boats, giving each of us our own part: *Breaking Wind, Relief, Silent Passage, Squeeze,* and *Fresh Air,* trying to establish radio contact with each other. Our show goes like this:

Breaking Wind, Breaking Wind, Breaking Wind—Silent Passage.

Silent Passage, we are *Breaking Wind.* We're looking for *Fresh Air....* *Fresh Air, Fresh Air, Fresh Air,* we are *Breaking Wind.*

Breaking Wind, Squeeze. Fresh Air is trying to reach you. I'll relay if you'd like.

Squeeze, Squeeze, Squeeze ...Silent Passage. Breaking Wind is coming through a little scratchy, but I know they're looking for *Fresh Air* and *Relief.*

Relief here. I heard *Breaking Wind* was scratchy.

Relief, Silent Passage. But I thought I heard *Breaking Wind* coming through with *Squeeze.*

Silent Passage, Breaking Wind, can you hear me?

Breaking Wind, loud and clear. How about *Relief* and *Fresh Air*?

Breaking Wind is getting through to *Fresh Air* now.

Breaking Wind is getting *Relief.*

Smilla pretends to enjoy our performance.

Three hours later, we enter the eastern hemisphere.

We reel in a big mahi-mahi, five feet long and fifty pounds or so, but don't land him. After we get him close enough for these guesstimates, he sees us and decides to stay where he is. He takes off on a 300-yard run and breaks off that much line with our favorite plug.

We enter the reefs surrounding Fiji at dawn, but it takes until afternoon to reach Savusavu. A huge piece of ocean makes up Fiji and it includes hundreds of islands.

A Tearful Goodbye

Bula. Say boolah. Fijian for hello. It's the best greeting we've heard yet. It's cool to walk down the street with people saying bula to you, and to return a bula to them; better than hola, bon jour, malo, even hello. Bula.

Savusavu is a city with a downtown about 400 meters long and a bunch of shops with loud music pouring out of them. The shopkeepers and the music are mostly Indian, the music occasionally punctuated with pop or hip-hop.

Greggii makes himself known here. Lorrie and I go for lunch at the Copra Shed Marina restaurant, and the staff asks where Greggii is. People always grab him and hug him, and if he isn't with us, they ask where he is.

This happened in Tonga too. I'd go to the market, and the woman at the back stall would ask where Greggii was. One time she asked me to tell him his order would be there on Saturday, when we never knew about his ordering anything. This woman said the stuff would be ready, and that it was going to cost T$7.00, the exact amount Greggii was due in allowance. When Saturday rolled around, Greggii and Lorrie went to the market for some last-minute things, and when they got home, Lorrie was a little upset with Greggii because she didn't know he had stuff on order from this woman. Then, she was a little upset with me because I did know. Greggii came home with a war club and a god of love carving, which looks just like the god of the sea and all the other gods—a nice haul for a six year old with seven Tongan dollars in his pocket.

On Sunday, we go to the Methodist church. We don't understand anything except what little they say in English for our benefit. What impresses me most is the church bell. Every church we've been to since leaving home has had regular bells. Bing-Bong, Bing-Bong, Bing-Bong. After we sit down in this church, which we think starts at 10:00 but in fact starts at 10:30, we hear a loud *Thunk...Tink-Tink...........Thunk...Tink-Tink...........Thunk...Tink-Tink*. We go outside to a little gazebo where a woman swings a club against a big old hollowed-out block of wood, emitting a loud, pleasant *Thunk...Tink-Tink* (67).

During our friendship with *Smilla*, we knew this time would come. We agree that *see you later* is better than *goodbye*, and that seems to help. Their plan is to leave *Smilla* in Fiji for the cyclone season, ours is to make Australia. They will return to Sweden for several months.

On our last night together, we go to dinner, where we try to discuss our own relationship to Christ with them. Helén has joined us for church several times; not that we've been going a lot, but when we have gone, she's joined us. She tells us Thomas has hard feelings toward religion of any sort, Christianity in particular.

Thomas doesn't let us get too far before he makes it known we are offending him. We want to present them with a Bible, but Thomas refuses to have one on *Smilla*, or even to accept it to ease the umbrella of discomfort we opened. Thomas says, "That *book* is responsible for more bloodshed than anything else in the world. *Ever*."

Long after Fiji, and after hashing it around in the air of different cultures, I begin to understand Thomas's view.

Too often, the Bible is used to justify actions toward others rather than to guide individual lives. Jesus' teachings are personal. If He wanted to, He could have addressed those Big Bad Romans, or justified a Jewish empire based on the evil in Samaria or Egypt or anywhere else, but He didn't. Nowhere did He advocate political involvement.

He speaks to me personally, about my life, my sins, and my relationship with Him. And He speaks to you personally about the same in your life. The only time the Bible instructs me to worry about your sins instead of your salvation, and you to worry about mine, is when those sins interfere with building His Church.

Thomas knows that whole nations, powerful nations, my nation, two millennia after Jesus taught, are using His name to build empires that bow to new Baals with innocuous names like *The Economy*, *Globalization*, and *Free Trade*.

God is 100% in charge of salvation. But I wonder if the profit gained by those contracted to wipe out evil in intentionally misrepresented worlds, with the noisy evangelical support that accompanies it, hasn't condemned millions of people like Thomas to blindness toward God's love and grace, and interfered with the building of His Church. Simply put, Thomas sees the United States' heavy-handed approach to foreign policy as Christianity in practice and, from that perspective, doesn't want much to do with Christ.

Thomas and Helén give us a DVD of photos of our time together and say not to open it until we get to our first anchorage. We return to *Faith* with both the DVD and the Bible.

We planned to be underway by 10:00 AM, but *Faith* won't start. Our cranking battery is dead. I try jumping from the house batteries, but those are useless for cranking. Then I try jumping from the generator battery, which doesn't work either. Finally, after we monkey-around with our portable charger hooked to the generator, the engine starts.

We sail out of Savusavu to Koro Island, in the middle of the Koro Sea, about a third of the way toward Fiji's main island of Viti Levu. We stop for the night without going to shore.

When we open the DVD of photos of our time together that Thomas and Helén gave us, a note tells us they don't understand how friends can talk about religion, casting further uneasiness on our first day apart.

We all feel something right now, but can't figure out what. Sure, we're sad, because that's the way with goodbyes, but it's more than that. A flood of emotions engulfs us as we recall the past nine months, from that first baseball game at the Panama Canal Yacht Club. God laid in our path this family, these friends who coached us into this life and stood by us when we were ready to hang it up. The bond we've groomed, and that they've groomed with no less effort, bears a bountiful harvest in a friendship we will cherish forever.

In the morning, we leave for Makongai. Fifteen old buildings and the foundations of a once large village surround the anchorage. The leper colony and hospital used to be here, but the concrete stairs are all that remains. A quarter mile away, following a path cleared in the jungle on what used to be the village's main road, there's a graveyard with a hundred graves marked by concrete crosses and European names. Kara, a Fijian who lives here with her husband and baby, tells us all these people worked at the leper colony. Kara and her husband work in the turtle and giant clam sanctuary that has taken its place in the abandoned buildings.

In Savusavu, we learned of the kava ceremony from a British expatriate who had lived on his own boat there for several years. Kava is the root of a pepper tree, and it plays large in Melanesian culture. We left the Polynesians in our wake at Tonga and are now in a part of the world populated by Melanesians and Indians. This latter group was imported as slaves to work the cane fields in colonial Fiji.

We learn to carry kava on board, a collection of woody roots that bundles easily in a page of newspaper, so that when we get to a new anchorage, we can go to the village chief and present this bundle while asking permission to anchor. It's all cloaked in ceremony, most of which we probably get wrong, but people everywhere seem to appreciate an honest attempt.

Following Makongai, we anchor in the lee of a small island, and with our kava in hand, we dinghy to shore and ask for the chief. Since he's away, we're escorted to a substitute chief. We present our kava to the substitute chief's assistant, who looks it over and hands it to the substitute chief. After inspecting it, he nods to the assistant, who in turn gives us permission to anchor and invites us back for the kava ceremony at 7:00 PM.

The kava ceremony includes all the men in the village and us. The kava is ground with a large mortar and pestle, and placed in something like an oversized sock as a filter. Then, over a large bowl, water is poured through it. After that, the sock is tied on the end to simulate a large tea bag, and stirred around in the bowl to get all the good stuff out.

Then, half a coconut shell is filled with a ladleful of this concoction and drunk by the most important guy in the room, the substitute chief. There are twelve men, plus our family, and this filling and drinking goes around several times with the guy managing the kava bowl asking, "High tide or low tide?" with every cup. It tastes like mud and has a slightly narcotic effect, but we don't get much more than a good night's sleep from it.

In the morning, we motor-sail to the town of Levuka on the island of Ovalau, Fiji's oldest colonial era settlement as well as the colonial capital.

We spend the next several days moving and the nights at anchor, as we move west along the north shore of Viti Levu, Fiji's main island.

Our last stop on Viti Levu is Lautoka, where we anchor near the port terminal and clear out at Fiji's Customs and immigration. We walk into town to run errands and stay long enough for the tide to come in. Our dinghy is tied to the main pier, where semi-trucks load on or off the cargo vessels and where cars ferry officials, dock-workers, and crew to and from the city. The pier is built on concrete pylons, allowing water below. When we return from town, our dinghy is wedged under the pier from the rising tide. I must work from somebody else's dinghy to let all the air out of ours so it will float low enough to be freed from under the pier. I go to *Faith* to re-inflate it before retrieving everybody.

Musket Cove, a fine resort, is our last stop in Fiji. The beach is lined with *bures*— say BURR-ray, or bungalows—and a store, a laundermat, a couple of restaurants, and three pools; all manner of water sports are available. We're tied to their dock to clean *Faith* inside and out. Across the dock from us, on a sandy spit, is a bar where we eat several meals. To eat there, you bring your own food, light a fire in the grill with their firewood, cook using their bar-b-cue tools, eat it on their plates at their tables, and buy your drinks from them. Cokes all around cost about $7US, and it's the nicest dining-out we've had in a while. It's hard to blame them for the service though.

We're at a nice resort in Fiji, but it could be Florida, Hawaii, The Caribbean, or anywhere else with sunny beaches and white guys being served by people who aren't white guys.

At Musket Cove, we meet a great couple from Melbourne, Australia. Again, it's Greggii who makes the introduction after meeting their two boys first.

In the sand near *Faith* and the self-cook restaurant, Greggii sets up a booth to sell headbands and crafts he weaves from palm fronds. He meets Brendan and Andrew there and teaches them how to do it. The boys end up selling a few pieces to some passersby, and each of them makes a couple of dollars for his efforts.

After Greggii introduces us to Craig and Toni, the boys' parents, we're talking about how we stay busy on *Faith*. I tell Craig I just finished reading a fascinating book about Jewish immigrants in America and how they started selling pots and pans from pushcarts in Pennsylvania to adapt to change, and become some of the leading business-people in the world.

Toni says she understands. They're Jewish, which I don't know until they tell me, and her grandpa started his business the same way in Australia. On their last night of vacation, it's Craig's birthday. We celebrate together at a pig-on-a-spit, luau kind of thing. They go vegetarian when they learn the menu isn't available, saying they aren't completely kosher but do draw the line at pig. To me, it's just another adventure, going to a pig roast with practicing Jews and having our blond six-year-old teach their children about making money.

Fire in the Sky

Fiji is ringed with reefs, and we travel fifteen miles before going out the pass. After we're out, a boat from Musket Cove radios to ask if we know something about the weather that they don't. We checked the weather beforehand, but never heard of the front they tell us about. Soon, the winds rise to thirty knots to continue for the duration. The seas are bumpy and confused. Some come from behind, some from ahead, and some waves hit us square on the beam with a *whump*, spraying water over the decks. Lorrie and I are in our second change of clothes because we didn't duck quickly enough.

During this miserable passage, it blows like stink all the way to Tanna, Vanuatu.

At night, from eighty miles, the sky glows from Mt. Yasur like a big orange beacon. Mt. Yasur is Tanna's active volcano.

We approach the mouth of the bay at Port Resolution, named after Captian Cook's second barque, and *Faith*'s engine battery is dead. We heave-to—adjust the sails to hold us nearly dead in the water—and let the generator charge the engine battery for two hours. At three, we motor into the bay and anchor five miles from Mt. Yasur.

Faith rocks uncomfortably from a swell entering the bay, but we're too tired to reanchor. In the morning, we motor farther into the bay and drop both a bow and stern anchor to orient *Faith*'s bow to the swell. That eliminates most of the rocking.

We go to the village near the beach and meet Rani, the chief, who visited *Faith* earlier this morning and talked to Lorrie while I still slept (33). Vanuatu's culture is more removed from, or less conditioned to, our own than any place we've visited. The inhabitants live in palm frond homes, with palm mats for walls and thatched roofs. The floors are dirt and the cooking area is in a separate hut; in a third hut is the toilet. They live in family groups of ten or so homes per group. We see neither men nor children over five years old. The children are in school, and the men are out doing important men-type things. Tanna is a land of subsistence living, where fruits and vegetables are gathered for each day's consumption. Most of the living part is handled by the men, who spend inordinate time goofing off and drinking kava, and the subsistence part is performed by the women, who do the work.

Our arrival in Vanuatu marks the crossing of two other borders as well. We are now in an area where the World Health Organization cautions about malaria, and we are sailing into areas less protected from the sun because of depleted ozone. *Faith's* anti-malarial prophylactic is doxycycline, which does not sit well in our stomachs and causes additional sensitivity to the sun. For it to be effective, we must continue taking it for two weeks after we depart Tanna.

Rani's son runs the shuttle service to Customs and Immigration because he has the pickup truck. He's available on Mondays to make the run. The village of Lenakal is a two-hour ride each way. With some restaurants, shops, and a bank, it's Tanna's commercial center. We're instructed to bring our cockpit cushions for the uncomfortable ride. The path we walked on from the beach, where we left the dinghy, to the village, is about as good as roads get on Tanna.

We board the pickup at 7:00 AM for the two-hour journey with five other yachties and several Tannans. At one time, there are three in the front seat, and thirteen of us piled in the back. We stop to pick up anyone walking along the road, going the same direction. It's easiest to stand up and wrap your arms around the naked frame of the canopy they attach when it rains. We ride through the ash field of the volcano, up a mountain, across a plain, and down the other side to the port. Fun and excitement and bruises are shared by all.

On the way back, we visit Mt. Yasur. One thing we don't miss about the U. S. is all the concrete walkways, barricades, and signs to control our access to cool things. We drive to the base and are left free to roam. We hike a short distance to the volcano's rim to witness the best fireworks we've ever seen. In the States, they'd have a sign saying, "Danger, big hot flying rocks can cause serious injury or death." In Vanuatu, they assume you know it.

All of a sudden, *kawhummp*, and the earth shakes, and big orange blobs fly out by the hundreds, high into the air, and then land all around the inside of the rim, mostly on the far side from where we are (68). Most of these rocks probably aren't much bigger than a twenty-seven-inch television, and when they land and shatter, it sounds like a hailstorm. The volcano is less than a kilometer across at the rim, and a large number of twenty-seven-inch-television-sized rocks lie outside the rim, even as far as the parking lot. We stay alert. The heat creates a column of rising air that is replaced by a fierce, cool wind on our backs. We're coated with ash and sand. It is in our eyes, our ears, our hair, our cameras (we got some great shots), and our pockets until we get back to *Faith*.

When we visited Lenokal, we cleared into Vanuatu and got departure clearance at the same time. The morning witnesses *Faith's* departure for New Caledonia.

Going Down Under

New Caledonia brings us farther from the ozone's protection, and we decide to worry about malaria later, rather than to crisp up like French fries in this wonderful French territory. We quit taking doxycycline, and quit worrying.

Several months ago, while in the Marquesas, we met a German man who was hitchhiking across the Pacific on boats. He worked as crew, and joined Scott and Stacy on *Willy Flippit* for the run from Nuka Hiva to the Tuamotus. They enjoyed Bernie's help and presence. He stood watches, did the dishes, and cleaned their propeller, among other things. He's been walking the docks in New Caledonia and finds *Faith* when we arrive. We agree for him to join us for the passage to Australia. He's from Munich, speaks French and English well, and is a great asset and friend on our passage to Sydney.

Greggii and Bernie hit it off, with Greggii doing his best to wear him out. Bernie is a physicist for Osram, the world's leading light bulb manufacturer. He banks his time off for several years to accumulate a year of leave for the adventure of hitchhiking on boats. This time, he ends in Australia to fly to Thailand for three weeks before going home.

Bernie is an ideal crewmember, eating breakfast on *Faith*, then going somewhere during the day and returning for dinner. He saves us from feeling we need to entertain him. On our first day in Ile des Pins, he hitchhikes around the island, the next, he sits on the beach all day, and the third, he combines the beach with a hitchhike to the village (74).

He's a lot like me in the stubbornness department, which I use to break the monotony of our passage, Matrimonial spats aside, I generally enjoy a good argument no matter how distasteful the position I defend. It seems I take an almost perverse pleasure in the most evil posture for entertainment's sake.

To get things going, I say, "It seems like things are going pretty well for us in Iraq."

He says, "Do most people in the United States really support President Bush?"

"What do you mean?"

"Don't Americans understand? He unilaterally invades a sovereign nation and kills innocent people, because of nuclear weapons he knew didn't exist."

"Look Bernie, I think you're a little confused. Nuclear weapons aren't the issue. The issue was to enforce a peace treaty that Iraq agreed to, limiting their military buildup, and allowing inspections."

To needle his sensitivities, I continue, "Just think, Bernie, if the Versailles Treaty was enforced by Britain and France, East Prussia would still be part of your country."

The entertainment value of this conversation increases dramatically, and *Faith* picks up an extra knot from the wind originating in the cockpit.

We end the conversation and agree to disagree, an easier task for me because I never disagreed in the first place.

Emily and Amanda begin to show an interest in sailing. They take watches, each staying on for a couple hours at a time. It's too rough to fish, but the water is as blue as any we've sailed, and the sun shines. We haven't seen any other boats in the four days since leaving Ile des Pins. We have sunshine, blue and following seas, blue skies, and fair winds.

Faith is making good progress toward Sydney when a blow develops from the south. It's mostly forty knots, but peaks at fifty-four. We alter course and point downwind toward Coffs Harbour, 240 miles north of Sydney (Australia map, page 83), to wait for better weather. Bernie, Emily, and I are in the cockpit, and Lorrie, Amanda, and Greggii are below for the blow. We bury the toe-rail and *Faith* heels several times to where the upper cabin windows get a good rinse.

Greggii hollers out, "Hey Dad, watch this!" He and Amanda sprayed their socks with furniture wax and are climbing up the floor and skiing from one side of our living room to the other.

I don't see Lorrie and ask later, "Where were you?"

"I was right there," she points, "under the table, praying."

Customs boards us on arrival at Coffs Harbour and confiscates all of our fresh food. Ever since Captain Cook's first contact, and his gift of rabbits, Australia has had problems with exotics in the fragile, isolated environment, and makes every effort to control them, including the confiscation of fresh food from visitors. We knew this and planned accordingly to minimize our stores.

Much of the landscaping at Musket Cove is old, dead, giant clam shells. They don't harvest live clams. Greggii found one that wasn't part of the landscaping (we think) and brought it on board. We know about endangered species treaties and that, even though this clam has been dead for a long time, we aren't supposed to have it. Greggii spent more time than he should have on our passage, finding a good hiding place for it. Proceeding into the final questions, the Customs woman asks about a whole list of endangered species including ivory, tortoise shells, and whale bones. Greggii asks, "What about giant clam shells?" The woman knows our six-year-old Greggii poses a minimal threat to the world's wildlife, but rules are rules, and he loses his shell after he shows her a hidden hatch in the aft cabin.

Bernie leaves us from here to continue his adventure before returning to work.

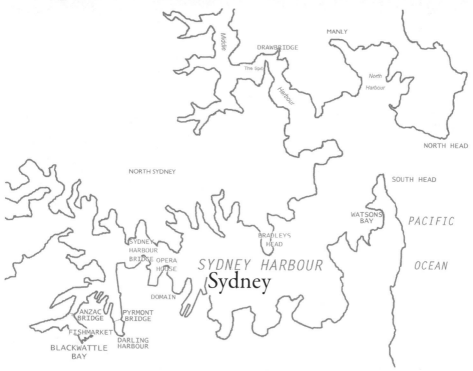

Sydney

SYDNEY HARBOUR

PACIFIC OCEAN

MANLY
DRAWBRIDGE
The Spit
North Harbour
NORTH HEAD
SOUTH HEAD
NORTH SYDNEY
WATSONS BAY
BRADLEYS HEAD
SYDNEY HARBOUR BRIDGE
OPERA HOUSE
DOMAIN
ANZAC BRIDGE
PYRMONT BRIDGE
FISHMARKET
DARLING HARBOUR
BLACKWATTLE BAY
Middle
Harbour

W e learn it was the appropriately named Southerly Buster that sent us to
Coffs Harbour– a front that turns the weather upside down for a couple
days at a time. When the weather returns to normal, we begin our move to Sydney.
Because we choose not to sail overnight, the first night finds us at Port Stephens.
The wind acts a little funny again, so we spend two nights here.

The sailing is work as we make our way down the coast. We're again in the mid-
latitudes, where weather patterns are different and continually changing. With
Christmas and the southern summer approaching, the weather is as unsettled as
springtime in Michigan.

We leave Port Stephens and sail to Newcastle, where we're surprised by Maggie
and Maddie, whom we last saw in Panama. They're living here on *Geneva* after
their engine failure forced a non-stop crossing of the Pacific. Carl works across the
river as an electrician for Australian Defense Industries.

Before their troubles, they were looking forward to sailing into Sydney Harbour; we invite them to sail there with us.

We leave early for the ten-hour sail, and make it between the heads—promon-
tories marking the harbour entrance—by mid-afternoon. In many miles and many
different sailing conditions since leaving Hampton, Virginia, nothing prepared us
for Sydney. New York doesn't come close in the amount of on-the-water traffic.
We were in New York in the fall, when other things are more important. We're
now in Sydney in the spring, and everybody is flocking to the water: a cruise ship,

a number of ferries, tour boats, sailboats, powerboats, fishing boats, canoes, kayaks, tugs with barges, airplanes with banners, and helicopters—all in an aura of celebratory confusion. As we round Bradley's Head, the Sydney skyline unfolds. Modern skyscrapers, glass and steel, and now the Opera House, and the Harbour Bridge. Many experiences in life are made better when shared with other people—it's good to share the excitement of Sydney Harbour with Carl, Maggie and Maddie (16).

We pass the Opera House and sail under the Harbour Bridge toward Darling Harbour (70). There aren't many anchorages in Sydney, but we find one in Blackwattle Bay, just out from the Sydney Fishmarket. Blackwattle Bay, separated from the main harbour by the Anzac Bridge, becomes our home for the next three months (book cover).

Carl, Maggie, and Maddie take the train back to Newcastle. We settle in.

An officer from Waterways knocks on *Faith's* hull our first morning in the anchorage. Waterways is New South Wales's on-the-water regulating, enforcing, and maintenance organization. He asks if we have a holding tank. Lorrie says yes. Are we using it? Again, yes. He then tells Lorrie that the fine for not using a holding tank is AU$750.00. Lorrie doesn't think it's the right time to say how we've been using it since the valve was turned the wrong way somewhere on the far side of Panama and the tank got filled up. The macerator pump—to dump the contents overboard—has been broken as long. We aren't using the holding tank for anything new, but since we can't empty it, it *is* in use.

This begins a new routine on *Faith*, as Waterways sneaks up behind boats in the anchorage to monitor them. We begin hollering to each other, "Can I flush?" or, "Can I pump out the shower?" as the need arises, and someone pokes their head out of the companionway to make sure a Waterways boat isn't around.

We're anchored in a small pool in the middle of this magnificent city. We walk in the park where a sign says "No Swimming," with a sketch of a big shark on it.

Sydney bustles with the excitement of the approaching holiday. Lorrie, Emily, and Amanda find Christmas-type things they can do only without Greggii and me—which is fine with us. Greggii and I have important things to do ourselves.

One of our first important things is to eat at the Fishmarket. It's filled with stalls, take-away joints, sit-down fast-food places, and at least one fancy-linen tablecloth place that we see only from the outside. We're partial to the take-away joints. Today, we order a fisherman's platter for two. Greggii and I sit with baby octopus heads in our mouths, smiling at each other with all these legs arranged in a poorly groomed handlebar mustache sticking out of our mouths, and wonder why the girls don't want to be around us.

Then we cross the Pyrmont Bridge. This swing bridge is the first in the world to be powered by electricity. The center balances and rotates ninety degrees on a support structure to let boats in and out. Its age doesn't show because this section of town was all polished up between the time they were awarded the Olympics and the time the 2000 Games played. I don't remember the Sydney games because I gave up on them earlier. Between the pro basketbawlers, Salt Lake City bribing their way in, and television's control of information flow, I don't pay much attention anymore. But in Sydney, they're proud of having hosted them, and that seems a good thing.

After crossing the bridge, we go to the Australian Maritime Museum, mainly because it's free. We ask a security guard what time it is and he says 4:47. Then we ask when the museum closes and he says 5:00. We spend our thirteen minutes fascinated by a whale boat, the first display. Instead of regular school, we plan to return tomorrow on a field trip.

After two days in Blackwattle Bay, we're greeted by another Southerly Buster. We make sure our anchor is holding and notice that one of the untended boats lets go and blows across the bay. Emily and I and a Swiss man from a neighboring boat retrieve it before it blows into the pylons of the Anzac Bridge, our gateway to the main harbour. We tow it back and meet David Maxwell, the owner, later in the day. His apartment overlooks the bay and he notices his boat isn't where he left it. We become friends with David and his girlfriend, Virginia, during the months that follow (19).

One morning we motor-sail eight miles through the main harbour, go under a drawbridge, and into another river. The harbour is a zoo. The Big Boat Challenge is a race of ten of the corporate-sponsored boats in the Sydney to Hobart Race. We come under the Harbour Bridge and are in front of the Opera House when all these boats head our way, along with several hundred spectator boats, ferries, tour boats, and helicopters. We're against the grain for a while, and then they all turn around and overtake us as they head back. We generally like more blue between us and anything that can significantly change the shape of our boat. The boats from Nokia, AAPT, and Skandia pass in front of us, each less than a couple boat lengths away, along with their respective photographer boats, fans, and others.

We anchor in a pool surrounded by vegetation-covered cliffs. Echoes of screaming cockatiels create an eerie aura. *Faith* is alone here. You wouldn't know the city of North Sydney dwells outside the encroaching horizon.

Returning to Blackwattle Bay, we walk to the Domain—a large grassy park. The event is *Carols in the Domain* with celebrities singing Christmas Carols for live television. Tonight's event is larger than last year's, which was attended by 100,000 people. They sing real Christmas Carols—as opposed to wintertime-happy-songs masquerading as Christmas Carols—accompanied by a fireworks and laser show. The finale is *"Joy to the World;"* singing it with 100,000 others and fireworks is a rush. Some entertainers use the stage to give personal testimonies of Jesus in their lives.

The best way to see the Sydney Opera House is during a performance; we go see *Carnival of the Animals* as the Australian Chamber Orchestra accompanies a cartoonist who reads poems and draws animals. The show begins with the orchestra playing centuries-old music. After the second song, Greggii asks, "When's it going to be over?" He then starts sketching and shows me his drawing of all the instruments: the violins, the ivories, and the oboe. Since he's trying to be quiet, he explains what each is by mimicking somebody playing it. He and I have serious ants in the pants until the intermission, but once the cartoonist takes the stage, we enjoy it. Michael Leunig is a poet, philosopher, cartoonist, and observational commentator—an Australian fixture the likes of the late Jeff MacNelly at the *Chicago Tribune*.

Boxing Day, December 26, is a legal holiday. The holiday is celebrated with movie premieres, after-Christmas sales, and a day off. In Sydney, Boxing Day marks the start of the annual Sydney to Hobart Sailboat Race. This race began when a bunch of sailing mates were in a pub with plans of sailing to Hobart and decided to make a race of it. Today is the race's 60th start.

We walk a kilometer to the bus stop for the forty-five-minute ride to Watsons Bay, then hike to the top of the South Head and stake out our vantage point for the start. We arrive at 9:30, unpack our blankets and picnic stuff, and watch the harbour fill with thousands of boats jockeying for position. Only last night, Lorrie helped me decide not to take *Faith* out. Good call.

The race countdown begins at 1:00 PM for the 1:10 start. What a spectacle: the sails, the boats, the ferries, the crowd! Out of 110 entrants, 109 start. There are two starting lines, one for the big boats, called super-maxis in the reredundant flair of corporate and journalistic English, sponsored by Nicorette, Konica-Minolta, Skandia, Targé, AAPT, and others, and one for the cruising class, the mom-and-pop boats that made the race the event it is and have as much fun as ever in spite of all the media attention cast toward the corporate hijackers of the race.

The racers sail north into the wind to exit the harbour. When they come out of the heads, about two-thirds of the fleet hoist their spinnakers in winds too strong for them; the super-maxis must, as they are under contract to display the billboards designed on them. The super-maxis lead a large number of boats not too different from *Faith,* who are not under such contractual obligations. In fact, *Faith*, in her past life as *Antipodes of Sydney*, entered the race twice.

One spinnaker shreds and several boats broach—turn to windward out of control because of too much sail. One of the super-maxis must be towed back because her swing-keel breaks.

Hobart, Tasmania, is 650 miles south. To get there, the race crosses the Bass Straits. The weather, beautiful today, may change tomorrow morning in a system that's predicted to be the worst since 1998, where six people were killed, five vessels out of the seven that were abandoned sank, and forty-four contestants out of ninety starts finished the race in eighty-knot winds and twenty-meter seas. *Faith,* as *Antipodes,* retired early that year.

Thousands of people line this ridge overlooking the Tasman Sea and the Sydney Harbour in the sunshine of an eighty-five-degree day.

While on the South Head, at 10:00 AM, we hear about a tsunami in the Indian Ocean. It's feared as many as ten thousand people have been killed. Later we learn the impact of what happened this morning: nearly a quarter-million people dead, in areas we find ourselves in the coming years.

With the sunrise over the Sydney skyline, we leave Blackwattle Bay on New Year's Eve to come under the Harbour Bridge and anchor two hundred meters from the Opera House. There are already a hundred boats in this little bay. The New Year's Eve fireworks show from the Sydney Harbour Bridge and from barges towed into the main channel is the first big New Year's celebration in the world. Tonga is actually first, but Sydney has the resources for a major celebration, and sees midnight sixteen hours before Eastern Standard Time.

Carl, Maggie, and Maddie join us for the fireworks, and we tour some of Sydney's other attractions with them including the aquarium and the zoo in the days that follow.

Since leaving Fiji, we've remained in contact with Thomas and Helén from *Smilla*. They left Fiji to visit their families in Sweden, and determined that they no longer feel at home there. They are considering a move to Australia. As part of the process of making such a move, they plan a month in Australia, two weeks of which are here in Sydney, to weigh their options. They arrive in late January, in time to celebrate Nicole's birthday with Emily and Amanda at a live production of *Dirty Dancing*. We sail on *Faith* together for several days in the harbour, visit Bondi Beach, and relive the good times we shared in the Pacific.

In early February, we revisit Carl and Maggie in Newcastle. *Faith* gets hauled out for a coat of antifoul and repairs where her hull was sacrificed to the reef in Tahiti.

Valentine's Day coincides with *Faith's* haul, and the first job at any shipyard is power-washing the hull to remove the barnacles and other maritime attorneys racking up billable hours on her. The shipyard is next to a small strip mall. One of the fine restaurants in this waterfront strip-mall has all the tables out, covered with white linen, fancy folded napkins, and lit candles in the center, just waiting for those special dates to arrive. A brief phone call from the restaurant to the shipyard puts an end to work on *Faith* until the morning. The restaurant doesn't see the romantic side of barnacle fragments on their Valentine's tables.

Our fresh paint gains us a knot of speed, and after launching and hugging good-byes to Carl and Maggie, we're on our way north to the Great Barrier Reef.

The Great Barrier Reef

From Newcastle, we sail and motor to Southport, just south of Brisbane. Southport is an expensive, souvenir-ridden, spit of land that we *must* see, according to people who like that kind of stuff. The kids and I enroll in a half-day surfing class and are documented as beginners on the certificates we receive. Being from Michigan, I put surfing somewhere close to horseback riding on my passion list.

To get to Bundaberg, a small, laid-back city famous for the rum by that name, we go through the Great Sandy Strait in a channel with minimal markings. We run aground more than once and must poke around in several spots to find the channel. We're early in the season for moving north, and nobody's around anywhere outside of the cities. Getting into trouble, like a serious grounding, would not be good.

We celebrate Greggii's seventh birthday on Whitehaven Beach, Whitsunday Island—part of an island group called the Whitsundays. We wake-up and eat breakfast, Greggii opens his presents, and then we go to the beach for sandcastles and a few foot races Greggii has planned. When the sun gets high and hot, we return to *Faith*, and resume our party on the beach when it cools again.

Northern Australia has two seasons: the wet and the dry; the transition between the two is now. We're learning a monsoonal trough means a lot of rain.

The water-maker quit working, so I take off the fill plug on deck that we fill our water tanks with, make a little dam out of rags, and watch *Faith* drink until she's sated from the rain.

After Cairns, we go to Cooktown, so named for Captain Cook's visit, where he rebuilt the hull of the *Endeavor* after nearly losing her to the reefs. Early in our voyage, I read a book on Captain James Cook. This led to another, and the more I read, the more fascinated I become with this guy. What we're doing is easy due in large measure to his pioneering travels and the charts he made. He had no way of telling what he was getting into except the colors, a shift in the wave patterns, or clouds on the horizon.

Next, we visit Lizard Island, which may be home to the most exclusive resort in the world. It's populated by lizards in the wild, celebrities in the resort, campers in the two campsites, and us. The campsites have a two-year waiting list.

We walk to Cook's Look, the peak of the single mountain where Captain Cook hiked to find a passage through the reef. It's a long hike, but it offers a view of the patchwork of pink reefs, golden sand, and aqua and blue depths in the Great Barrier Reef. On our way down, Greggii thinks it's a race. I holler for him to watch out for lizards, monitor lizards that grow to a meter long. The next thing we hear is a shriek from his direction below us on the steep path. I holler, "Gregg, are you all right?"

"Li-li-li-lizard!"

When we catch up to him, he's frozen in fear, a good thing so as not to scare the lizard too badly. This way we can all get a look as it warily watches us gather at the source of the scream. Greggii doesn't run ahead again.

As we sail north of Lizard Island, about halfway to Cape York, Emily catches the biggest fish of our voyage—a beautiful tuna, fifty pounds being as good as any other guess (51), which she insists on cleaning herself because "I caught it, and I'm going to clean it."

The tide lifts our dinghy off the shore at one deserted beach, and with all the crocodiles and sharks Australia has marketed, and with the few sharks we see at this beach, I find a new talent for speed swimming in the fifty meters it's blown from shore.

The only other boats we see are shrimpers and little freighters running the

Cairns to Thursday Island circuit. We go to one of the shrimpers and buy two kilograms of the best shrimp we've ever eaten for AU$20.00.

Going to shore at Cape York requires us to walk the last hundred meters in ankle-deep water over a tidal shoal. As we arrive at a little park that marks the end of the road, a prominent sign informs those arriving by road of the large number of crocodiles in the area. It would be nice if there were a sign facing the other way to inform those arriving by boat. A brisk pace takes us back to the dinghy unmolested.

We've been flying our spinnaker across the Gulf of Carpenteria for three days. Greggii and I lie on the back deck to check out the stars. Since he and Lorrie discussed the solar system earlier in the week, he knows about the planets in the manner you'd expect of a first-grader. Jupiter is bright so I show him that. Our spinnaker is deep blue with the Southern Cross as its design just like the Australian flag. We're oriented to see the Southern Cross on the port bow and its mirror image on the spinnaker starboard. Then we look at Orion, The Crow, The Big Bear or Dipper, The Southern Cross, Sirius, Betelgeuse, and a couple other stars. He's interested and asks, "Where's my anus?"

"Uranus?"

"Yeah, my anus."

When we get to Darwin, *Faith's* raw water systems must be treated after having been in foreign waters. There are problems with certain mussels, and they don't want vessels bringing them, or any other exotics, in.

The marina into which we're going must be entered through a tidal creek at high tide—it's dry at low—and they have a lock system to maintain the water level. The tides are seven meters.

Visit from Darwin

Australia is a land of cities, and cities are where the pace of commerce lies: Sydney, Newcastle, Southport—or Brisbane, to which Southport is a suburb—and to a lesser degree Darwin. From Brisbane to Darwin, the pace returns to the reasonableness of the wilderness. Oh, there are cities and commerce between these places to be sure, but Cairns, Bundaberg, Mackay, Cooktown, and the rest resist the compulsion toward fast society. They rely instead on their location for survival. The residents of these places know they don't need to change their pace of life to suit the needs of commerce; after all, they have the rail sidings, the fuel, and the locations demanded by commerce without making such change.

Our lives since Panama have been spent soaking up our surroundings at the blistering speed of eight knots, and that, only during rare moments of optimum conditions. The pace of life in Australia prepares us for a change in our own pace.

From Darwin, we take a six-week trip to Michigan, a holiday from our sailing lives. We leave *Faith* at Bayview Marina, under the watchful eyes of friends we meet. We fly to Sydney, then Los Angeles, then Chicago, then Grand Rapids.

Michigan seems much the same since we were last here; it is we who are different. We feel dissociation with what was the fabric of our lives until nearly two years ago. Society, our society, is moving well without us, and after the initial closeness of welcome hugs, we start looking to what's next for occupation. Living in the moment, so easily managed on *Faith*, surrenders here to a cultural value to live anywhere but in the moment.

The timing is fortuitous as Emily graduates from high-school. A call to the Home School Building in Grand Rapids gets her into a graduation ceremony for twenty home-schooled kids in the area. This provides us occupation because with the ceremony comes the planning, preparation, and execution of her graduation open house, an ice cream social.

It's hard to explain the emotions we feel. My mind tells me I'm home, but whispers in my being tell me I'm only visiting. There's a discomfort being this far from our home, floating in Darwin.

Our return to *Faith* takes time, because we purchase tickets only so far as Sydney—like purchasing tickets to Los Angeles to get to Detroit. Virginia, who befriended us on our earlier stay in Sydney, lets us stay at her home in the Sydney suburb of Newtown, while we organize our trip to Darwin. She works most days and golfs on weekends, so we don't see her much.

We purchase cheap seats on the Ghan, Australia's north-south railroad from Adelaide to Darwin. On Saturday afternoon, we board the Indian-Pacific Railway at Sydney's Central Station to arrive Sunday morning in Adelaide, where we transfer to the Ghan.

Australia's interior is like Arizona's, except where Arizona is buff colored, everything is red in Australia. Red dust, red clay, red dirt, and red rocks. The plants along the way are mostly mounds of silver, to yellow, to olive-green grasses, and shrubs and trees of the same colors, in contrast to the green farms between Sydney and Adelaide.

Around noon on Monday, we arrive in Alice Springs for a four-hour stop, sufficient time to walk into town and restock our on-board food supply.

We arrive in Katherine on Tuesday around 8:00 AM and stay for another four hours, where after a brief look around, we taxi to a lake for a couple hours. It's just something to do, and while we're walking around, we scare up several wallabies.

We saw kangaroos in the sheep fields just outside Adelaide, but haven't seen any since; they're more acclimated to the mid-latitudes. Wild camels are reputed to be along the route, but we don't see any.

There are several ways to buy passage on the train. The Gold Kangaroo sleepers are the nicest, followed by the Red Kangaroo sleepers, then followed—literally on the tracks as well as in quality of accommodation—by the Red Kangaroo daynighter seats. These are not much more than wide airline-type seats with legroom. Our seats are in this last category.

These seats are also where the backpackers sit, along with most of the families like us who are using the train for its transportation more than for the romance of rail travel. All the people in the Gold and Red Kangaroo areas look as if they've reached a successful point in their lives when they can afford the sleeper cars at two to three times the fare; many of them look like they can fall asleep practically anywhere.

I think the only guy that gets a good night's sleep in our car is the guy honking up a good snore behind Lorrie.

It's Tuesday night, and it's good to be home on *Faith*.

I spend several days installing things I purchased in Michigan for *Faith*: ventilation fans, a switch for the sail and trim instruments to connect *Faith's* navigation electronics to the computer, and a number of other odds and ends. Now our job is the navigation of paperwork for Indonesian visas and cruising permits.

Part III. Worlds Apart

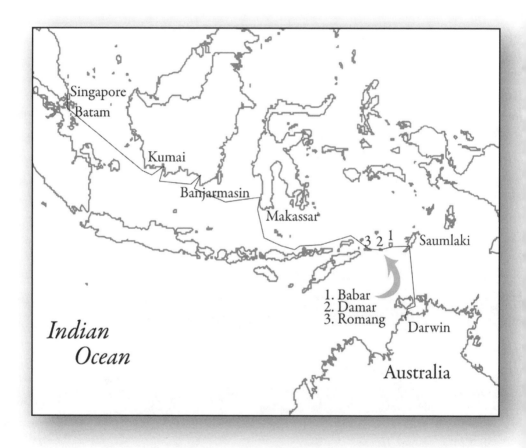

Singapore
Batam
Kumai
Banjarmasin
Makassar
3 2 1
Saumlaki
1. Babar
2. Damar
3. Romang
Darwin
Indian
Ocean
Australia

Indonesia
22 July to 14 October 2005

Prejudice

The exact contrary of what is generally believed is often the truth.

Jean de la Bruyere

Landfall is not marked by a negative element, so much as we experience a leveling of the pleasanter aspects of bluewater sailing. The air loses a degree of crispness, the tone of the water a degree of its brilliance, either of its own, or as it reflects the sky. Land emerges through the haze of a horizon in which we are no longer alone.

Today's landfall is the island of Jamdena or Yamdena, depending on whose charts are looked at. Our preconceptions of the otherness or nothingness of Indonesia cast their own shadows on the water.

Two days after leaving Darwin, the anchor settles, and the Port City of Saumlaki becomes our home. Both words, *port* and *city*, are overstatements. Saumlaki is a large village that becomes a port of entry only while officials are here for the annual Darwin to Saumlaki Rally for Cruisers. We pretend participation.

Because *Faith* is the first boat to arrive, the people of Saumlaki think we're the winners and congratulate us all around. Although we enjoy the attention, we tell them the winners are yet to arrive and that *Faith* is not part of the rally. We learned of it two weeks ago in Darwin and made Saumlaki our destination then.

As we work the wobbles out of our legs on the restaurant deck of Harapan Indah Hotel that doubles as our dinghy dock, we meet Dani, the hotel's owner, who directs me to the port office.

I walk out onto the sidewalk and along the narrow street in Saumlaki's main business district to find the officials for clearance. The sidewalk is maintained differently or not at all by the individual shopkeepers; it's rarely level, often broken, crowded with people, and radiates the anger of the midday sun. As I enter the immigration office, a young man there, mute from the language barrier, escorts me to the side of the building, points to a canoe paddling toward *Faith*, and indicates I must go back. I return to find a boy in a small canoe and a man aboard *Faith,* speaking with Lorrie. He's pleasant, in the pleasant manner of someone who wants something, which becomes more apparent during his cursory search, asking, "Is that for me?" or, "Do you have gift for me?" I tire of saying no, and when he points to a ball-cap and asks again, I say, "Yes."

Some officials in Indonesia spend considerable energy in their quest for rewards, but aside from the mid-level annoyance, our experience suggests if your papers are in order and you respond to their questions honestly, or at least believably, you can refuse a bribe.

While we are in Indonesia, a story unfolds in the *New York Times* about the American corporation Freeport McMoRan Copper and Gold, Inc. The company made US$20 million in payments to police generals, colonels, majors, captains, and entire military units.

> Freeport said in a written response to The Times that it had "taken appropriate steps"... "There is no alternative to our reliance on the Indonesian military and police in this regard," the company said. "The need for this security, the support provided for such security, and the procedures governing such support, as well as decisions regarding our relationships with the Indonesian government and its security institutions, are ordinary business activities."
>
> *Below a Mountain of Wealth, a River of Waste*, Jane Perlez and Raymond Bonner, December 27, 2005, New York Times.

The influence of western businessmen, who far outnumber other western visitors, might partially explain Indonesian officials' expectation of gifts; after all, they are *ordinary business activities.*

Indonesia spans an area of the globe two-thirds the size of the United States; most is ocean. Comprising over 13,600 islands and over 700 languages, Indonesia, I assume, is the most difficult country in the world to govern. That they have a national government of all the disparate pieces is remarkable, and the idea of entities from financially blessed parts of the world dictating their terms of exploitation becomes less unbelievable.

In Indonesia, people must declare their religion on their identification card; atheism is not a religion. With 88% of its population of 240 million professing such, Indonesia is the world's largest Muslim country. This is often a matter of birth, not choice. The remaining population claim Hindu, Buddhist, Christian Catholic, and Christian Protestant as their religion. Many continue to practice animism in addition to their professed faith.

Indonesia has Bali, with a recipe to attract Australian, European, and American tourists, and that recipe is our reason for a different route. We have our whole lives for places catering to white-guys, but we'll probably never return to Saumlaki, or Babar, or Damar, or Romang, or Makassar, or Banjarmasin, or Kumai.

We struggle to draft a concept of Indonesian culture, and realize the futility of it. The one element that spans all areas of Indonesia is the government, though the more populated areas share a common tongue: Bahasa Indonesia. Indonesia has no dominant culture, but instead attempts to unite hundreds, maybe thousands of disparate cultures—cultures with less in common than all western nations have with each other.

We find an enchanting land struggling for identity between ancient and modern cultures—ancient cultures with individual identities on each island group, or on larger islands, identities separated by terrain, and a modern culture with some elements attempting to maintain tradition, some attempting to maintain a cohesive nation, and some attempting to move the nation toward production on a global scale, all overlaid with outside influences extracting Indonesia's profits.

Television is recent in Saumlaki, and American television is part of it. In addition to the unifying element of language, Indonesia has the struggle of this cultural leveler. *We never knew what we didn't have* is an emerging theme. While transportation and communications have homogenized the United States into a cultural marshmallow, the export of American programming is expanding the marshmallow and dramatically changing the world.

As Americans, we live in invisible test tubes of about an arm's length called *our space*. We feel uncomfortable when someone violates it. In Indonesia, and in all the non-western cultures we visit, personal space does not exist, and we learn not to miss it.

Wherever possible, we use local transportation. Sitting in a van full of people different from us, who speak differently, act differently, dress differently, and smell different may not sound like a picnic, but it does offer a hint of the flavor of humanity. When we finish this journey, that will be something we miss—the closeness of people. On our return, everybody will respect our space, and the world will be lonelier on that account.

While we are dining on deck at Harapan Indah, Nelis introduces himself and sits with us. He teaches English at the Catholic school and wants to practice his English with us. Here we are, shocked by the otherness, uncomfortable with our loss of space, and annoyed that the restaurant lets people in to pitch all sorts of things, when Nelis asks us to help teach English at his school. That's all it takes and an instant bond is forged with this timid, yet determined, young man (3).

The school brings excitement, anxiety, and apprehension. After the welcome, all we can do is begin teaching. I recognize the dumb looks the students give me as the same dumb looks I gave my teachers when I was clueless. At seven years old, Greggii is better than I am. He doesn't see teaching as a task, an accomplishment, or an obstacle as I do. He simply tries to communicate and succeeds. So do Emily and Amanda.

In the days that follow, the *real* Darwin to Saumlaki Rally boats filter into the harbor. One of the rally events is to go to the same school and teach, and we again go as a family with the new arrivals. This visit begins with the headmaster giving a warm, forty-five-minute welcome speech to the volunteers. The students hold welcome banners and sing songs to greet us.

Saumlaki has two groups of people: normal folks like us and politicians. The officials mark events with ceremony, and we join the Darwin to Saumlaki boats for the political shenanigans. The week is spent in ceremonial one-upmanship.

One morning, we take a tour bus to a village where a special welcome is planned. Along the way is a village, the streets lined on both sides with smiling, waving school children crying "welcome" and "hello!" They're spaced two meters apart for a half-kilometer, each waving a plastic Indonesian flag on a stick. The next village is where the event is planned. The people here brought all their crafts to the community center for display and are preparing for a parade as we motor past. Then, the bus abruptly turns onto a sandy side street and deposits us on a beach some distance from the village. We determine that our bus was hijacked so one of the muckety-mucks can hold his own ceremony.

We're entertained by long speeches and a short demonstration of traditional dance by boys and girls in costume.

The best part of the afternoon is when we steal away to the community center for the crafts show, where we buy a beautiful, intricately carved, wooden sailing boat model made out of ebony (page 91). We've been warned not to use water to clean it just in case the ebony is stained onto it. The villagers here are not allowed to attend the ceremony, and are hurt by the officials having taken the reception from them and cancelling their parade.

We each experience a degree of digestive discomfort from the newness of Indonesian cuisine, and Greggii's peak discomfort coincides with one ceremony that we attend. After dinner and before the speeches, he has a violent bout of diarrhea. Indonesia is in the process of adopting the sit-down style toilets we're familiar with, but they're not universally available. The restrooms for tonight's ceremony are the squat-over-a-hole-in-the-floor-and-hope-you-don't-hit-your-shoes style. I hold Greggii's hands to balance his squat. Toilet paper is also gaining acceptance, but again, this facility is traditional, fitted with a tub of water and a *gayung*—a hand-dipper. Too timid to ask, I assume you simply splash yourself clean. I leave Greggii, scared, sick, and crying, and go to the serving table for napkins. Greggii and I work together on the cleanup and return to the hall. When our hosts hear of his malady, an ambulance is called. Neither Greggii nor I am too hot on the idea of going to the hospital, so I ask the ambulance guys to take us back to Harapan Indah, where Dani lets Greggii sleep in a quiet room until the girls return.

Another event is hosted by the most prestigious of all, a governor of sorts, who after the ceremony, dances with many of the women. Emily dances with him a couple times. Later we learn he's in trouble for spending US$2 million of government money to purchase the *MTB Express,* a ferry boat to service the islands between here and Ambon. It doesn't seem a bad price until you see the rusty hunk of scrap iron by that name. We learn later that this man has his housing and food provided in a medium security facility. It's unfortunate that a simple phone call to any number of foreign firms would provide the name of the right palm to grease to make his troubles disappear.

An emotional undercurrent develops in our lives, urging us to scratch deeper into our beliefs about who we are and why we're here. We can't know it now, but our struggles are social, and will haunt us for two years until we reemerge in the West, a place that so masterfully created our distorted perception of the world.

Cruising guides speak of the bribes for the officials. The Western press thrives on stories of bombings in Bali or Muslim terrorism in general. Sailing periodicals continually feature piracy. Only days earlier, we sat *safely* at the dock in Australia, mining misinformation.

You know, a lot of the places you're going don't value human life like we do.

I brought to Saumlaki a distrust that I didn't previously possess, or at least I kept it hidden enough not to be aware of. I'm ashamed of my meanness and rudeness that springs from this distrust, that only becomes more apparent with our time here. We're engulfed in fears.

The madness is that our preconceptions fuel my distrust when the reality we experience is wholly positive.

We let our prejudice blanket reality.

What we *know* about the world, what we *think we know* about the world, and the reality we experience create confusion in each of us in our own way.

Emily questions who she is and her fit in the world. While her friends launch into the world of university life or work, she jumps into a future of unknown worlds with her family on *Faith*.

She's frustrated with her inability to articulate ideas; and the conflict between the Indonesia that never existed for her in America, and her experience of Indonesia is especially difficult to express. She learns that the world looking out from America is a fiction designed to vilify others to maintain our American notion of entitlement to their resources and profits.

Amanda has the most difficulty. Our visit to Michigan coincided with the end of the school year, and she joined her class trip to Cedar Point, an amusement park. She returned in tears from the meanness shown toward people of color by some of the friends she grew up with. For the past year, Amanda has had few friends that are not people of color. She also came home in tears from the end-of-the-year dance, failing to understand the shallowness of some of these kids, hiding behind stuff and afraid of doing anything because it might not be cool. "Dad," she cried, "they just stood there!!"

From Saumlaki, still clinging to the belief that somebody at home understands what we're doing on a boat on the other side of the world, she calls a friend of hers. This call makes it clear they don't. All I can offer her is a shoulder to lean on and an ear.

It takes a while, as these things do, but once she starts, it's easier. With tears flowing she begins, "I hate America and never want to go back! It's so sad, because I look around at my friends here, and they are just real, genuine people, and their only hope in life is to be just like Americans!! My friends at home have lost their personalities to be the coolest, and my friends here, who don't have any of the stuff that makes Americans cool, want to change into them.

"Do you see their school? Did you hear how they're so proud of it for being a new school? Dad, it's four walls, a tin roof, concrete floors, and a bunch of broken windows, but they are so excited about learning! They've got nothing! Beat up desks and no books, but they *want* to be there. At home, we've got carpeted floors and everything, and they were so rude when I tried to share our trip with them. Here, when the teacher talks, you can hear a pin drop. When we sing songs, every one of them is proud of their voice. Nobody's ashamed. It's not like in America, where everybody is so self-conscious that they barely hum. They have practically nothing here, so the only thing that shows up is their own personalities, which are beautiful. At home, everybody hides behind stuff, whether it's nice clothes, cars, or any of the other things so they don't have to let anybody see who they are."

She continues, "I mean, Dad, just think about it. It's like looking into a hallway with fifteen doors, seven on the left, seven on the right, and one straight ahead at the end. In America, all we care about is getting to that door on the end, and we'll claw and kick our way to get there because everything in America is about getting to the end. My friends here? All of them would look in every door along the way, knowing that every door holds a treasure. Even if that treasure is disappointment, they will be so much richer when they get to the last door."

As she becomes saturated with the drug from the neuro-whachamacalits triggering her tears, her argument loses coherence, but I have a general idea what she means.

Greggii's seven years haven't allowed him to build preconceptions; to him, Saumlaki and everywhere else is normal.

We have this emotional stuff going on and still can't pinpoint it. Amanda comes close, but even that isn't quite it. Going forward, we explore with new eyes the worlds we contact.

One morning, Emily meets a teacher at the dock. This woman came to teach Emily how to make *rujak*—a salad of local fruit in a sauce of peanuts, palm sugar, asamjawa (tamarind pod pulp), and chilies. They first visit the market to get the ingredients, then return to *Faith* to sit in the cockpit and cut and prepare the fruits, then move to the galley to assemble the *rujak*.

Amanda loves arts and crafts. She goes to the school for a day devoted to crafts, and returns with a wall hanging of cane and felt and some beautiful flowers made of palm fronds ironed and stained into poppy petals and leaves bound to wooden stems.

Greggii uses Saumlaki, like everywhere, to burn excess energy playing with the local kids. He takes his scooter to Harapan Indah and rides it through the hotel and around the deck, taking turns with the hotel staff. A special friend is Kenzo, the nine-month-old son of Dani. It was in Kenzo's room that Greggii slept after the ambulance dropped us off.

The sounds, the colors, and the aromas, most but not all pleasant, are reasons I enjoy the *pasar*—the market. Buyers and sellers speaking loudly or softly in a tongue more foreign to me than the braying or bleeting or cu-clucking of the live merchandise, the fish and squid hanging in the sun in different states from fresh to cured, the animals and their waste, tobaccos, rolling papers, CDs, clothes, shoes, and the spices: chilies and cloves and nutmegs and cinnamons and garlic, and open-air food preparation with those same chilies and garlic over wood fires, and people and melons and trinkets and mud squishing inside my sandals from the recent rain orchestrate the market (45).

The vendors, in addition to their wares, display something else—something of an almost spiritual nature when you're as removed from production as Americans are. There are some products that originate elsewhere, but for the most part, the vegetables are grown in the seller's garden; the fish are caught by the seller; the livestock is raised only a few kilometers from the market; and, the pirated DVDs are burned by the vender. They demonstrate a pride of craft in selling products of their labor, of themselves. The absence of middlemen—those traders and deal-makers that replaced craft in America—to isolate the buyers from the producers is not a bad thing.

Nelis is a growing presence. He sleeps on *Faith* several nights and often joins us for dinner. One night, after dropping him off at the dock, I'm returning to *Faith* and hear high pitched cries close on the starboard bow of the dinghy. I have a torch in hand, but don't use it until I power down and turn hard to port. A couple families in a small wooden craft are as relieved as I am that we didn't crash. I holler, "I'm sorry!!" Their response, amid the chatter of scared children being comforted by parents on their crowded boat is the same, followed by Indonesia's ever present, "Mister."

While our relationship with Nelis grows, and while we still face the demons of an Indonesia defined in America, we ask him to join us as a guide and translator for our remaining time in his country. He accepts.

This fills our last days in Saumlaki with another round of ceremony. We share our request with the headmaster at Nelis's school, who holds a goodbye ceremony during the school's 17 August *Freedom Day* party. He invites us to his home for dinner to give his family's blessing to Nelis's future. The teachers at Nelis's school visit *Faith*, and then his parents join us for dinner. If our meatloaf and scalloped potatoes are the shock to their systems that Samulaki cuisine was to ours, they'll probably became intimate with their own porcelain for a few days after we leave. While Nelis's parents are on *Faith*, they ask us to Nelis's uncle's house to allow him, by tradition, to pray for Nelis, us, and our journey.

His uncle is the mayor of Saumlaki. He speaks ceremonially for several minutes, at times growing tearful about Nelis leaving Saumlaki. We finally get around to his praying. Nelis brings him a bottle of *sopi*—the distilled spirit of nectar of coconut flowers.

Nelis's uncle pours a glassful of this potent concoction, grumbles a prayer in *Bahasa Tanimbar*—old local language—and walks outside to pour it in the street ceremoniously. Nelis explains later that the prayer is to his ancestors to watch over our safe passage, and that the first round of sopi is for his ancestors to enjoy.

The uncle returns and fills the glass for his first son, who drinks it, then for his second son, and finally for himself. Then he prays a Catholic prayer followed by the Lord's Prayer in Bahasa Indonesia. Prayer is followed by dinner. We eat alone in the kitchen, where Nelis's uncle's family serves us and then waits in the other room for us to finish. They will eat after we leave.

Knowing it's Nelis's last night in Saumlaki, I turn to him on our way back to *Faith*, and ask, "Would you like to stay at your parents house?"

"No dad, I can't."

"What do you mean?"

"I am no longer a part of that family. I now belong to your family, dad, and you too, mom. You are my family now."

"Because of that ceremony?"

"Yes."

To prepare for departure, I work on *Faith*. The generator overheats and the water-maker blows a hose. Indonesia is the one country we've landed in where water quality may be questionable and we lose the generator *and* water-maker. We need a water truck to fill us up, 1000 liters for 30,000 *Rupiah*—slightly more than US$3.00—and Dani, the apparent master of all things on Jamdena, helps us organize it.

I take the high-pressure line from the water-maker to Sumbar Teknic, an all-purpose hardware and construction equipment shop that is also the only place in town to change American currency to Rupiah. I change $150.00 and receive nearly a million and a half Rupiah. I then show the man my hose; he scans the faces of guys goofing-off in his store and picks one to take Nelis and me to a workshop where the broken fitting is brazed together. The welder does a good job, but while he's brazing, the rubber hose inside the stainless braiding melts.

Our move to the dock for water elevates our highly stressful busy-ness to complete confusion. Ships line the outside of the T-dock so we raft to the outside of the *MTB Express*. Nelis's mother and father board us, which means climbing their way over a cargo boat, then through the *MTB Express* and then onto *Faith*. I help and find them frailer than before; the goodbye is painful. They bring Nelis's brothers and some nieces and nephews.

Dani is at the wharf offloading a cargo ship. He says the water truck won't have enough hose and we need to come inside the T-dock, so we move. Many people walk the wharf to check us out. When the water truck arrives, we weave the hose through the crowd.

As we begin filling, Emily and Amanda arrive with their friends from school. Everybody appreciates the spectacle we provide as a diversion from the aura of sadness on the dock. When we first came inside the T-dock, the depth was 9.7 feet. While we are taking water, the ebbing tide raises the seabed to 8.4 feet. As soon as the water's in, it's time to say goodbye because the bottom will rise two more feet in the next hour and *Faith* draws eight feet. I don't want to add a grounded boat to the sad entertainment.

There are no dry eyes on *Faith,* or the dock. We hug our last goodbyes, push and fend off, and leave with water between the encroaching bottom and the keel. Fifty people crowd the wharf as we cast off, a brilliant array of fading faces of *Faith's* first port in Indonesia (71).

Babar: Organized Tourism

C learance in Tepa, the main village of Babar, is the most difficult of any place we've been. A lot of this difficulty has to do with Joseph.

Joseph introduced himself to us at Harapan Indah. He sat down between Nelis and us while we were talking, and Nelis deferred to him because Joseph was older—not old, just older. Joseph monopolized our time, first urging us to go to Babar, then simply hanging around to annoy us. I finally told him we didn't want to spend our remaining time in Saumlaki with him.

Aristoteles, also from Babar, was one of the guides in Saumlaki for the rally. It is here that we learn Aristoteles works for Joseph.

Nelis and I take the dinghy to the beach and are met by Aristoteles. It's coming slow, but I'm realizing Aristoteles is a good guy in a tough spot. Until now, I haven't really trusted him. These things take time, and in Indonesia, things that take time take longer because of language and prejudice. It doesn't help that Aristoteles accompanies us to the harbor master's office where we're greeted by our long-lost, self-proclaimed good-buddy, Joseph, who immediately takes charge of us and our clearing-in process. The assistant harbor master tells us we don't have the right clearance paper from Saumlaki, the one the Saumlaki harbor master said wasn't necessary. Rules are rules, and we need to talk to his boss.

Joseph then tells me he'll take me to the district manager's office, then to the police, but Nelis must wait because he has shorts on. Probably the best place for him to wait is here at the harbor master's office. I tell Joseph that since Nelis is going with me and since I have shorts on, we'll both change. Joseph says it's okay because I'm a tourist, but Nelis is Indonesian and can't go in shorts. I insist that we want to honor Babar's customs and we will be right back.

Aristoteles meets us again at the dinghy landing and takes us to the district manager, who welcomes us to Tepa. Next, the police. The assistant chief wants to board *Faith*, "to check it out." After the police, we march to the Army post. We haven't yet been to a military post for clearance. Then, back to the harbor master's, where we arrange to meet him in the morning.

While waiting for the assistant police chief, Nelis, Aristoteles, and I stroll the shore, pleasantly conversing about something not memorable. Joseph approaches and hands me a letter from a local school, inviting us to a cultural exchange in our honor. The letter reads:

Welcome Ceremony
From: Art and Cultural Group
For: Mr. Gregg and Family
At : Christian Junior High School
A boy student with traditional Cloth stop front to Mr. Gregg. He is handshake and sing welcome traditional song. After that he is step back.
Two girls student with traditional Cloth brought a bottle of Coconut wine and a glass, and areca nut plus kind of plant.
First: Mr Gregg as the chairman will drink little wine
Second: Chairman must eat little areca nut with some kind of plant.
The Guest step front to traditional Dancing group. Soon they do the attraction to say welcome.
The Guest fisit the EXJIBITION place together with District Govermant.
Asking and reply program
Rest time to enjoy some drinking
The end Ceremony
Note: Special for the traditional Dance, the guest will to pay Rp. 150,000

Joseph transforms before my eyes from a medium annoyance to a pain in the butt. We aren't special, and I don't want Joseph having people treat us special. I explicitly told him that when we first met in Saumlaki.

We talk to Aristoteles about a tour of Babar, and he finds a man to drive us around for the day. While finishing the details of our tour, we decide to go to the school's welcome ceremony. The easiest thing would be to refuse, but Aristoteles is caught in the middle and Joseph's reputation would suffer. I don't like Joseph, but he doesn't deserve to lose face in his community. We must go.

Emily meets a girl in the village of Tepa, Esthy, who asks Emily to church, where she is practicing her singing for Sunday's service. Our family also practices, accompanied by the keyboardist, Joseph. He dubs us the *Faith Family Singers from America* and tells everyone we're singing for Sunday worship so the church will be full. We begin to feel like pet hamsters.

Joseph behaves himself for our tour of Babar. Heri, an off-duty policeman, is our driver. I don't know he's a policeman until later at the sopi distillery where Greggii, with seven-year-old innocence asks, "Dad, is it okay if I shoot a gun?"

In my forty-eight-year-old innocence, noticing the slingshots, bows, and bb guns lying around, I say, "Sure Gregg, go ahead and shoot a gun."

Greggii raises my protective antenna when he asks again, "Dad, are you sure it's okay if I shoot a *real* gun?!!"

"Uhhh, what gun do you want to shoot?"

He takes me to Heri, who pulls his gun out of a holster near his butt. It doesn't look like a very comfortable place to have a gun strapped, especially while he's driving.

I tell Greggii, "No, you're not going to shoot that gun."

Then I look at Heri and ask, "How good are you?" pointing at the gun.

With a smirk, he says, "Pick at target."

Since Greggii started this dialogue, I tell him to pick a target.

Up to this point, everything is quiet except for the sound of the bubbling coconut flower nectar in the fifty-five-gallon drum, and the crackling fire. In a coconut grove, the trees grow twice as high as on a beach, and Greggii says, "That coconut, way up there."

Heri takes aim and shatters the stillness, followed by the sound of bubbling coconut flower nectar, the crackling fire, and a *thunk* when Greggii's target hits the ground. Heri severed the stem. I'm impressed. Greggii adds, "That was cool!"

The distillery is a pavilion-type structure constructed of bamboo with a palm frond roof to keep out the rain and exhaust the smoke; an open fire, two steel drums, and bamboo piping are assembled under the roof. The prominent feature is two parallel, eight-meter-long, sloping bamboo poles, the lower ends of which drain into used water bottles to capture the product (38). The sweetness of the sopi dripping into the bottles is exceeded only by its potency.

We then go to caves where the islanders hid, were found, and were massacred by Japanese soldiers near the end of World War II. This massacre occurred shortly before Indonesia's independence following four-hundred years of colonial rule, first by the Portuguese, then the Dutch, and then, only briefly, by the Japanese. The caves are a local treasure and we can't venture far for fear of disturbing the human remains.

Nelis tells Joseph how hot it is as we prepare for the welcome ceremony and asks if it would be okay, just this one time, to wear shorts. We can't contain our laughter. The ceremony is everything the invitation said it would be, and discomfort is shared by all as the officials, the students, and we stare at each other thinking about the pleasanter things to do later.

We go from the school to the church for our final practice before tomorrow's worship. Joseph has everything all arranged: the order of the two songs, where we and the other singers will stand, and how we're to teach part of one song.

Surprises are coming naturally from Joseph, and Sunday morning brings another. We will sing alone, without the girls that practiced with us, and we aren't going to teach anything; to complicate things, his accompaniment slows to misery. In the afternoon, the crew of *Faith* convinces the captain of *Faith* to talk to Joseph; I make no attempt to conceal my anger.

In the evening, we're joined by Aristoteles for dinner at Heri's house. *High-Tide Heri* we call him, because all through yesterday's tour, whenever we'd stop and wherever sopi was poured, Heri made sure his glass was filled to *high-tide*. After all, he needed his energy to drive us around and deaden the discomfort of that gun strapped to his butt.

Nelis and I are at ease and cocky when we visit the harbor master, who tells us our clearance will be 75,000 Rupiah, about $8.00, because of the *mistake* with the paperwork made in Saumlaki. It isn't much, but the ATM in Saumlaki did not work, and we don't have much money to get to where one will work; we don't even know where that will be. I say, "Forget it. We'll just sail back to Saumlaki for the right papers," and walk out the door with Nelis.

Making a brisk pace back to the dinghy, I tell Nelis, "don't look back." I know the harbor master is following and wants nothing more than to get our clearance papers into my hands so I won't end up at his district headquarters in Saumlaki telling them he wants compensation for a mistake they made. When he catches us, his sweaty brow and pained eyes betray the smile on his face as he hands us the papers and wishes us a pleasant voyage.

Our comfort crashes when we see Joseph waiting at the dinghy. He says the police chief wants Nelis to pick up a letter from him, and he wants Nelis to go alone. I swallow hard. Nelis blanches. He does have enough composure to say he'll be right back, after changing out of his shorts. We go back to *Faith* with our port clearance in hand, and rather than changing clothes, we decide changing location would be better. While the harbor master, Aristoteles, and Joseph are joined by other witnesses, *Faith* raises anchor and shrinks into the horizon.

About two miles from our anchorage in Tepa stands a small, high island we use to screen us from view of Tepa. We circle into its blind side and drop the anchor. Two fishermen from the small village here give us lobsters in exchange for tee-shirts. Damar is less than a day's sail, sixty-six miles away, and our port clearance is dated two days hence. Believing it imprudent to arrive in Damar before officially departing Babar, we stay in this small village and eat lobster for a few days.

Spicing Up Global Trade

During our sail to Damar, the seas are up, the wind is down, and the rigging bangs all the way. On arrival, the bay narrows quickly and is fed by a small stream from the north. Because the bay faces east, where the weather comes from, we nudge *Faith* into the stream. Several boys on shore gesticulate assistance. A reef juts out ten meters from shore and we lower the anchor into the arms of those boys, who now stand ankle deep on it. They carry it to the beach and wrap it around a hunk of concrete. We can't leave at high tide because their work with our anchor is done at low tide when the beach is dry, whereas it is nearly two meters under at high.

Emily, Greggii, Nelis, and I go to shore where a growing number of boys and girls wait for us. We walk to the village on a weather-beaten structure born into service as a wharf for Dutch traders. Before reaching the village, we're greeted by the aroma of Christmas. The sidewalk is a patchwork of drying cloves on cane mats (37). They're green, yellow, red, brick-colored, and brown, depending on how dry they are. It takes three days of sun for the clove flower, harvested before it opens, to dry for market.

This little flower on this little island plays large in the history of global trade. A route west from Spain was sought when Magellan travelled, and this island was colonized by the Portuguese. Later it was the Dutch who colonized, evangelized, and settled the area, building the eastern trade center of Batavia, now Jakarta, to consolidate the products of the Spice Islands for shipping west. That's what we learned in school. What we didn't learn in school was that, at the same time, traders and evangelizers from the Middle East and China were doing the same.

We pass mat after mat of cloves on our way to the village chief's house, where we're welcomed by his wife and told he's in Ambon. She serves us strong, smoky coffee and several-day-old donuts, which Greggii seems to like. While visiting, she rummages nervously through books and stacks of paper to produce a letter. We watch as she unfolds the envelope and see it holds her shattered heart. She asks us to send it to her daughter, Miss Dina Cecelia Andersen, Bismand Street 2500, Okland, America, an incomprehensible address. Nelis helps us ask for more information, hopefully without betraying our doubts, but Bismand Street 2500, Okland, America, is all she has left of Dina Cecelia. We'll post it from Singapore.

We walk back to *Faith* for lunch with two boys who have the gumption to ask if they may come with us. Then Nelis, Amanda, Greggii, and I return to the village with the boys and a mission: to get palm sugar, cloves, and plantains for Emily to make her plantain desert.

One of the boys takes us to his brother's house for the plantains. We ask about cloves and he tells us a kilogram is Rp25,000, about US$2.90. We buy three kilograms. I've never seen a kilogram of cloves before (a kilogram of dried cloves is the size of a volleyball), but now *Faith* has more than any supermarket in the USA.

In Damar, life isn't as complex as we make it at home. The *wow factor* to the people of Damar is *Faith* and us. Our *wow factor* is them and the cloves. Amanda, Nelis, and I sit on the porch of the guy who sold us the cloves, and Greggii sits on the steps to look at the twenty faces gathered around. Sitting is a key component of doing business in many parts of the world. If they're supposed to be doing something else, it doesn't matter. Tomorrow always comes.

We return to *Faith* to rest after our overnight sail from Babar.

Greggii wakes me to say some people are here. By the time I put pants on, two policemen are on deck. The younger one carries a machine gun. It looks like a toy, except for the real looking barrel with a big hole in it. I sit down inside the cockpit and he—looking big on account of the gun—sits on the edge of the cockpit with his legs facing out and his back to me. When he rests the gun in his lap, I notice, as these things tend to be noticed, that it's pointed somewhere between my chin and my ear. I've never had a gun pointed at me and I don't handle it very well. I get angry, which in hindsight, doesn't seem too clever of a response. He moves it around and for a few minutes it points somewhere else, but it always settles back to where

I look at the business end. After looking down the barrel more than I think necessary, I move next to him, so close that he doesn't have room to wiggle. I learn that security results in bridging cultural barriers with a close relationship.

While I dodge unfired bullets, the older man clears us into and out of Damar. Nelis explains we aren't in the mood for bribes, or fees, or gifts, and we all have a leisurely cup of coffee and a bowl of popcorn while they wait for their boat to pick them up again.

On shore, a boy shows us some clove gardens. A garden is a plot of land on the south slope of the weathered volcanic mountains. Interspersed among the coconut palms are the cloves, growing on cylindrical trees, eight meters tall and four meters in diameter. The flower is harvested between late July and early September.

The mountain we're exploring has many small farms worked by different farmers. Many combine to harvest one man's farm and then move to the next man's. Whole families work together on the rugged mountainside.

When we return to *Faith,* another boat, not much larger than *Faith,* arrives at the anchorage—a traditional sailing boat with many people on board. They enter the small stream under sail—they don't have auxiliary power—going behind *Faith* to anchor close to and upstream of us. This boat is an Indonesian trader and ferry boat, wooden and rigged with blue tarps for sails, bringing supplies and people to the island and departing with cloves for the world (31).

The people aboard this trader along with a number of people on shore wave encouragement as we raise *Faith*'s anchor to depart.

Black Magic

A twenty-meter fishing boat is above the line of sand at the beach in the green shade of the palms. Framed and planked, the boat is far from complete, and less than five meters outside the builder's house. This builder's beach is where we land in Romang.

On our first landing, an angry man approaches to spew a litany of grievances in our direction. I don't understand, so Nelis intervenes. After their brief sidebar, the man meekly addresses me in a tone more conducive to friendship that I grasp with equal ignorance. Nelis explains that Romang's inventory of natural resources includes ingredients for bombs and that East Timor rebels have used this anchorage to acquire them. Apparently, we look like mercenaries, here to cause trouble on behalf of the rebels. Or something like that.

The second, softer exchange is his apology after Nelis's explanation.

We are in Romang because Nelis's father taught here and Nelis lived his pre-memory youth here. Two miles away is the village of Jerusu and the school. The road is the width of a one-lane road anywhere and is well travelled by students. There are pedestrians, horses, donkeys, and chickens, but no cars. A number of people we meet were Nelis's father's students. Nelis tells us it feels like home with his dad's friends, the school, and the house where his sister was born.

Lorrie and Greggii stay behind to do the laundry in the elbow of a fresh-water stream.

When we return from Jerusu, we bathe in a different bend of the stream. I learn bathing occurs in a different bend after the discomfort of watching Greggii bathe in the middle of a group of women doing their laundry. The feeling just isn't right, and before someone else jumps in, we're directed to more privacy downstream.

The neighboring island of Maopora is a place where devil-worship is practiced, according to Nelis. Nelis recalls a story he was told about his youth. At four months old, he was targeted to be made an innocent human sacrifice. His parents and their friends told him of how he was overcome with the devil and saved by God only through the prayers of many people here. Even now, in telling us about this and other occurrences on Maopora, like flying human heads, mutilations, and sacrifices to fire, Nelis is visibly shaken.

The anchorage in Romang is fine at low tide when the reef rises to break the swell, but unmanageable at high. We're taking fifteen knots of wind from the east, and one-meter waves from the sea, and then again when they echo off the shore. *Faith*'s target, should something fail, is the beach less than a quarter mile away. The only consolation is that the bottom is mostly sand, provides good holding, and will damage our egos more than *Faith*'s hull if we do end up on it.

When Lorrie and I take the dinghy to get the laundry we left to dry, a breaking wave sends us tumbling. Lorrie, yet to experience the terror of flipping the dinghy, is unsatisfied with the sensation. Out of her concern for the welfare of our family, she always looks for scary things to happen; when I suggest she enjoy her moment when something scary actually *does* happen, she gets more upset. I can't win. An hour passes before she talks to me, so I work on the dinghy outboard in relative peace. I'm amazed I can take the cover off the Yamaha, dump several liters of water out, pull the cord, and have it start again. Lorrie's going to take more energy.

We spend time looking for Lorrie's glasses that disappeared during our spontaneous swim. After several minutes of looking, we decide God has a better handle on their location and ask Him for help. Two hours later, Lorrie finds them—a hundred meters from where we flipped.

Makassar: City Life

When we left Hampton, Virginia, we had a plan to sail around the world in two years. As early as Panama, Thomas and Helén from *Smilla* began encouraging us to slow down: "Yes, you can sail around the world quite comfortably in two years, but you will not see much if you do."

Having heeded their advice, we mark our two-year anniversary of life on *Faith* on a passage to nowhere. We have no destination mainly because we're suffering an outbreak of indecision. We have a general idea of what direction we want to go, and sooner or later we want to end up in Singapore.

Several days out of Romang, somewhere in the waters north of Flores, we choose Makassar, on Sulawesi. Arriving in the wee hours, we pass hundreds of fishermen in small canoes, flashing torches so we can see them. We anchor in front of the Makassar Grand Hotel at two o'clock and are asleep by three-thirty.

Shortly after 7:00 AM, Sampu wakes us. He's a water-taxi driver who turns out to be a great resource and friend (32). He takes us to shore and watches over *Faith* from the water-taxi dock there, and becomes our get-things-done intermediary. He takes us to the ATM, the first that works for us in Indonesia, and then to the Harbor Master for clearance.

After the Harbor Master, we hire three *becaks*—BEE-checks, tricycles with covered and cushioned seating for two in front of where the owner sits on a bike seat to pedal—to ride around town. The trip is an adventure when we start on a five-lane one-way road, crowded with traffic, going the wrong way in a middle lane for several blocks. During our trip, we purchase eight 32-liter plastic jerry cans that our driver lashes on top to nearly double the height of our becak.

In the morning, Nelis, Emily, and I meet Budi at the water-taxi terminal. He's taking us to immigration. Budi is the harbor master who cleared us in and is concerned about people in Makassar who might take advantage of us. Budi thinks Immigration is open seven days, but today it's closed. We do talk to Pa Tre, who invites us back tomorrow morning at 9:00.

As a family, we go to a supermarket, not huge like grocery stores in America *now*, but like they were before general merchandise and processed products of questionable nutritional value dominated the aisles, back when a variety of *food* was important. With the exception of pork, which is nonexistent on account of Makassar being mostly Muslim, it's ironic that we have more choice of basic foods here on the island of Sulawesi than at the supermarket in Michigan. Lorrie's ecstatic and purchases some cheeses, breads and deli meats.

We go for our visa extensions: Budi, Nelis, and I, and our taxi driver from yesterday, Reza. We fill out three forms per passport, plus a large amount of information on the outside of each folder. Before we left *Faith*, I printed copies of several documents to ease the process. Pa Tre tells us to return for the passports that afternoon; it's normally a three-day process.

By helping us as they did, Budi and Pa Tre cause us to question the motivation of a nation that would have their citizens, us, believe that here is among those *places in the world where they don't value human life like we do.*

Budi and I ride his motorcycle to pick up our completed passports, and my eyes get a good dust and smog burn. There are a few simple rules to driving in Indonesia, but nobody follows them. It seems the general rule is to win. The horn plays an important role when borrowing part of a lane from oncoming traffic and is always politely acknowledged by horns of the oncoming traffic. Most amazing is that nobody cares what the other guy does. I read somewhere that Indonesian driving is like a school of fish. No fish swim in a straight line, but they don't bump into each other either; every fish moves to let the other fish move. There's no frustration, just a bunch of people with smiles or dust masks on their faces enjoying the ride.

We rent a room at the Hotel Pantai Pagura for Greggii to play in the pool and for everybody else to be off *Faith* while I tackle the engine room. Nelis, Emily, and I spend the night on *Faith* while Greggii, Amanda, and Lorrie spend the night on land.

Monday morning, I ask Nelis how he slept. "Not very good, dad, I want to talk to you about my feelings for Emily." That remark chases the remaining grogginess from my veins.

We don't discuss it now, allowing me time to exercise my imagination. It also gives me time to formulate lame responses to what my imagination conjures up. Soon, Emily wakes and says, "Dad, you should know that Nelis wants to talk to you."

"I know, he already told me."

"I told him to talk to you, because you're pretty good at talking about things. He said last night that he has feelings for me, and I told him that I don't share those feelings."

"Is that all?"

"What do you mean? I told him we could be friends, but that's all."

I give my imagination the rest of the day off.

Lorrie, Nelis, and I eat lunch on the pool deck at the Pantai Pagura. Nelis lays his heart out on the table so that Lorrie and I can skip the menu and make a feast out of the poor guy if we want. We order from the menu. Nelis tells us how he feels about Emily and knows she doesn't feel the same. He asks us for advice. I tell him he has three options: to go home now, to continue and enjoy the rest of the trip with us, knowing things won't change, or to continue with us, hoping for a change. I say I'll resist the last option, but no matter which option he chooses, he's stuck for now with a broken heart.

He wants to finish the trip.

With everybody comfortable at the Pantai Pagura, I work. Sampu helps navigate Makassar's industrial area, where we find a shop to make new lines for the water-maker. I have an extra made for when it breaks again. Sampu then helps with fuel and water. This is where the jerry cans come in. Fuel costs twenty cents a liter. We hire a becak to cart it to the dock in our new cans and Sampu brings it to *Faith*. For Sampu's services through the week, we pay him US$100 which he treats like a gold mine.

We depart on a two-day sail to Bamjarmasin, on the south side of Borneo, and find a dirty, smoky, coal shipping center where we stop for two days before moving to Kumai.

Kumai: The Ancestors

Afraid to enter Kumai at night, we anchor five miles out. Drift nets lazily slither in the currents, and we wake at daylight with a net draped over our anchor chain. Raising the anchor and believing ourselves free, I start the engine and wrap a basketball-sized wad of net around our propeller shaft. While cutting it free, I think of crocodiles, not having distanced ourselves enough from the eco-tourrorism of Australia. I cut the bulk of it free, thinking our feathering propeller will cut the remaining bits while we're underway.

We motor up the broad river to Kumai, dodging floating islands as big as coal barges, broken from shore and drifting in this tidal river to the sea. The tide causes the river to flow both ways, affording these islands several missed opportunities to hit *Faith* as she lies at anchor.

Harry's Yacht Service provides fuel, taxis, watchmen for yachts, and anything else necessary to make an excursion up the river as easy as possible for visitors to Kumai.

Orang is Indonesian for person; *utan* is forest; orangutan—person of the forest.

Our transportation is two, twenty-foot long, covered wooden craft called klotoks, so-named by the sound of the long-stroke, single-cylinder diesel engine. "KLOtok-KLOtok-KLOtok" (35).

We ascend the river on JJ's boat *Britannia* and *Cahaya Purnama,* belonging to the father and son team of Emang and Enang. Our guide for the trip is Ennog. When we stop to see some long-tailed macaques, JJ tells us *Brittania* needs some

114

work done and to all get on Emang's boat. Against my better judgment, because the food is on *Britannia*, we leave. We klot-klot upriver for two hours and expect to see JJ coming around the last bend any moment. When we do turn back downriver to look for him, he catches up with us in minutes.

Spread for lunch on *Brittania* is tempura-style fried tofu, rice, and veggies. We're running behind, so while we eat, JJ motors toward Camp Leakey, where, at 2:30, they feed the orangutans. We're not disappointed. We stay at the feeding station for an hour and then walk back to the ranger station, where a mother and baby are. A big male there is ogling the mother. The rangers don't want him near her any more than we want him near us.

Orangutans know their hairless cousins keep food in backpacks, and JJ carries a backpack. On a boardwalk leading to the klotoks, an adult female approaches. Most of our party is ahead and JJ and I are last. She meets us in front of JJ, who asks me, "You want to go first?"

We learn that orangutans are eight times as strong as humans. The females average about a hundred pounds; the males range up to 260. They're not—with the exception of a sex-starved or domination-challenged male—normally aggressive, but it's prudent to give them room. "No, JJ. I kind of like being behind you."

We jokingly jostle for position when JJ says, "I have an idea. How about I give my backpack to you and walk past her? Then, you throw it over her head to me."

JJ is a happy man with a permanent smile who's worked as a guide for fifteen years. I have confidence in him and say, "Sure, let's try it."

It's a good strategy, but it doesn't work and she's still between us and *Brittania*. After a while, she gives up and bounds off through the woods.

We sleep under mosquito nets on top of the klotoks, boys on one and girls on the other.

Breakfast's aroma wakes us at 5:30. At 7:30, we're back at Camp Leakey for a tiring walk through Borneo's natural tropical forest.

Next, we go to the information center to learn about habitat, rainforests, the impact of the illegal cutting of timber, and deforestation. The conversion to biofuels means increasingly more orangutan habitat is destroyed for palm oil plantations.

We eat lunch and watch three other klotoks arrive. Ennog and I relax at the end of the dock on *Brittania* while Greggii, JJ, and the rest of our gang are at a picnic table on shore. One female orangutan, who comes to beg for stuff, amuses them.

I join Ennog on the dock when she approaches. She comes to me and holds my hand. Her fingerprint is like ours. While she holds one hand, I put my other on her back and face her. We sit for a moment like this, when suddenly she gets up, bounds over the dock, walks into one of the recently arrived klotoks, and comes out with a grocery bag of snacks. She sits on the bank and eats the roasted-in-the-shell peanuts she stole, out of reach of anyone who would rescue the food. Ennog retrieves the plastic wrappers.

We return to the information center. A female orangutan named Francis, with her baby latched to her side, grabs the hand of the woman from the information center who squeaks a half-hearted "help-me." I hold out my own hand, and Francis takes it with her other hand. The four of us—the information woman, Francis, her baby, and I—walk a hundred meters to the steps of the park director's house. As soon as Francis lets go, the other woman leaves. I sit on the steps with Francis on the ground in front of me. She has her hand on my knee, and her baby lies in the grass next to her. Then she lumbers over to sit next to Emily and plays with the cuff of her jeans, while her baby climbs the tree that shades them to practice swinging.

Four gibbons entertain Greggii by taking small green fruits out of his hand.

Amanda takes pictures of Emily and Francis, and then she too takes a seat next to Francis. She's wearing a crocheted hat that catches Francis's attention. Francis reaches her hand over to touch Amanda's arm, then brings her foot over to do the same, all the time looking at that hat. Slowly, she reaches up to liberate Amanda's hat before moving onto the grass where she plays with it and puts it on a couple times, hamming it up (55). When the novelty wears off, one of the keepers trades a banana for it and gives the hat back to Amanda.

We stay in Kumai for two days after our river trip. Relationships grow now. Camp Leakey and the river trip were great, but our relationship with Ennog and JJ was professional; they knew it and we knew it. Now that the professional part is fulfilled, we're free for friendship. I suggest to Greggii that the bike Santa gave him for Christmas in Sydney is rotting on *Faith*. The salt air does that. Maybe he wants to give it away, a suggestion he grudgingly agrees to. The next day we see his bike at Harry's, its chain unfrozen, its frame polished, and its broken seat fixed.

Emily and Amanda visit the pregnant wife of the man who watched over *Faith* during our river trip. Weeks later, Emily receives a text message from Ennog that this woman gave birth to a baby girl. Can Emily and Amanda help think of a name for her? They suggest Faith, but are told Indonesian names are longer. The next message tells us this girl is named Faith Emily Amanda.

Batam: Worlds Apart

Our passage to Batam sees our latitude in degrees north—on top of the world again!

From the ferry terminal in Batam, we say goodbye to Nelis. Here we realize the impact of our travels with him, a Christian from a Christian pocket of islands in this racially and culturally diverse nation of a strong Muslim majority. The worlds of Indonesia that unfolded for us were as foreign to Nelis as he was to us. And yet he came, to make himself a better English teacher and to give us better lives.

Batam is our last stop in Indonesia. When we arrive, *Faith* needs varnish work on her toe rails—the teak perimeter surrounding her deck. The other boats at the marina say there's a guy doing similar work on *Argonauta*, whose owners give Ardi a good recommendation.

At times, you question the value of relationships and wonder if they warrant the pain of parting; Ardi's is that relationship. He's the only brother Greggii will ever have (5). To Lorrie and me, he will never be a son in the same sense that Greggii is, but there is no other word to describe our relationship—our son from different parents.

At night, a young man waits at the security shed leading to the dock. He's Ardi, and has been told to talk to me. We discuss *Faith*'s work, and I ask if he can start tomorrow. He says yes. When I ask how much to pay, he replies, "up to you, sir." I learn later that many Asians know westerners put a higher value on their services than they do and that *up to you, sir* works to their advantage. I have this need to know these things ahead of time, so I suggest, "100,000 Rupiah per day?" (US$11.00). He agrees and we shake on it.

Packaged in my white skin, I possess this recently uncovered character trait called racism. When I deal with a non-white, or a non-westerner, I worry about being taken advantage of. This defies logic because my experience is, first, I've been taken advantage of so rarely that it should be a non-issue, and second, the only people who *have* ever taken advantage of me happened to be white westerners. Racism isn't based on logic or experience. Sadly, it just is.

Ardi starts work in the morning. He and Emily and I sand and sand and sand, then break for something to eat, then sand again, trying to get a coat of varnish on in the afternoon. I don't know why, but I can't have somebody work *for* me; it has to be *with* me. I can't say, "do the thing," and walk away, but I must say, "this is what we must do," knowing that *we* includes me.

After a couple days, Ardi refuses our food and drink because of the arrival of *Ramadan*—Islam's month-long, holy period of fasting during daylight. Lunch sees him disappear for an hour that I know is for some sort of high-end religious stuff. It will be over a year from now that Ardi tells us what happens during these lunch periods. He and his friends get together and fry up some noodles, and eat them. They're Muslims, demonstrating their own shortcomings in keeping their faith, but I can't think of a better bunch of guys to illustrate my own relationship with Christ—same behavior, same God, different religions.

Two days after the advent of Ramadan and sometime after Ardi comes back from his clandestine noodle affair, he begins to act squirrely. He won't look me in the eye, but finds a more important attraction in the lifeline, or teak deck, or mast, or something.

Then, to compound his agony around me, he hangs around after work and helps fold laundry, all the while acting as if he wants to say something.

The poor guy is a basket case.

We're walking back to *Faith* after dining on shore, and Ardi's waiting for us at the security booth.

As he and I move aside, he says, "Sir, me talk Emily. Is okay you, Sir?"

"Now?"

"Is okay you, Sir?"

"Where?"

He walks with me a couple feet so we can see a concrete bench under a security light, clearly visible from *Faith*, and points to it.

I look over to Emily, not more than fifteen feet away, and ask her, "Emily, do you want to talk to Ardi on that bench over there?"

"OK."

I ask, "How long?" indicating a spot on my wrist where a watch would be if I wore one, which must look silly to somebody else who doesn't wear one.

In the precise generality I love about Asia, he says, "Not long, Sir."

Emily returns to *Faith* an hour later. She says, "Ardi was in bad shape all afternoon, ever since I told him he had to ask you before I'd go with him to talk somewhere."

Ardi it seems, is following Nelis down that same painful path.

I say, "Well you know, Emily, I trust you, and if you choose to talk to somebody, that's fine with me. They don't really need to talk to me first."

"Dad, that's not the point. I figure I can learn how much somebody wants to talk to me if I make them talk to you first. A test. Ardi's scared of you, dad, so I know he really wanted to talk to me if he went through that all day."

The crew of the good ship *Faith* are changing worlds faster than some people change their socks, and are exhausted when they tie off in the slip at Raffles Marina, in Singapore.

These past seven chapters about our interaction with Indonesia illustrate our experience with people and lands we grew to love more than any other of our voyage.

Events we thought were strange were nothing compared to a modern yacht appearing in an anchorage like Babar, Damar, or Romang. The last yacht that anchored there might have been last year, or ten years ago, or never. The only defense I have for my reactions to certain events is that of a father protecting his family.

...trips to fairly unknown regions should be made twice; once to make mistakes and once to correct them.

John Steinbeck, *The Log From the Sea of Cortez*

Part IV. Faith's Refit

Southeast Asia
14 October to 25 January 2007

Singapore: The Eastern Gateway

The Singapore Strait is no less a gateway to other worlds than the Panama Canal, a bottleneck of shipping from east to west and back again. The contrast with where we arrive from is startling. Singapore hustles, it bustles, and it shines with wealth. Indonesia has resources available for taking. Singapore does not. Instead, the economy is built on servicing those anointed to redistribute the world's resources, resources mistakenly created in the wrong place for proper profits and consumption to occur.

The transportation works; everything is clean. The reason is the pride Singaporeans have for their place—and their laws. The rules of the mass transit system say you can be removed, blacklisted, and fined for putting your feet on the seat, or littering, or eating, or for carrying a special fruit called durian on the train. Durian has an odor of its own that is offensive to some people. Chewing gum is illegal, and Singapore sparkles as a cooperative work of art in cleanliness.

Another contrast between where we arrived from and here is the speed of life. The worlds of commerce and service and consumption are driven at a blistering pace, and the people of Singapore are drawn to that world. In Makassar, Indonesians balance life between getting the job done, whatever it happens to be, and relational aspects of life: family, friends, and fun that form wholeness in the individual. In Singapore, they're plugged in, turned on, and tensed up as they fiddle with phones, handhelds, laptops, books, periodicals, letters, and other items tethering them to their productive existence. Life has richness in the culturally closed, religiously conservative, locally influenced Makassar that is lost in the worldly riches of Singapore, where joy is blanketed by drive.

Life on *Faith* allows us to be chameleons. We choose our pace and enjoy Singapore for two weeks. We find excellent foods from around the world, spare parts to keep *Faith* happy, and fun places to visit. Chinatown is exciting, Little India, breathtaking. We're in Singapore for *Deepavali*—the Hindu "Festival of Lights"—which the Indian population celebrates with parades and dancing and music. In Little India, Emily and Amanda experience *henna*—temporary stained tattoos—each coming home with art on their arms and hands.

Within days of our arrival, Ardi calls and says he will come on the ferry from Batam to see us. When he arrives, he and Emily go talk somewhere in the marina. Emily returns in the evening all excited to tell us Ardi accepted the promise of Christ and took Him into his life.

Ardi, until this time, was Muslim from a Muslim household in a Muslim country. His identity card says he's Muslim and that probably won't change. His parents support his decision, which cannot be assumed in a Muslim household, any more than a Christian family would support one child's decision to become Muslim. Ardi was, until we met him, carrying the waywardness of youth into his adult life (scars and a weak hand from motorcycle accidents attest to this.) His parents witnessed a change in him toward owning his responsibilities of adulthood.

Just as people riding sailboats around the world know other cruisers, Indonesians working on boats know others. Ardi knows many and never lacks for a place to stay or food to eat in Singapore.

Ardi—short for Suardi and with no last name—is Buganese, a people that originated on Sulawesi. Many Buganese, or Bugis, are born, live, work, raise families, and die aboard boats. Those that are able fish and trade for sustenance while plying the waters of southern Sulawesi and Kalimantan. Historically, they are fierce fighters, with certain rules and harsh penalties for breaking them. I heard this was where the term *bogeyman* came from, but minimal research debunks this, causing only a little chip of our romance with Indonesia to disappear.

Ardi was born in Batam after his family moved from Sulawesi. He has aunts, uncles, cousins, grandparents, and even a brother and sister in Sulawesi. We spent enough time in Makassar, on Sulawesi, and in the city of Banjarmasin, on Borneo, to witness an eerie undercurrent that Ardi confirms is part of Buganese culture. Because of the dream-like quality of our visit to Banjarmasin, our memories coalesce into better description now than was possible while we were there.

The smoke, that same smoke that invades Singapore and Malaysia from July to

October, originates in the hills near Banjarmasin from slash-and-burn agriculture in Kalimantan, the Indonesian province on the island of Borneo. Our time in the river that connects the coal-shipping center of Banjarmasin to the world was filled with smoke. Visibility was between two- and four-hundred meters, except during late afternoon, when onshore breezes beat the smoke back up the mountain. This smoke framed the eeriness of our visit.

While motoring through the smoke and water, in a river teeming with coal barges in need of paint waiting to be filled, and tugboats lying at anchor, we passed a coal barge being loaded with a dump truck tripping his load and a loader leveling it off efficiently.

Greggii, at seven years old said, "I just saw a man get killed."

"What?" I asked.

"On that barge. Do you see the truck? And the Bobcat?"

(Greggii calls every piece of construction equipment a Bobcat because I used to have one when I built seawalls; this Bobcat is a large loader.)

"That truck backed up and the back went up, and when the door opened, it hit the man. He fell down, and the Bobcat couldn't see him and covered him up."

Lorrie asked, "Greggii, you didn't *really* see that, did you?"

I followed, "Gregg, did you see that?"

"I...I don't know."

Five hours later, Lorrie said to me, "You know when Greggii said that about seeing a man get killed? I saw it too, but I was so shocked that I blocked it out and didn't believe it was real. I couldn't accept it. This is a spooky place."

We discussed it for a few minutes and knew we must talk to Greggii to tell him what he saw was real and to tell him he could talk to us about it.

Now, something evil took residence in our hearts, and we accepted a fatal industrial accident as normal for this part of the world. Worse still, we allowed our fears in this eerie place to justify not telling anyone; after all, it was too late now to be of any help.

We motored up-stream about five miles, until we came to an impassible bridge. We went back to the city and up another creek that took us to the center of the city, where another low bridge stopped us. After circling in indecision, we were motioned by a man to *raft-up*—pull alongside and tie to the outermost—to six Buganese fishing boats (34). The attentions of people on the other craft turned to us. Many of them walked onto *Faith* and looked in the open hatches. We were tired after sailing, so we asked if we could sleep now and visit tomorrow. Everybody agreed, and some of our new friends even returned to their own boats.

Within two hours, we were required to go into the river to circle, while two of the fishing boats shoreward of us departed. We retied, and rebegan our visit. The second time we untied to let a boat leave, we moved to anchor in the main river.

After dusk, we situated *Faith* in the main river amid the hulking shadows of empty coal barges, lit by the hazy yellow haloes of distant dock lights in the smoky air. While the droning of diesels, the drumming of steel hulls, and the din of industry coalesced in the smoke, Lorrie and Nelis slept in the cockpit with wary eyes for badness. After midnight, a boat carrying three men approached. They identified themselves as part of the Navy Base. With Nelis to translate, they asked, "Have you seen any criminals yet?" The *yet* suggested inevitability; not if, but when. They asked us to move downstream, close to the Navy Base, where they would keep an eye on us. We hoisted the anchor and were again sleeping by three, after paying each of them US$5.00 and some cigarettes for this service.

We woke at daylight to search for the reason we came to Banjarmasin: The Floating Market. We anchored out from it, and a man in a large, dugout canoe with an outboard, came to ferry us through the market. Emily, Amanda, Greggii, Nelis, and I boarded the unstable craft and went from boat to boat, buying watermelons, squash, tomatoes, and other produce. The boats were covered, wooden craft constructed to be floating market-stalls, bringing produce from gardens upstream to trade (44). One boat was a restaurant where we were served a breakfast of noodles. We returned to *Faith*, paid our escort, and departed.

In the choppy seas outside the river mouth, we bumped the sandy bottom for a mile. We didn't get stuck, and finally reached a comfortable depth. We're glad we stopped in Banjarmasin but several days passed before the experienced dread was shaken.

While Ardi explains his heritage, Banjarmasin comes to mind. Ardi affirms that much of our recollection, especially the boats we rafted to, contains cultural threads of Bugis life.

While here in Singapore, we attend a lecture on how to stay safe in the Straits of Malacca. We learn about weather, currents, and piracy in one of the world's piracy hotspots. We learn that 99.9% of the piracy in the straits is directed toward commercial vessels. In fact, in the previous five years, there was only one reported incident against a yacht, and that was north of the straits, in Thailand. When this attack is mentioned, one of the attendees says, "Yeah, but that's not the whole story," and tells of the sailor whose yacht was boarded because he forgot to pay his hooker, and the *pirates* were her friends helping her collect. I'm sure there are several morals to that story, but what I take is a healthy skepticism toward published accounts of piracy.

Ardi's goodbye in Singapore is more difficult than in Batam, but that's the way of goodbyes in growing relationships. During our final days in Singapore, we meet a representative of the Sail Asia Rally. This rally is to encourage yachts to stop in Malaysia, rather than sailing directly to the more popular Phuket, Thailand. They marketed the rally in Darwin, Australia, to participants of the Darwin to Bali Rally, but since we chose to explore more traditional parts of Indonesia independently, this is the first we hear of Sail Asia. A big selling point is a week's free berth at Telaga Harbor Marina in Langkawi, Malaysia. For anchor swingers like us, this is too good to pass up. Langkawi becomes a destination.

Malaysia: The Start of Something Big

The Rally offers freebies and a chance to meet other cruisers. Little do we know that we will spend over a year in Malaysia, and the friends we meet will be long term, and mostly Malaysian.

Our first night out of Singapore is spent at *Pulau Pisang*—Banana Island. During the haze of daylight, we count eight to ten ships plying the straits at any time; at night, when it's clear and they're lit, we count thirty to forty. We make the trip to Langkawi during daylight, anchoring at night, or in the cases of Port Dickson and Penang, staying in marinas. Port Dickson offers us access to the Dutch Colonial city of Melacca; Penang played large in British colonial times.

We arrive for Sail Asia's reception on Langkawi, an island on Malaysia's border with Thailand. The rally offers two bus trips: one day, they herd us all onto a bus for several hours of shopping; the next, we take an island tour, including a stop at *Telaga Tujuh*—Seven Wells—the waterfall named for the seven pools carved into the rock. At the base of the mountain is an ice cream shop. When Amanda starts eating hers, a macaque jumps up to steal it. These naughty monkeys are the size of a dog whose bark is closer to *yip* than *woof*.

Telaga Harbor Marina is the terminus of the rally. All of us except Lorrie rent scooters to explore the island. We take off, Emily and Amanda on one and Greggii and I on the other, and make good fun of it until we get to the busy city streets of Kuah, where Emily takes over driving instead of Amanda and tips over. Both girls get skinned up a little, Emily on her elbow and hip, and Amanda on her elbow and knee. Never one to let something like this pass, Lorrie gives us a dramatic "I told you so." We give her plenty of practice in the *I told you so* department.

Arriving in Malaysia puts us more than halfway around the world from our start. Actually, we were playing with orangutans at the halfway point. *Faith* has taken us 19,000 nautical miles and has been our home for over two years. She shows signs of being a little tired, so I invite a man from Wavemaster Langkawi, a local shipyard, to look at having some work done. We agree to proceed and have *Faith* hauled-out in their yard.

Some flexing of the hull and deck where the mast penetrates the deck and attaches to the keel has annoyed me from the start of our voyage. The flexing has become more pronounced with time, and Wavemaster proposes a fine solution of tie-bars to fix it.

Having an aversion toward missed opportunities—the opportunity here being cheap labor—I also contract exterior paint and interior varnish for *Faith*.

We aren't in Langkawi long before Ardi comes for his first Christmas.

I hail from a family of huggers, and once Ardi clears immigration, I grab him and give him a big bear-hug. His terrified reaction tells me he isn't from a family of huggers. We give him the extra bed in Greggii's room.

I hire Ardi for work not contracted with Wavemaster.

Malaysia, a Muslim country with a few Buddhists, Hindus, and Christians, is a tough place to buy Christmas decorations. We bring our three-foot tree to the apartment to celebrate our third Christmas abroad.

By New Year's, Wavemaster has used up fifteen days of the forty-five day contract to complete *Faith*. I'm warming to the idea that the forty-five days they promised might be a *make-the-sale-happen* fiction.

Ardi stays into January and February. He too feels the pain we experience as *Faith* moves farther and farther from completion. Her mast is off, the windows out, and the deck stripped of hardware—a skeleton of a life we recently lived.

Malaysia: The Work

Malaysian and Indonesian overlap enough that each can speak most of the other's language. Ardi helps me at Wavemaster because he relates to Malays in ways I cannot.

During our first months here, I'm another rich, white, American. While my perception of them relies on an American definition of Islamic cultures in general, their perceptions of us are generated by America's exported culture—the small screen, the big screen, and the music—as part of sophisticated trade agreements. They must wonder where on *Faith* we keep our guns, loose women, and fast cars.

Our respective perceptions of each other are an obstacle to understanding, but Ardi helps establish a working relationship. Another obstacle in quality work is the nature of Malaysia's workforce, or at least Langkawi's workforce, Langkawi being the only area we have work done. (Too often we wrongly expand small pictures into large ones.) The recent decision to pursue a production-based economy is burdened by a lack of history of productive employment. Some of the young men working on *Faith* have taken vocational training to learn the mechanics of a craft, but none possess a history of craftsmanship; there is no mentoring or apprenticeship where the art of a craft is passed. The art is the more important quality.

Ardi understands. On the interior varnish, where the Wavemaster employees simply sand, then varnish, Ardi shows them that a little finesse often makes the difference between me rejecting or accepting the work (72).

Our work takes ten months to complete.

130

We're trapped, but realize too late that Wavemaster is only the bait. The trap is our creation, as we fall into feeling like victims, robbed of God's plan for our lives. We try to escape on rungs of anger, frustration, and self-pity, but find the quality of our lives deteriorating. On days we choose to be victims, we waste God's grace. Ardi is with us and becomes part of our family. We continue to mesh in the midst or even because of the frustrations. And we're blessed with lasting friendships.

One friend is Joe. Joe is an ethnic Indian Malaysian. He's one sinner I look forward to spending eternity with, because he's a Christian who acknowledges his own sinful nature, without getting too hung on everybody else's.

We meet Joe when a fire explodes in my mouth. Asking around develops a consensus that Joe Pharmacy is best equipped to deal with problems of this nature.

As we approach the pharmacy for our first visit, a curious sight greets us—shoes—and a sign telling customers: "Please give your shoes a rest." Cleanliness and professionalism mark the atmosphere inside and Joe greets us warmly.

"Do you boil the water?" is his question on hearing my symptoms.

"No."

"You have something going on in there, fungus," he says as he takes a tiny tooth-paste-type tube from a glass case near the counter. "Put a dab of this on your tongue and work it around to put the fire out." He walks to a case on the opposite wall, and returns with some anti-fungal pills. "One of these every day for a week—you will be okay. From now on, my friend, boil the water."

During this dialogue—in which gaps are filled with talk about sailing, about Langkawi, and an invitation to his church—friendship again begins to blossom.

As our friendship develops in the following weeks, so too does Joe's ability to look me in the eye and tell me quite bluntly to quit feeling sorry for myself. I can play victim all I want, but he knows better.

He's Roman Catholic because "That's where God told me I could do the most good." Jesus came to him the night he opened his pharmacy, years before, after friend of his, a Hindu priest, came to his opening and offered to bless the store. Joe, caught off guard and not wanting to ruffle his friend's feathers, accepted. That night, Jesus appeared and asked, "Joe, why do you persecute me?" He tells me he spent the rest of the night crying on his knees in prayer.

Joe offers Emily work in the pharmacy in the capacity of a student volunteer, and she does for four months. With Ardi's coaching and the work there, she learns to speak Malay. She learns other things as well because a lot of the Malaysians who come into the pharmacy figure the white girl can't speak Malay, and they discuss private things with Joe. When Emily feels brave or bored, she finds entertainment in speaking up during a Viagra-type conversation.

Under Joe's professional instruction and supervision, Emily fills prescriptions and dispenses pharmaceuticals. The pharmacy has no narcotics, which are dispensed through hospitals and doctors, but nearly everything else, from antibiotics to contraceptives to performance-enhancers-in-the-sack, is sold over-the-counter. Malaysians as individuals must be either smarter or more cautious than Americans, who need several costly layers of protection from these same medicines.

Alcohol is treated in the Koran and the Bible similarly—drunkenness is forbidden in the Bible, intoxication is forbidden in the Koran. Many Muslim societies have a *no-alcohol* stance similar to many Christian churches. The result, apparent to Emily, is that Joe leaves untapped a substantial market for cough syrup, only to watch one dejected soul after another slink out of the store without a purchase after reading the ingredients of the syrup he offers. It's a tragedy that Christians and Muslims can't cherish our similarities—accept that we all worship the God of Abraham, that Moses climbed the mountain for the same playbook for us all to follow or break as we're so inclined on a given day—and trust God to sort out the rest.

During one of her phone calls home, Lorrie learns that her mother has been diagnosed with ovarian cancer. Lorrie feels helpless and guilty, halfway around the world from where her mother might be dying. She goes home for six weeks, but returns with more questions than before. At times, I feel the radiance of her rage for putting us in this seemingly hopeless situation.

Emily grows into a young woman with a man in our home who professes his love for her. Yes, early in our time with Ardi, he tells both Emily and me that he loves her. First Nelis, now Ardi. Emily must be especially attractive to Indonesians. Her heart becomes a basketful of conflict and turmoil. She spends time, energy, and prayer to learn how to behave. She needs a recipe to respond, a guide that tells her *if this happens, do this,* but none is forthcoming. Early in her teens, Emily pledged to wait for God's provided husband. Now, during our frustrations and angers, she must take ownership of decisions easier made as a child.

I must work every day to make sure the progress on *Faith* is acceptable. This gives me purpose and a sense of self. Lorrie has her own concerns with our household and her mother. Emily has a close friend in Ardi, in spite of the chaos she allows him to wreak on her emotions.

This sense of purpose and relationship can't be said for either Amanda or

Greggii. Ardi's relationship with them is that of a brother. He's a friend to each, but that doesn't fill their needs for social interaction. They both hurt.

Amanda tries to connect with her friends on the internet and with email. A few connect, but most of her old friends have moved in different directions, and she watches from a distance as relationships fade. She's spent her most formative years, between twelve and fifteen, living in a world of otherness and possesses an uneasy comfort in it. She personalizes my comments about America's demonizing this otherness, without having the ability to discern rhetoric from substance.

Greggii finds kids to play with, but he fills positions and isn't fully included as a person. He knows he doesn't belong, but is allowed to play the game. His best friend during this period is Ardi. They share a bedroom with two twin beds, littered with toys that boys buy to fill needs that can't be filled, so they sit on the shelf. I know I can look at my own shelves full of toys, and name the holes in my soul that each was to fill when I purchased it.

The cloud of victimization continues while *Faith* gets her facelift. The brightest spot is Ardi. He calls Lorrie "mom;" he calls me "sir." I never get used to being called sir, but can't get him to call me *Gregg* or *dad* either. "Sir" becomes a joke, and months later, on my birthday, he buys me a tee-shirt with "Sir" embroidered on the pocket.

He tells us we're his family unlike the family that raised him. There are cultural differences between us, but he enjoys inclusion in the closeness of our family, a mutual feeling.

One cultural difference is that every time Ardi goes back to Batam, he returns broke.

I learn this because he doesn't eat lunch when he returns.

"Why aren't you eating, Ardi?"

"I can't buy today, Sir."

"Don't you have any money?"

"No, Sir."

"What happened to the money you've been making? You don't have any of it?"

"My brother, he need some, I give him. Last time, my father, he need some, I give him, Sir."

In a wave of western wisdom, I say, "Ardi, what if I pay you only half of the money you earn, and Emily keeps the rest in an envelope for you? It's your money, Ardi, but you can't give it away if you don't have it on you. Then, when you want it, it's there for you. It's your money. Even if you want to give it to your dad and brother, it will let you think about it without having it in your pocket when they ask."

"Thank you, Sir. That is good."

While we learn about each other, Ardi reveals another side. Sara is a two-year-old girl, Ardi's daughter in every sense except blood. It happened that Ardi got drunk, and a girl said that she conceived Sara after being with Ardi while he was drunk. Not wishing to care for her any longer, she then gave Sara to Ardi. Ardi soon learned the impossibility of his being her father, either by counting months or being told otherwise.

"Why do you keep caring for her, if she's not your daughter?"

"She need me. In Indonesia, very hard for her without me, Sir."

In May, Amanda learns Jacob, her friend from home who joined us in St. Lucia, will visit from June 26 to July 22. We expect *Faith* to be ready for Jacob's visit. The nearer his arrival becomes, the more we realize that *Faith* will not be ready.

Anticipation of Jacob's visit causes a ray of sunshine to pierce the cloud we're building. We're excited. This is our life, where God put us right now, and somebody wants to check it out.

Broken Bones—I Told You So

Following months of daily routine, back and forth to Wavemaster to work on *Faith* on the scooters we now rent by the month, Emily, Amanda, and Ardi go to McDonalds for lunch (4). Emily calls fifteen minutes later and asks me to pick them up at the police station. They're caught driving without licenses. She must first convince me the call isn't a prank.

"Here dad, do you want to talk to him?"

"Yes."

After our initial greeting, the policeman says, "Do you know they drive without driver's license?"

"Yes, they were going to get lunch for us. What do I need to do?"

"They cannot drive without license in Malaysia. Why you let them drive without license?"

"They were going to get lunch."

"Do you want me give them ticket?"

"No, I don't want you to give them a ticket."

"OK, I will let them go with warning. Don't let them drive without license."

They return shortly with lunch, saying at first the policeman wanted them to push their scooters home, then softened and said they could drive home. Emily then asked if they could pick up lunch before coming home, and the policeman allowed them this also.

On Sunday, a friend from another yacht comes to visit. He asks how work is

135

proceeding on *Faith,* and we ride to Wavemaster so I can show him. Emily and Ardi follow.

On our way back to the apartment, he comments on how well I drive like a Malaysian. That's not necessarily a compliment, but I'm given to taking it as such anyway. Then, in the middle of showing off, I screw up. We're following a slow bus belching black smoke in our faces. I start passing the bus blindly—driving is on the left here and this is a left curve—when suddenly a construction barrier appears. I hit the brakes to get back in my own lane, but a dusting of sand is in front of the barrier and we go into a slide, heeling heavily to port. As soon as we hit the clean, traffic-washed pavement, the tires bite and we slam over hard to starboard. Damage to the scooter would have been worse if my right, upper body didn't cushion the shock.

This happens in front of the hospital, which is the last place I think I want to go. We flag a taxi for home, and my friend follows on the scooter. He had the good sense to eject early and was unharmed.

I pay the taxi while several people assemble to size-up my condition. My social skills aren't up to the task and I feel like throwing up. I free myself from the discussion and get into the elevator with somebody's assistance and ride it to our apartment. It's a glass-bubble-type elevator that overlooks the pool where Lorrie is; I signal for her to join me.

In the apartment, I sit on the bed. Lorrie comes and helps me lie down, causing an excruciating sensation in my right, upper back. There's no getting comfortable.

Lorrie calls Joe to ask if he can help. He comes in a half-hour with Ace bandages and anti-inflammatory pills. He looks me over and confirms my suspicion that my shoulder is dislocated. He then calls a masseuse who can put my shoulder back in the traditional way. Traditional means not medical, usually of Chinese influence. The masseuse is on the mainland but will return on the six o'clock ferry.

We go looking for a clinic that's open on Sunday, but most are closed. We see one that's open, and Joe says the doctor's good, but might have beer on his breath. At least he's open. The doctor surprises Joe with his sobriety and says we need an x-ray to see what's in there.

I want to go back to the apartment and wait for the shoulder undislocater guy to show up, but Lorrie presses the x-ray issue. Joe now takes her side. I'm looking forward to getting my shoulder reconnected so the pain can go away, but fortunately, I lose this battle. As we enter the hospital's driveway, I point out my tire tracks and the construction barrier to Lorrie.

The x-rays are taken, the first time with the metal pin in the Ace bandage glowing like a candle. Joe and I know no good can come from editorializing about Langkawi's medical services, but my mishap elevates Lorrie's significant stress level and she's on a roll.

Five minutes later, we're summoned and shown several broken ribs and a broken shoulder blade, right in the spot that hurt so badly when I lay down. The doctor on staff calls an orthopedic surgeon, who tells us over the telephone that all I can do is wait for healing and for the pain to go away. Another revelation is that my shoulder is not dislocated.

I can't imagine the pain if the traditional shoulder relocator guy had been available. All I know about dislocated shoulders comes from *Lethal Weapon,* where Mel Gibson slams his own shoulder into a wall to fix it. I have visions of this guy doing that to all my broken bones.

Joe helps situate me at the apartment and I sleep in the living room chair, still unable to lie down. Monday and Tuesday are painful.

My doctor in Michigan wants me to confirm that I haven't punctured the chest cavity, so on Tuesday, Emily and I ferry to Kedah, twenty miles or one-and-one-half hours away. It's calm. When we arrive at Kedah Medical Center, an urologist friend of Joe's introduces us to an orthopedic surgeon by the name of Dr. Singh. I see a lot of Dr. Singhs on signs outside different offices and ask if they're all related. "If you Sikh [pronounced sick], you Singh," is his response. This floor has many Sikhs and the men of this faith all take the Hindi name for lion.

Dr. Singh looks at my x-rays and tells us I broke the number three, four, and five ribs. My shoulder blade has a tear from the bottom to two-thirds of the way up. He also says a couple of the lower ribs, that don't show up on the x-ray, are probably broken too, given the amount of pain I have there. Wow. I broke at least four bones, probably more. He confirms there is no damage to the chest cavity.

A cost is eventually incurred when stupidity is exercised on the road. The monetary cost in not-America is considerably less. The x-ray cost one hundred Malaysian Ringgats, the consultation with Dr. Singh, sixty. That falls in the neighborhood of US$40.00 for both.

The seas are up on our return trip and my bones curse me all the way.

In spite of the pain, breaking a bunch of bones helps put things in perspective. I've been fighting, mostly at Wavemaster over things I can't change. *Faith* has been out of the water for six months, and the frustrations have multiplied to where nothing is more important.

Breaking bones forces me to let go.

Southeast Asia: Bangkok

Our travel with Jacob begins on a ferry from Langkawi to Satun, Thailand, a canopied pickup truck with benches to the bus station, a bus to Hat Yai, another pickup to the airport, and an Air Asia flight from Hat Yai to Bangkok International. We change our currency to Thai Baht.

Our first night is spent in a seedy hotel near the airport. Amanda, Jacob, and Greggii walk to McDonalds, while Ardi and I opt for a hawker place with the World Cup on the big screen. Germany beats Argentina in penalty kicks. The World Cup becomes part of our routine. In Langkawi, nursing my broken bones, I had nothing to do but watch the games, and I grew fascinated with the sport the world calls football.

In the morning, we move closer to downtown. Hiring a van works better than last night's taxis because we got separated; our taxi, with Amanda, Jacob, and me, got lost. Not for long, but enough for Greggii to have thoughts of losing his dad.

We arrive in the Sukhomvit district at a backpacker's inn called Sam's Lodge. It's clean, it's new, and the fact that the bathrooms are shared for all rooms on the floor doesn't matter because ours is the only party on the third floor.

The Chatuchak Weekend Market sits on thirty-five acres, and has more than 15,000 shops and stalls. Emily and Ardi explore on their own, as do Amanda and Jacob. Lorrie, Greggii, and I enjoy the day until Greggii gets tired, which tends to suck energy out of anybody around him. He thinks a foot massage will help. I agree. There we are, Greggii and I in adjacent chairs, getting our feet worked over.

Greggii laughs and wiggles because it tickles. I grimace and groan because it hurts.

The difference between a *tuk-tuk* in Bangkok and a *becak* in Makassar is the motor on the tuk-tuk. Ardi, Emily, Greggii, and I ride in one, and Lorrie, Amanda and Jacob ride in the other. Our drivers take us to the Tourist Information Bureau, where our visas and travel arrangements can happen under one roof.

To kill time in Bangkok, we take the cheesiest tour of our voyage—the Damnoen Saduak Floating Market. We hear 'floating market' and recall Banjermasin, but Damnoen Saduak has more souvenirs than anything else. Most of the produce is cut up and packaged in plastic wrap, rather than natural skin. The tour buses are lined up and there are more white guys than Thais.

We finish the market early and wait at a Cobra Show—not part of the day's planned activities—for the other vans to arrive so we can continue to the next highlight on the day's schedule. Our *private* van for the day is part of a group, and six vans are traveling together. Greggii and I are bored to tears and don't look forward to the rest of the day's tour, so he and I head into the Cobra Show. Greggii's interaction with the show is worth every Baht. A large jumping snake jumps into the glass in front of us, and he practically jumps out of his skin (Greggii, that is).

After watching football until 4:00 AM, we wake up at 5:45 for our transfer from Sam's Lodge to the bus depot to begin our trip to Cambodia.

We wait an hour at the travel office before transferring to the bus depot to sit in the van for a half-hour until the bus comes. We board the bus to find that it has one fewer seats than people on board. The operator makes arrangements to buy somebody off to fix that problem, and we all get seated for a less than comfortable ride to the border.

When we're close to the border, a group holding orange squares of paper for their tickets are told to leave the bus for a transfer; then, a few minutes later, those with tickets like ours are told to leave for a different transfer, not in the calm manner of somebody concerned about customer service, but in a loud, barking, "Get Off The Bus, Now!" manner. The flags go up, but my protests are answered only with louder barking.

We board an open truck to transfer to the border.

Southeast Asia: Cambodia

A van waits on the Cambodian side to take us to Siem Reap on the worst road in the world—it's our roughest passage yet.

Lorrie's protective instincts are mobilized in a no man's land between countries. We were warned about children who hold umbrellas for us in the tropical drizzle as we cross, rifling through our pockets while we're distracted by this generous gesture. Lorrie sees the umbrellas coming and the children choosing their targets, and asserts herself to keep them away from us.

I exhibit nastiness four hours later when we stop at a little store to use the toilet. It's after six and we see no end to this miserable road. Amanda asks me to buy some bananas, so I go and ask how much for a bunch. The woman quotes a price. I don't know why, maybe nervousness, maybe anger, maybe fatigue, probably all three, but I just laugh at the preposterous idea that she charges the equivalent of seventy-five cents for a bunch of bananas. I get back in the van, and when our driver returns, I ask how much longer to Siem Reap. When he says two hours, I get mad and holler, "Get us to Siem Reap—NOW!"

I scare the guy, and he tears out and goes too fast for this terrible road.

Getting angry was a mistake—it usually is. I say I'm wrong, but he speaks very little English. "You good, you okay. Me bad." I think he understands. Then I ask him to slow down, pointing to the van around us, "no break." Soon, we end up feeling and hearing part of the van dragging in the road. We discover that the spare tire has abandoned us and we're dragging its bracket. We turn around and find the tire a short distance back, and continue at a more reasonable pace.

When he asks about reservations, I tell him the Golden Banana. We don't have reservations, but I don't want *him* choosing our accommodations. We call the Golden Banana from the edge of Siem Reap to book rooms, and the manager gives our driver directions. We arrive rattled, exhausted, and relieved, at 9:30 PM.

After waking late, we eat breakfast and walk the town, the highlight being the tour of the rehabilitation center where prosthetic limbs are fitted. Sixty percent of the patients are here because of landmines and *UXO*—unexploded ordnance. Cambodia is loaded with landmines, causing 898 deaths in 2004, down from 3,400 in 1979. The family farm of our guide is on a list to be cleared, but is at least fifteen years away as populated areas and road construction take priority. No one we meet at the rehabilitation center speaks in terms of what should be, or of expectations, or in any of the terms of blame I find myself trapped in when I face disappointments or obstacles.

Cambodia owns a horror-filled recent history: The Vietnam War, when Americans chased a fantastic threat to our way of life all over the eastern half of the country, followed by two murderous regimes—3,000,000 murdered under Pol Pot's reign of terror alone. Of all the people we have met in our journey, Cambodians have faced the most circumstances outside of their control from which to form a basis to blame others, and yet, we witness quite the opposite. We witness a joy that comes from receiving each day as a new gift from which to grow, an acceptance, not of the wrongs committed against them, but of the promise that tomorrow will be better than yesterday.

In the morning, we board three tuk-tuks to take us to the temples. Tuk-tuks in Cambodia are motorcycles with a trailer for passengers.

While Europeans lived like Mel Gibson in *Braveheart,* Asians were building the temples and governments and cities we witness the remnants of today, Angkor Wat being one of the more famous (75). The residences and palaces of wood did not survive, but the temples and walls are made of stone and have survived 800-1,200 years.

In the afternoon, we visit the Landmine Museum, founded by a man who, as a boy, worked for the Khmer Rouge to walk in front of the soldiers and locate landmines, and who survived whole to tell the story. He was expendable because, at eight years old, he couldn't carry a rifle. Most of the museum staff are victims of landmine accidents.

Hiring the same tuk-tuks with the same drivers the next morning, we go further afield to a waterfall and the River of 1,000 *Lingas*—penises—but while we see carvings on much of the riverbed, the Lingas are either somewhere else or suffering the effects of the cold water.

The tuk-tuk drivers receive commissions from the tourist restaurants they take us to, where Cambodians can neither afford to eat nor desire the western tastes. After twice refusing to eat at their selected restaurants, I tell one of our drivers we want local fare. I give them the same amount of money we would pay at a tourist joint, and tell them to make as much money as they want, but provide us with a local meal.

One driver calls his brother to arrange things.

After the waterfall, we stop at Banteay Srei, my favorite temple. Greggii has had his fill of temples, and Lorrie stays with him while he sleeps in the tuk-tuk. The sandstone is pink, the carved stones comprising the walls are well preserved, and the place radiates the genius of the artisans that crafted it.

From Banteay Srei, we go to dinner. A small store sits on the road and the building next to the store has bottled petrol for sale. Behind each is a house, and behind the two houses is a small farm with a large garden, some animals, and fowl. The first order of business is to disable two ducks and a chicken with a slingshot, then to pluck and slaughter them.

While waiting for dinner, we visit the matriarch. At least, judging from her looks, and the way the family ignores her, we think she's the matriarch. In a chair, with a blanket over her legs, she fails to keep the bright red spittle of betel-nut juice from soiling her front, while the blanket conceals any other soiling. If she has any teeth, they're still in a glass on her nightstand, a long-term effect of chewing betel-nut. I don't know what draws us to her except maybe the contrast she provides, not only with us, but with the rest of her family. Her head is shaved, reflecting her position as a Buddhist nun. Language prevents deep understanding, but an indefinable sharing occurs; she seems to enjoy our visit as much as we enjoy visiting her.

An hour later, woven mats are placed on the concrete patio where the matriarch sits and it's time to eat. Rice, chicken, ducks, spicy sauces—everything is good, one highlight of many for us in Cambodia.

On our last day in Siem Reap, Emily and Amanda again go to Angkor Wat, with paper to lay over the carvings and shade with crayons to pick up the relief. They get some nice impressions before being warned by small children that the police are coming to tell them not to do it.

Southeast Asia: Vietnam

. . . We have been too often disappointed by the optimism of the American leaders, both in Vietnam and Washington, to have faith any longer in the silver linings they find in the darkest clouds. . .

Walter Cronkite, CBS Evening News, February 27, 1968

In Phnom Penh, we keep Greggii occupied and away from the two places we wish to see: The Killing Fields and the Toel Slang Genocide Museum—a secondary school turned into a torture prison and death camp during the reign of the Khmer Rouge. Emily summed our emotions that day in a college term paper, "Dehumanization: War Weapon and Justification for Genocide," (November 24, 2008):

> The day was hot and dry. It was impossible not to inhale the dust. I was in Phnom Phen, Cambodia, visiting The Killing Fields. The ground was ridden with teeth, broken bones, and shreds of clothing. I had to walk carefully to avoid stepping on these remains of the victims of the Khmer Rouge genocide. I came to a large tree with a sign next to it that read, "KILLING TREE AGAINST WHICH EXECUTIONERS BEAT CHILDREN." Then I walked over to a large *stupa*—a Buddhist shrine—that contained layers upon layers of skulls that had been unearthed from an excavation. Questions were flashing through my mind such as: "How did this happen?" "Where could the evil behind something like this

143

come from?" I left Phnom Penh and life continued. The shock of what I saw and the questions I had were still with me, but faded over time.

After Phnom Penh, we board a bus bound for Ho Chi Minh City, the old Saigon (76).

I was born two years too late to participate in America's conflict in Southeast Asia, but I grew up with Walter Cronkite providing nightly coverage. By age thirteen, I knew I didn't want anything to do with what was going on here; this conflict grew up my generation; to some degree, it grew up our parents' generation.

The begging is not as pronounced as in Cambodia, but many people make ends meet by selling lighters, books, and other items we don't need. The prices are quoted in dollars, Vietnam being one of the few places we visit in the world where US Dollars are preferred over the local currency, *đồng*.

We go to the War Remnants Museum that was previously called the War Crimes Museum until American diplomatic pressure caused the name change. The exhibits did not change with the name, however, and four themes are apparent: massacres, especially My Lai, the outcomes of Dow Chemical's Napalm and Monsanto's Agent Orange on people (Monsanto claimed then that Agent Orange was safe, just as they claim now their pesticides and genetically modified foods are safe), paintings by children of how the world *should* be, and the American photo-journalists who put the war's atrocities into American living rooms in an era when atrocities on *both* sides were the responsibility of journalism.

I think we finally found one of the *places in the world where they didn't value human life,* but that was at a time when their values were imposed by outsiders.

The Cu Chi Tunnels are one of the places the Viet Cong and guerillas lived during the war. Cu Chi is just outside of Ho Chi Minh City, where over 240 kilometers of tunnels were maintained with health clinics, war rooms, sleeping quarters, and cooking facilities. There are also several primitive but effective booby traps on display, many made from unexploded U. S. bomb casings and other abandoned hardware.

While the U. S. put people on the moon, had the most sophisticated weaponry in the world, and the talent to abuse it as effectively as anyone anywhere, the war was won with primitive methods used by a determined people.

A taxi is our first experience in Hanoi. We ask to go to the Viet Anh Hotel. The driver gets on his cell phone as soon as we're out of the airport, chatters in Vietnamese, and then takes us to an area where the main racket is hotel rooms. A man in a maitre de or bell hop uniform runs out of a building with a business card from the Viet Anh Hotel.

"So sorry, Viet Ahn no room."

"Is this the Viet Anh?" I ask.

"Yes, Viet Ahn, sorry, no room."

"The Viet Anh is on Ma Mai Street, all these signs say 'Heng Buam Street.'"

"Signs bad. Viet Ahn, no room."

Our driver then takes us to a second place, and I refuse to let him take the bags out of the taxi. We've been had, and I tell the driver to take us to the Viet Anh Hotel. We pile back in, and drive around a little longer, before arriving at our original destination on Ma Mai Street.

Too tired to do much else, we try going to the Water Puppet show. It's sold out, so we buy tickets for tomorrow afternoon.

In the morning, we take a walking tour. Emily and I go one way, and Lorrie, Jacob and Ardi go another. Emily and I complete the walking tour of Hanoi's Old Quarter in mid-afternoon by sampling a couple traditional Vietnamese coffee shops. Vietnam has great coffee, and we're both a little wired before long. On the way home, we stop and sample Bin Hoi, the cheapest beer in the world. A one-pint mug costs fourteen cents.

As a family, we walk to the Water Puppets Theatre for a fun show. The reflection of lights off the surface of the shallow pool hides the underwater mechanical apparatus that brings the puppets to life. When we exit the theatre, we find a woman squatting on the sidewalk over a small kettle of boiling water. We're curious and after watching her boil an egg, we try it. The egg is already opened when she hands it to us, revealing an almost developed duck. Jacob and Lorrie abstain, but the rest of us find it palatable. Like everything in the exotic food world, it tastes like turtle.

On 20 July, we fly from Hanoi to Bangkok, then from Bangkok to Hat Yai, then taxi to Satun for the return ferry to Langkawi.

Light at the Tunnel's End

The Wavemaster circus continues. They hired a new foreman while we were away, and he and I spend several minutes developing a seething dislike for one another.

I poured my heart into *Faith* and into the guys working on her for eight months, but this new manager's sole goal is getting *Faith* out of the shipyard, regardless of quality.

The crew of workers on *Faith*, consisting of Ayip, Hashim, Halim, and Khairy, is devastated by his insistence they lower their newly acquired quality standards. Ardi is upset. I'm livid. I go so far during one of our early arguments to bang a big ratchet on some steel scaffolding. An echoing *clang* rings through the building. The new foreman then takes off his hardhat and bangs it on the same scaffolding, I suppose to demonstrate his own anger. The hardhat's made of plastic though, and emits only a mild *thud*.

Joe tells me, "Don't sweat it so much, Chief [his nickname for me]. You will never get quality work done here, and you must accept it. It's only money and your job is to take care of your family." I manage *Faith's* completion without any more major flare-ups.

On 29 August, Halim's crew attempts the final coat of paint on *Faith*. An hour later I'm told he wants to see me. When I get there, the timid Hashim says, "Sir, your system not work."

There's a class structure in Malaysia, with workmen avoiding confrontation with foremen, managers, and especially owners. I'm glad he knows me well enough to be straightforward.

He's right. Halim, Hashim, and I then plan to change the system, sand again in the morning, and apply a finish coat in the afternoon.

On Wednesday, 30 August, *Faith* has all of her paint.

We begin installing deck fittings, and I stay late to paint the antifouling on her hull over the next couple days. Six days after the paint, we drag her out of the barn to install the mast. After twelve days, on 11 September 2006, *Faith* goes for a swim. The remaining work is interior, and rather than the dusty confines of the hot shipyard, we tie her to Wavemaster's pontoon.

I'm beyond the point of frustration yet still this side of despair, a point where the quality I advocate isn't as important anymore. Maybe Joe has something to do with that, or maybe the time has come to get on with life. Yes, we have to finish her. Yes, the work must be done right, but perfection will not be achieved, and as de facto project manager and foreman—the new foreman has been instructed by Wavemaster's general manager to cooperate with me—I am the one to determine which areas aren't that important.

I spend a day in the engine room reconnecting the engine exhaust and the hoses to the bilge pumps. In the engine room, I sit on the engine, hard and lumpy. I never work long here before springing a leak, usually on an arm—from a hose clamp, a sharp end of a bolt, or something new I never thought of as wound inducing.

No matter how simple in my imagination, work in the engine room is hard. This discomfort, pain, and hard work add up to a shirt that's wringing wet with sweat twenty minutes into any job in here. By noon, I smell like week-old gym shorts. By five o'clock, my nostrils are numb and I'm self-conscious of how badly I must stink to anybody whose nostrils are not. Lucky for me, everybody else has been sanding all day, and the most they can smell is the dust in their own boogers.

Lorrie brings the kids to spend time with me before Emily has to work at the pharmacy. We decide Greggii must give up his room in the bow cabin so Emily might enjoy a measure of privacy more fitting of a twenty-year-old woman. Greggii tries to resist but knows he's fighting a losing battle.

Lorrie and I think his attitude might benefit if he stays with me on *Faith*.

After he regains his composure, he says, "Dad, have you ever lost something you

147

really loved?"

"Are you talking about your room?"

"Yeah, I mean, what if you lost mom?"

I think he exaggerates the importance of the bow berth, but I'm pleased with his ability to articulate his feelings.

Before bed, he asks me to wake him before sunrise. He wants to fast during the daylight hours of Ramadan like the Muslim population of Malaysia. Experiencing the world through the eyes of others is a goal of our journey on *Faith*.

Greggii wakes at 5:00 to make a bowl of instant noodles, and spends a minor eternity trying to convince me to start the day, but finally gives up and we both get a couple more hours sleep.

He wakes again at 8:30 full of energy, and burns a lot of it chasing fish around the dock with a makeshift net we made from half of a five-liter water bottle with a hole in each side where we shove an old boat hook pole through.

His fasting resolve diminishes by 11:00.

"Dad, I can't fast, have we got anything to eat?" Lorrie, Emily, and Amanda arrive soon with lunch.

Emily stays to work on *Faith* today and to spend the night.

Her first job is to send me up the mast in the boson's chair to set all the cotter pins we only barely set before in case we didn't have something right. We then replace the lazy jacks—a set of lines to guide the mainsail on top of the mast when lowering it.

Emily says, "It's not fair that you and mom won't let anyone in our family ride a scooter. You and mom are the worst drivers in the family. You drove like a madman on the scooter, and mom drives the car just as bad." She's right, but I'm not going up against mom on this one.

Amanda is next to stay on *Faith,* and it rains all day. We spend our time inside, sorting nuts, bolts, washers, screws and other miscellaneous stuff in *Faith's* parts' bins. It's the most tedious task that needs doing. After fifteen minutes, the screws all look alike, and identifying the differences in threads, diameters, and lengths makes our eyes dizzy.

Lorrie calls to tell me of a matching exercise Greggii had in his schoolwork today. In one column was the word *star* among a list of words, and in the other column, the word *box*. Greggii saw them and knew they belonged together. Here we are, half a world away from Seattle, and there's a *Starbucks* at the ferry terminal.

Doing What's Important

I arrange to work tomorrow, Saturday, with Hashim, Ayip, Sujiman, and Ardi. We're getting close, and I can almost taste the day we sail away.

I get home, and as I walk into the apartment, Greggii says, "Dad, I've got a surprise for you!" He was at a friend's house, and learned of a fishing contest from 10:00 to noon tomorrow.

I'm not the first parent to know the overwhelming importance of what I planned, while realizing what I hold so important pales next to the importance Greggii places on my taking him to the fishing tournament. I ask Ardi to cover for me on *Faith* so I can go with Greggii. After the contest starts, Amanda and Lorrie bring us some fresh prawns for bait, and some water, an umbrella, and other necessities. Soon, it gets hot enough to force Greggii and me to shore to fish from a shaded boardwalk. Greggii's only catch is a needlefish, not enough to win the contest.

One night, we're sitting in Ardi and Greggii's room, when Amanda comes in and says she wants to do something with Ardi, who's barefoot on his bed. She sits down, grabs his foot, and asks if his mother ever did *first-little-piggy-went-to-market*. We soon reason, with the aid of Ardi's puzzled look, that *first little piggy* is not a Muslim tradition.

I have lunch with Peter. Last names are unimportant in a trip around the world in a sailboat. Relationships get deep fast and don't often last long. Nineteen months ago, Peter and his wife, Becky, were riding on his motorcycle when the frame collapsed onto the rear tire, locked it up, and sent them into a slide. They slid into an above-ground water main and Peter flew over it. Becky hit the pipe. According to Peter, when I met her, it was the first time since the accident that she could sit up for guests. While we were in Vietnam, I received word of a memorial service for Becky. When we returned, I asked him to lunch.

He tells about the cremation and his hands-on experience of it, including the tradition of picking out pieces of bone from the ash with chopsticks, which he was never very good at, so he picked the pieces with his fingers and put them into the urn. He says that helped him in his grief.

Lorrie has an encounter with another cruiser in Langkawi. After exchanging cruisers' pleasantries, Pat, from Ireland, suggests that as a U.S. citizen, Lorrie has influence over U.S. Global Policy. She decides she has somewhere else to go and departs.

Later, I explain to Pat the futility we face in effecting change at home. I tell him only ten percent of the U.S. population holds passports. Subtract from that the ninety percent of them using their passports for business or diplomatic purposes, and subtract from that the ninety-five percent using their passports to go to some exotic land to have their western desires pampered, or to force beliefs on the people there. We're among very few motivated to see the world as a collection of sinners just like us, and maybe, to have the opportunity to share the world we experience with a few people when we return home. Before long, Pat and I become friends.

In Cambodia, we witnessed true joy, even in the kids on the street, one step away from begging. They've been through so much pain, and still exhibit basic joy. The same is true in Vietnam, and Vanuatu, and Indonesia. While we don't like the hustles and scams of some of these places, there's a higher degree of joy than in places where stuff is purported to bring happiness.

When we began our voyage, we knew God was leading us somewhere or toward something, but we had no idea where that was. I always dreamed God would use us to train our children to make a difference, never knowing what that difference might be. We witness daily that the world is not a scary place, as American opinion-makers want us to believe.

It's full of people everywhere, created in God's image, whose biggest responsibility is to provide a safe environment for their families, with a moral compass not unlike our own. Our perspective has been turned upside down over the past nearly three years.

People everywhere simply want the freedom to love and to be loved.

We have our health, we have each other, but most important, we have God leading the way.

And then I get a phone call as I prepare for bed on *Faith*. From Ardi...

Letting Go

"Sir, how are you?"

"I am good, Ardi. How are you?"

"I am in Singapore now to meet my friend talk about job, so he give me job in the boat and have good salary $1200 US a month. He will go Phuket also! So what do you think?"

"I don't know what to think, Ardi," I say as sadness engulfs me.

"I need your help. What can I say to Emily. I don't want she get angry with me."

"I need to think. Can I call you tomorrow?"

"Yes... Sir I am very like with your family. You make me like your kid. I feel very bad to tell you about this. But I am promise we meet again in Phuket."

My heart is heavy. Ardi is not Greggii, Amanda, or Emily, but Lorrie and I agree he's someone we care for like one of our own. We loved, and love.

The next day is an emotional trial. Lorrie brings Emily, Amanda, and Greggii to *Faith* to talk about Ardi.

Emily spends most of the day in tears, shifting between sadness and hurt before settling on anger as the day progresses. Anger is part of the grieving process, and hers grows because Ardi said he was going back to Batam to check on Sara so he could sail to Phuket with us. Now our world is changing.

The day's bright spot comes when Andy, the rigger, tunes the rig—the mast, the boom, and the hardware holding it in place. To do this, we take a brief sail late in the afternoon. What an exhilarating feeling to hoist the sails and make way through the water on the wind once again.

A brief blanket of diversion drapes itself over our sadness.

Emily supervises Amanda as she drives the car around the boatyard a couple times for her first driving experience.

Then, Amanda takes Lorrie for a spin while Greggii chases fish around the pontoon, and I show Emily the progress on *Faith*. While inspecting the forward cabins, we hear Greggii screaming, "Help!" Rushing out of the companionway, we find him terrified and swimming around *Faith*. We just finished installing *Faith*'s ladder, so I run back and put it down while Greggii is hollering, "Dad! Jump in and save me! Sharks!" If you want to invite someone swimming with you, that's probably not the best way. Further, I don't think there are any sharks around, and I tell him to swim the ten feet to the ladder.

Planning on being at Wavemaster for forty-five days, we never called the apartment our home. We spent our time there not quite living out of a suitcase, but far from living at home. We stored most of our stuff at Wavemaster, and as soon as a room on *Faith* becomes finished, we move our things for that area back on. I negotiate with Brendan, Wavemaster's general manager, to arrive at a fair settlement to our contract, accounting for the delays. When the last of the work is finished, we're ready to leave.

On 21 October 2006, we return to Telaga Harbor Marina, taking many of the guys who worked on *Faith* with us for the one-hour trip in a grey drizzle.

We invite every Wavemaster employee who worked on her out for a day of sailing, swimming, and fishing. The guys build a fire on the beach on which to grill the fish they catch. It's a great day, and while we're out, all of them sign a special birthday card for me. It was a miserable ten months of our lives that we spent at Wavemaster, but I realize today how much I'm going to miss it (8 & 73).

Ayip, the lead carpenter, made the most progress toward craftsmanship during our time here. He started on *Faith* when we first hauled out and stayed for the duration. He has a great sense of humor, takes pride in his work, and grows animated with frustration when his work fails.

Hashim was hired from a competing shipyard halfway through *Faith*'s incarceration. His job was the interior varnish, and he's good at it. Hashim offered information only when pressed but opened up as time progressed. He takes care of his sister's and Halim's two boys a couple nights a week, and brings them to visit Emily at Telaga Harbor and to fish from the dock.

Halim was hired a couple weeks after Hashim from the same yard (74). He knows yacht finishes and was responsible for *Faith*'s exterior. His approach to work was deliberate and scientific. After the original subcontractor put several coats of paint on badly, I wandered over to look at a job Halim just completed on another boat. I talked to Wavemaster's general manager about having him paint *Faith*, and that became the plan.

A'Chong is Ayip's helper. He's Malay but his given name is difficult, even for Malays, and he looks Chinese so his moniker stuck. He started on *Faith* when she was first hauled out, and drifted in and out of fits of productivity. As work and time progressed, his productivity escalated. He figured out that since he had to be there anyway, his satisfaction increased with his input.

Khairy was hired as a helper during our stay. He's a twenty-year-old kid with a great smile, who enjoys being a part of something, it doesn't matter what that something is.

Zubir was the foreman when we first started. He's a hard worker and a great guy, but we got off to a bad start. I don't remember what went wrong, except that it was more my fault than his. Our friendship grew with time, and he also brings his family to visit us at Telaga Harbor.

And then there's Brendan, my lifeline to sanity during our time at Wavemaster. Brendan is Australian, married to Pei Pei, an ethnic Chinese Malaysian who gave him another daughter during our stay. He's Wavemaster's general manager, and gave me an ear to cry to when things got too bad. Not a week passed that I didn't go running to his office at least twice, but often that many times a day to seek help on some problem we encountered.

Joe and Christina from the pharmacy, with their girls Angelina, Tina Belle, and Cecilia board *Faith* to sail around Langkawi with us (17). Joe says his family, in the twenty years they've lived here, has never seen Langkawi from the water. We go to a group of islands south of Kuah-town, never travelling more than ten miles away, and see narrow turquoise channels between rock-faced cliffs colored with tropical greens.

Lorrie hosts a surprise fiftieth birthday party for me at *Sunday*, one of the finer restaurants in Kuah-town. God blessed me with a fantastic family and great friends during my first fifty years, and I have no reason other than life-expectancy to believe they won't be with me for the next fifty years. Lorrie arranges the best gift: Ardi comes from Singapore to celebrate my birthday. He stays until we cast off for Phuket.

Family

We are Circumnavigators

1. Beginnings, Anguilla

2. From left: Gregg, Amanda, Greggii, Emily, and Lorrie

3. Nelis, Nelis's mother, Emily, and two students from Nelis's school

4. Ardi, Emily, and Amanda

5. Ardi and Greggii

6. Phuket, Thailand, sampling the selections at a night market bug-booth

7. Aden, Yemen, Middle East
cuisine is among our favorite

Cuisine

8. Langkawi, Malaysia, beach barbeque
with Wavemaster workmen

9. Greggii showing Roots the anchorage, Rosseau, Dominica

10. Greggii and Kuna children in Panama watching Scooby Doo

11. Joseph brings Greggii a pinata for his sixth birthday

12. Coco, Raimana, and Taiana, in Apataki, Tuamotus, French Polynesia

13. Bicycling around Maupiti, French Polynesia, with Thomas, Helen, Nicóle, Nadine, and Lucas

Friends

14. *Smilla's* family welcome to Ua Pou

15. Greggii, Emily, and Amanda with Davina
Toau, Tuamotus

16. Sailing into Sydney Harbour with Carl, Maggie, and Maddie

17. Joe and Christina, with Angeline, Tina Belle, and Cecilia, join *Faith* for a tour around Langkawi waters

More Friends

18. Werner, from Legend II, helping Emily prepare Faith for the Red Sea passage

19. With David and Virginia, Sydney, Australia

20. A woman in Sana'a, Yemen, applying a henna tattoo to Amanda

21. With Dr. Ahmad Shono at the UN Hospital in Asmarra, Eritrea

22. Emad, of Stephen's Children, helps me while in Cairo, and shows us the city

23.

On Passage

24.

25. *Faith* at anchor in the Tuamotus (photo credit, Thomas Lindblom)

26. Our home under sail

Faith

27. *Faith* under sail in the Gulf of Aden (photo credit, Pat Murphy)

Boats

28. Galle Harbour, Sri Lanka, navy gunboat

29. Thailand, long-tail

30. Thailand, fishing boats

31. Damar, Indonesia, inter-island ferry

32. Makassar, Suluwesi, Indonesia,
Sampu's water taxi

33. Tanna, Vanuatu

34. Banjarmasin, Kalimantan, Indonesia, Buganese traders and fishermen

35. Kumai, Kalimantan,
Indonesia,
Klotok for river trip

36. An *Uhu* in Anachakuna,
San Blas Islands, Panama

37. Damar, Indonesia, Cloves drying in the sun

38. Babar, Indonesia, a sopi distillery, coconut flower nectar is transformed to liquor

Industry

39. Cairo, Egypt, recycling industry, where all saleable materials are removed, and the garbage is turned into donkey fodder.

40. Isabela, Galapagos Islands, Luis (right) *Faith's* watermaker motor is the smaller item on his bench

41. (below) Aden, Yemen, sorting sesames for the mill to turn into oil

42. Galle, Sri Lanka, Harvesting rice with a hand sickle

Commerce

43. Port Sudan, Sudan,
fresh market

44. Banjarmasin, Kalimantan,
Indonesia, floating market

45. Saumlaki, Jamdena, Indonesia,
fresh market

46. Spice Market, Finike, Turkey

47. Menswear Shop, Salalah, Oman

48. Sana'a, Yemen, Emily posing

49. Dolphins in the Gulfstream

50. Wahoo

Marine Life (and death)

51. Cape York, Australia, Emily and dinner

52. Tuamotus, French Polynesia, Giant Clams

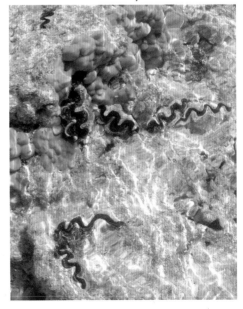

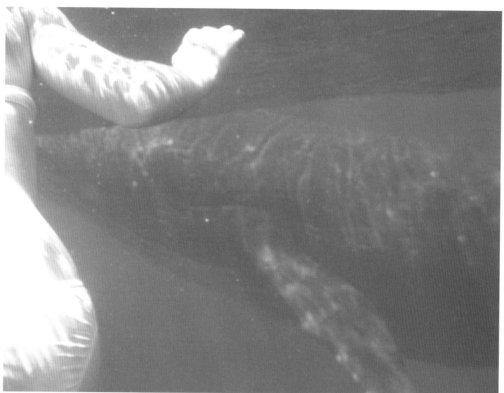

53. Vava'u Group, Tonga, Emily swimming with the whales (Photo courtesy, Nicóle Lindblom)

54. San Cristobal, Galapagos Islands, a sea lion looking in from *Faith's* transom,

55. Tanjung Pantung National Park, Kumai, Kalimantan, Indonesia, Francis and Amanda

56. St. Croix

Places

57. The drawbridge opening, St. Maarten

58. Dominica

59. St. Lucia

The Caribbean

60. Anguilla, with Claudell

61. The Panama Canal

63. Toau, Tuamotus, French Polynesia, copra drying

62. Galapagos penguins near where *Faith* is anchored in Isabela

64. Ua Pou is a postcard

65. Church service in Papeete, Tahiti

66. Moorea, Society Islands, French Polynesia

67. Church bell in Savusavu, Fiji

68. Mt. Yasur, Tanna, Vanuatu, The Volcano

The Pacific Ocean

69. New Caledonia, with Bernie

70. Sailing into Sydney Harbour

71. Saying goodbye to Saumlaki, Indonesia

72. Performing interior work on *Faith,*
Langkawi, Malaysia

73. The workmen of Wavemaster Langkawi
Yacht Service

74. Halim and his family (left) and Hashim join
us on *Faith* for dinner

75. Angkor Wat, Siem Reap, Cambodia, with
Jacob and Ardi

76. Vietnam

77. Sri Lanka, tea plantations and waterfalls

78. Salalah, Oman

79. Sana'a, Yemen

Asia to the Red Sea

80. Easter Service, Massawa, Eritrea

81. Suakin, Sudan

82. Seperation Wall, near Bethlehem, West Bank

83. Kekova Roads, Turkey

84. Serifos, Greece

Mediterranean Sea and homecoming

85. Coming Home

Frolicking Sea Trial

We sail four hours to Koh Adang, Thailand, and tie to a mooring ball. On our second night here, a swell on the beam develops. Size isn't as important as rhythm and the swell's orientation to the hull. A two-thousand-pound mast, seventy-eight feet up and a seven-ton keel, eight feet down form a pendulum and *Faith* gets rocking. She likes it after being still for so long, but for the rest of us, trying to sleep with all the stuff we can't live without banging around in the cabinets, and with our own centers of gravity oscillating from right to left and back again on three second intervals, we don't like it.

I go on deck to quiet things down—a banging spinnaker pole and several halyards—and notice a strong current holding our orientation to the waves. I monkey around with the rudder in an attempt to reorient *Faith* to the swell and succeed. Lorrie comes out of our cabin to tell me how smart I am. She's tired, and I don't want to delay her by explaining the difference between intelligence and luck.

When we leave Koh Adang, we go to a small island adjacent to Koh Tanga where the snorkeling is reported to be good but isn't. Unable to find a comfortable place to anchor near the island, we go off-shore to where the charts show a shallow patch of sand and anchor in open water for the night.

In the morning, when we're underway again, we catch a small Mahi Mahi and clean it for our Thanksgiving dinner. Lorrie tried to find a turkey in Langkawi, but there weren't many birds in the first place because of bird-flu, and the larger resorts bought the turkeys that did get there.

We spend the night at Koh Rok Nok.

Lorrie comments that travelling with Greggii is like travelling with a new crew member. His year in Langkawi helped him forget much of what we did before, and everything brings a fresh sense of wonder.

After dark, a boat comes close, passes slowly, and anchors nearby on the reef. They suspend a bright green fluorescent tube and I assume they're hunting lobsters. I develop an itch to investigate and, thinking they might speak Malaysian, I ask Emily to go with me. We approach after they turn off their light and find three men and one woman, all about my age, on two boats rafted together. They speak Thai.

The boats are twenty-five-feet long, both powered by *long tails*—an engine, usually Honda, with a horizontally mounted fifteen-foot-long shaft leading to a propeller on the far end, hinged at the transom (29). The propeller is dipped into the water for forward propulsion. We ask about lobster and get dumb looks, a sign we mispronounce the word from our translation book. Then I draw a lobster that looks more like a prawn and they say no, they have none. They're fishing and take us forward to show us their cooler, loaded with Wahoo. We purchase one about one-meter in length.

One word describes our time: *frolicking*. That is, all of us except Lorrie, who's never been a good frolicker. Unfortunately, she maintains the American notion that the world is a scary place and we can't convince her otherwise, in spite of our difficulty finding those *places in the world where they don't value human life like we do.*

It seems when things are going okay, and an easy day is in store, something breaks. I learn of one project at night when the generator runs hot. The main culprit is a broken hose clamp, allowing the captive, fresh, cooling water to escape. Normally a hose clamp is simple, but on a marine generator hiding under a storage shelf, it grows tricky. I remove the stuff on the shelf, and then the shelf itself. This exposes the generator's sound cover. The front and back snap on with big clips; the top and sides require unbolting. Once exposed, the hose clamp is easy to find; it's where all the water is spraying out. With access, I also find a broken temperature sensor, a worn fan belt, and a bad gasket. I'm sure there's some spare gasket material on *Faith*, but I can't find it. I make one out of card stock slathered with Vaseline. Some things surprise me when they work, and greased-up card stock is one of those things that logic says should not work.

I don't reassemble the whole thing, cover and all, because I want to go over it again when we get to Phuket.

In Phi Phi Don, nearly everything is new or under construction because of the Boxing Day Tsunami of 2004. We anchor in Tom Sai Bay. Thailand is like a lot of places where developers use disasters to root out undesirables; everything is going upscale, and the pre-tsunami backpackers and budget travelers of the old Phi Phi will need to find a different destination.

Phi Phi Don is a cross between Oa Pao, in the Marquesas, with its rugged topography, and Mackinaw Island, Michigan, with its commerce without cars. Large, two-wheeled carts are pulled by men to move ice, fish, scuba gear, and hotel linens.

Greggii and I pair up to go to a beach while the girls go their own way. There's a difference in the amount of skin to be seen in the conservatively dressed Langkawi and here. The thong is popular and Greggii brings a particularly well-concealed garment to my attention.

On our way back from the village after dark, the dinghy engine overheats and quits running. Lorrie and I differ considerably on problems like this. My first reaction, when Amanda told me a couple days ago that there's a lot of smoke coming out of the engine, was to ignore it; Lorrie's reaction has always been to spur me into action. I use ignoring to weed out annoying *potential* problems. This time the problem is more than potential and affords me the opportunity to go to the beach in the morning and become quite intimate with her lower unit.

When I return to *Faith* after rebuilding the cooling pump, there's a charter boat anchored next to us.

Charterers are different from us. First, *Faith* is our home, while their boat is not. Second, *Faith* is a symbol of the life we're living, while theirs is a symbol of a life they left. Third, this is how we engage our world, and how they disengage theirs. They're living their dream, just like us; the difference is the dream. Only now, there's a charter boat parked too close.

I run the water-maker long enough to blow a high pressure hose again, the second one of the two I purchased in Makassar. There are no hydraulic or pressure-pump guys on Phi Phi, so in addition to the generator, I add the water-maker to the list of things to do.

Phuket

Our patience for frolicking among tourists wears thin and we depart for Phuket to clear into Thailand, and to begin finding *Faith's* parts. Phuket is a small town with big-city swagger where nearly anything can be found.

Thailand had a bloodless coup last week that allegedly changed the rules for immigration and Customs, and every cruiser owns an inaccurate interpretation of the new rules. It took eleven days to travel from Langkawi to Phuket. In many places, this would raise suspicion, but in Phuket, it's the norm and we're surprised by the pleasant and helpful officials who walk us through the process. Sometimes I forget my rule of relating to new people: assume goodness until proved otherwise. Above all, don't attribute disagreeable hearsay automatically to the otherwise.

The trip from Langkawi was a good sea trial, but our list grew longer than we expected. I separate the list into things to do myself and services we need to hire. The hired services are to have the life raft recertified, the SSB radio and the email modem repaired so they can talk to each other again, and the main engine alternator fixed. The biggest job I'll do myself is to fix the generator. It's also the most critical because our water-maker and refrigerator won't work without it.

On the way back from the dinghy repair shop, we get ice for the refrigerator and freezer and hope we aren't losing much food.

Greggii hollers that Tom on *Juno* is coming into the anchorage. I go say hi and Tom, soft spoken and unshakeable like the Navy pilot he was in a past life, says he's leaving shortly to check on his refrigerator and to take in his own alternator. The man who has his refrigerator is good at these things, so I remove *Faith*'s alternator, split the cost of a car with Tom, and we're off.

Mr. Ponpoon looks at *Faith*'s alternator, and says it's burnt and needs rewinding. He can have it done early next week.

Again, there are parts of the world where people fix things. What builds my confidence in Mr. Ponpoon is his approach to Tom's freezer unit. Earlier in the week, he tried a certain regulator to get the voltage right for the compressor, but it didn't work. With the smirk of a little kid, he tells us to wait a minute and goes to the back room of his shop, his living quarters. He returns with the control and receiver from a remote-control helicopter. He says he was thinking about it last night and thinks he can get the voltage right by using the helicopter's receiver in line with the compressor, and jiggling around the controls to get the right voltage. It's a test to determine whether the compressor works. If it doesn't, repairing the refrigerator doesn't make sense. Anybody who lies awake thinking about trouble-shooting a freezer with a remote-control helicopter is my kind of craftsman.

I'm sleeping in the cockpit with Greggii; after a couple hours, my legs get cold. I grab a blanket and curl up, only to get colder and colder. Soon I'm shaking and go below where Lorrie takes my temperature and then takes my blanket. It's 100.7° under my arm. I take some ibuprofen and Lorrie rubs me down with baby wipes, which I've never understood having on *Faith* as we don't have a baby, but they help bring the fever down.

I develop a stomach ache, down low, and make several trips to the bathroom, fearing my current sensation is something worse than wind; it isn't, but it's accompanied by a less than pleasant odor. Lorrie makes sure I'm aware of this, thinking the fever disabled my nose. The next night, the fever creeps to 103°, and after a bunch of ibuprofen, a shower, and Lorrie stealing my blanket again, we get it back down, this time followed by a bout of sweating.

I think it's a bug, but Lorrie calls it food poisoning. When I tell her it's just a bug, she says, "Come on, Gregg, let me believe it's food poisoning so I know it's not contagious." We agree on food poisoning.

Ardi will leave Singapore shortly. Mr. Trond, the Norwegian owner of the boat Ardi works on, and three others will make the trip to Phuket with him.

Once I feel well again, Emily gets sick. She doesn't improve as the night passes.

She never develops a fever, but her mind plays tricks on her. Every time she thinks she can sleep, her mind throws some problem at her she thinks needs solving. Noting she's still awake at two, I tell her to sleep in my spot because there are no problems there. She does, but less than fifteen minutes later, I hear her walking in the galley, then a *thump,* and she's on the floor at the base of the companionway ladder, crying, and asking, "Where am I?" Lorrie's in the master head and Emily has to throw up, so she's trying to get to the saloon head. Emily remembers wanting to throw up, but doesn't remember getting up, walking, or falling. The next thing she remembers is being on the floor. Finally, after a visit to the saloon head, she sleeps.

I rouse her at 8:30 to give her some slices of apple and a glass of water, and ask if she wants to run errands with me. She looks a little haggard, but not too bad. I want her to go with me for several reasons. First, if she's still sick, I can monitor her, and she'll be on shore if we need a doctor. Second, I always enjoy her company; she's easy to have along and gets hungry for lunch about the same time I do. And third, her space and time away from *Faith* are important.

Amanda joins us and the three of us leave at 11:00 AM to go to see Roland, a local French man who has a half-dozen beat-up cars for rent, grab his tiny Diahatsu, and get on our way.

A woman we met earlier in Phuket meets us at a restaurant to give me the parts I ordered for the generator. She marks up a map with five places in Phuket City for marine parts. Our errands consist of getting water-maker hoses, spare belts for the engine and generator, engine oil for changes in each, engine degreaser to clean both, and a number of other items. We stop at the five places and successfully procure all.

When we reunite with Lorrie and Greggii at the beach, Lorrie's not feeling well. She probably has the same food poisoning I had earlier in the week. It seems to be running through *Faith.*

Ardi arrives and calls us from the pier in Chalong Bay. He's captain of a boat named *Chilli* and must clear in with Customs and the harbor master. He asks me to go with him, and again, the officials are helpful. We then go to breakfast together. In an unexpected gesture, Ardi sneaks up to the cashier and pays for our meals.

Our family goes to see *Chilli* at Royal Phuket Marina. First, we visit Roland to get his cheapest vehicle. The car, a four-seater, was built similar to a little pickup truck where two can ride in the back. It's another Diahatsu, smaller than any of our previous rentals, and we're laughed at everywhere. Thais like funny stuff and find the six of us in this tiny car amusing.

Then, it's Amanda and Ardi's turn to be sick; Greggii's ornery, probably because he doesn't like it when his *best brother in the world* is sick.

Ardi, Greggii, and I are on shore before sunset and we see a good-looking girl without her top on.

"Good view here, Sir."

"How are you feeling now, Ardi?"

"I feel better, Sir, hee-hee."

Greggii says, "Wow! That girl doesn't have her top on, didja see her? Huh, didja see her? She doesn't have any clothes on!!"

I hate pretending I'm not looking, and nobody's fooled anyway, so I say, "You're right Ardi, this is a good view."

"Hee-hee."

Three days before Christmas, we go to the pier to get water, and hit it.

The main pier comes out over 500 meters from shore. At the end is a tee-dock, going fifty meters each way. On the north side of the main pier is the fuel dock, where water is available. We approach with twenty knots of wind blowing us toward the main pier. Rather than go alongside, I let out the anchor and try going stern-to to the fuel dock. We have a communication breakdown between the captain and the youngest crew. I'm controlling the anchor from the helm to keep us away from things, and when Greggii sees what I'm doing, he helps from the bow. I quit putting out chain to see how it's holding, not knowing that Greggii continues to let it out from the bow. And out, and out, and out.

We have enough chain on the bottom so the anchor won't do any good if we get into trouble, and then we get into trouble. The wind pushes us into the pier. A man in a passing dinghy offers assistance and pushes the bow away from the pier after it hits a couple times. In so doing, *Faith* pivots on her keel and her stern hits.

Nobody's hurt, which doesn't offer as much comfort as it should, but we damage the *bow pulpit*, that stainless rail in front; the *push pit*, that rail in the back (just reconstructed at Wavemaster with the life-raft cradle in it); and two *stanchions*, those supports for the wire rope *lifeline*—the perimeter fence—in the middle.

Greggii and Amanda are crying, Emily and Ardi are too busy to cry, Lorrie is trying to comfort Greggii and Amanda, and I'm numb. And dumb. I can't believe it.

We re-anchor and lick our psychological wounds.

Ardi and I dismantle the parts to take and have fixed. We carry the parts around the area near where we're anchored, having heard about a steel shop that could allegedly assist us. Then we strap them into a pickup to take them ten miles to a shop in Phuket City. Nobody can do the work right away, so we give up.

Bearing in mind our upcoming visa run to Langkawi, I call Wavemaster to schedule us in after the first of the year.

Lorrie hears a friend on a kid-boat—a cruising yacht like *Faith* with children on board—whom we haven't seen since Tonga, on the radio. This friend is anchored in Nieharn Bay, about ten miles away, along with several other kid-boats. A Christmas Eve barbecue will be hosted for yachties at one resort there and we make plans to go there for Christmas.

Our fourth Christmas abroad is again in a place where it's a holiday. The decorations are up around town, we have carols playing, and the kids decorate *Faith* with popcorn strings, and construction paper mistletoe, stars, and poinsettias. The tree is as nicely decorated as any Christmas since we set out.

Christmas would be different had I not invited friends from another boat, who just arrived here this morning, to join us for dinner. Either our hospitality or their loneliness or both cause them to linger when we want to spend time with Ardi on his last day with us for a while.

And then, on the morning of Boxing Day, we feel the melancholy of the day after. Christmas has come and gone and so has Ardi, who returned last night to *Chilli* to await Trond's family.

Langkawi Visa Run

Thailand gave us a thirty-day visa on arrival. At the end of those thirty days, we must make a visa run to Langkawi, and now, to repair the parts damaged from hitting the pier. A visa run is the exercise of leaving a country to be issued a new visa on re-entry.

The night we depart, Amanda has a talk with me, unpleasant for both of us. She takes the time, in love, to address my demons. I would like to keep my demons, and the shame that accompanies them hidden, but as any good addict will tell you, that's not always possible.

We went to the Easy Beach Restaurant at Naiharn for dinner last night. My goal was to get to bed early to depart for Langkawi this morning. I had three Big Beers (660ml, or about two 12oz. cans). Everyone else wanted to go back to *Faith*, but Amanda wanted to go to the hawker stalls to get a tee-shirt for a friend of hers in Langkawi. Emily stayed with us.

While walking among the hawkers, looking for tee-shirts, and playing some arcade games, I had a couple more cans of beer. We saw live music at an outdoor bar setup, and sat down there. I had a couple one-liter pitchers of beer while sitting there. Amanda had to take me by the hand to get back to the dinghy and *Faith*. She spends much of our discussion filling in details I don't recall.

I think I understand why Grandpa Lou was an amoral person. Alcoholics have only three choices: quit drinking, live under a crushing burden of shame and guilt, or make a conscious decision to live without that shame. Grandpa chose the latter. I can't.

We again tie to the pontoon at Wavemaster Langkawi Yacht Center.

The fabrication crew is hard at work until the wee hours, but the work progresses sluggishly, probably because I have nothing better to do than watch.

When the work is done, we depart once more for Phuket.

Great news! An email from Lorrie's brother informs us that her mother's cancer is in remission. We pray a prayer of thanksgiving to God, and Lorrie sits stunned in disbelief for hours. We call to congratulate Sally and share our joy with her.

Our return to Thailand begins at Koh Muk. The draw of Muk is the *Hong*—a lagoon accessible only through a narrow, low-ceilinged, water-cave at the base of a hundred-meter high, vertical wall of rock surrounding us. There's a one-meter-deep pool near the cave we entered, defined by a soft, sandy beach about thirty meters long, from one side of the lagoon to the other. Behind the beach is lush, tropical greenery. The cave to get there is too spooky for Lorrie, so she has us paddle her back to *Faith* before we enter it.

After Koh Muk, we again sail to Phuket.

Just over there!!

That seems to be our destination and focus, and as soon as we get there, our burdens can be cast off and we'll begin to embrace life and the new world around us. It doesn't matter where *over there* is. For us today, *over there* is a physical destination. We're in Phuket, preparing to sail to Sri Lanka, so we must focus our energy there. As soon as we arrive, we can shed the burden of Southeast Asia and know that we're now *over there*. Maybe *over there* is a landmark age; at 16, I can get my driver's license; at 21, I can take a legal drink; at 55, or 62, or 65, I can retire. Perhaps it's a career goal, maybe that elusive promotion, or a financial break that's going to make the difference. The point is, it will never be *here*, because as soon as we arrive, another *over there* comes into focus. We can live our whole lives, forget who and where we are, which often is agreeable, I'll admit, and focus on another time or another place. The benefit of this focus is that it's not here; the drawback is the same. I can never live anywhere but *here*, and to spend a whole life dreaming about somewhere other than here is to not have lived.

Medical Services in Phuket

Per citizen, the United States spends more than half again as much as any other country in the world on healthcare, yet maintains outcomes in the lowest third of the top fifty industrialized nations, according to the World Health Organization. Perhaps this can be explained by the extraordinary influence we have conferred on our corporations in the shaping of public policy, or perhaps this stems from America's concept of the rugged-individual and the notion that those not sufficiently rugged possess a lesser claim to personhood and human rights.

Lorrie urges me to have a medical checkup before leaving Thailand.

The dentist is first, refilling and repairing a filling and a cracked tooth, scaling, cleaning, and polishing all my teeth, and providing the overall assessment that my teeth are still there.

Monday morning begins a complete health check-up consisting of a chest x-ray, an organ ultrasound, some lab work, a treadmill-stress test, and a consultation with a physician after lunch, when all the test results are in. It's a fascinating concept in medical care, starting when I arrive shortly before 9:00, without an appointment—you don't need appointments in Thailand. I'm handed a medical menu about the size of a large postcard listing the services offered from lab work to full-scale MRI, and the prices of each with little check-boxes next to them where I indicate which services I desire. Then, in an act defying the logic of what we *knew* was the best healthcare in the world before we left the US, the receptionist hands me a folder to carry around. It's incredible that, here in Thailand, they trust me

165

with my records. I'm escorted to another desk where the woman places an order for a chest x-ray in my folder and shows me to radiology. Ten minutes later, I leave radiology with a full-size x-ray dwarfing my folder, and I'm taken to the lab to pee in a cup and donate blood. Next, I'm wired up and jogging on a treadmill. A little before noon, I'm told to get some lunch and return at 12:30 for an interview with the doctor, who has all my information electronically in front of him, but who also looks inside my folder during our talk.

It starts at 9:00 AM and it's over by 2:00 PM; I walk out of the hospital with a complete report in my hands except for a couple things in either the urine or blood that they'll email me. I have a clean bill of health.

The costs: Dental, US$60.00, Physical, US$250.00.

Lorrie and Greggii missed the movie they went to see yesterday, and she tells Greggii I'll take him today. Missing a movie is easy in Phuket because the listed times have only a loose relationship with the time the movie plays. Greggii and I are fortunate to be an hour and a half early for the 2:50 showing of *Night at the Museum*, which starts at 1:50. Once seated, each of us with our own popcorn and Coke, I know I'm doing what I should.

During our final days in Phuket, we do something Greggii has wanted to do since Cambodia: Eat Bugs. At a night market near our marina are stalls selling bugs and grubs. Here we are standing around this guy's bug booth, and he's telling us to try anything we'd like. He has two kinds of grubs, a handful of things that look like cockroaches but aren't, grasshoppers, crickets, and other critters.

We—all of us except Lorrie—sample them before deciding the fat grubs and crickets taste best, and buy a mixed bag of them (6).

The hardest thing for all of us during our whole voyage is parting with Ardi.

The week finds us waiting for the right weather for the passage to Galle, Sri Lanka. I choose Tuesday, January 23, to depart. Ardi joins us on Monday to spend our last days together.

Neither the weather nor our hearts are right to depart on Tuesday, or Wednesday. As the week passes, it becomes clear we're postponing the inevitable; we must leave. On Thursday, Amanda, Greggii, and I say a tearful goodbye to him from Naiharn Beach, and Lorrie and Emily drive him back to the Royal Phuket Marina.

Part V. Pirates Not!

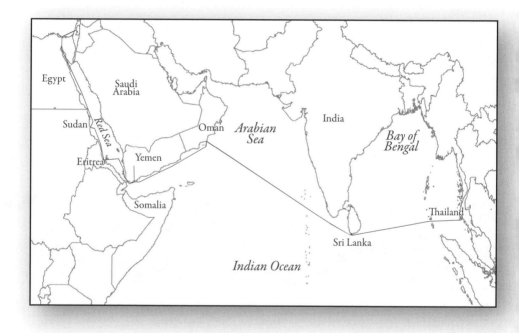

Phuket, Thailand through the Red Sea
26 January to 4 June 2007

Another Passage

We depart Naiharn Beach, Phuket, in the wee hours of January 26, 2007. Emily vacillates between bouts of sleep and bursts of tears for the first days out. She and Ardi stay in contact with email.

I think no one can comprehend making passage on a small boat in the middle of a huge sea alone, unless one has made such passage. I don't mean Joshua Slocum's kind of alone, because he truly was; I mean existing as the sole boat inside the horizon.

After having made such passage in good weather, which is rare, in bad weather, which is rarer still, and in no weather, which we experience more than any other, I believe there is here a magnificence in God's creation that has no parallel in any other endeavor.

No more day-sailing, but honest-to-goodness passage making, where the first days are filled with emotional excitement and physical discomfort. After initiation, when the queasiness of commencement departs, the dance begins. Our bodies, our souls, and *Faith* are again synchronized to the rhythm of the sea. With enough breeze to keep the rigging quiet, but not so much that we need work too hard, our journey begins anew.

The destinations offer education in love and hope; the passages offer education in faith.

Passage making is most pleasurable for me, but not as an end of itself. What joy would there be in that? Passage making, without expectations and anticipations, hopes and fears of unknowns lurking beyond the horizon could not hold the same wonder.

We zig and zag our way through the Andaman Sea, trying to keep a little comfort in what would otherwise be a straight run with wind directly on the stern. We always sail more comfortably with the wind 30° off, especially in these light breezes.

Once we pass through the Sombrero Channel in the Nicobar Islands, the breeze freshens and we set the pole to sail *wing and wing*—sailing with the main sail on one side and the jib poled out on the other—for several hundred miles.

Wing and winging comes to a halt when several things happen in rapid succession. The first thing is the loud crunch I hear while biting into, of all things, a candy bar hardened in the refrigerator. I remove the candy from my mouth to find my top-left-front tooth imbedded in it. It's a crown, but it broke right off with the original tooth peg and all.

I don't have time to think about it, because before I can show the rest of the family, the main halyard breaks, and the mainsail falls to the top spreader. We turn to windward, and while Lorrie readies the boson's chair for me to ascend the mast, the sail frees itself to fall the rest of the way down. During this time, I have Emily and Amanda furling in the poled-out Genoa. I just finish stowing the pole by locking the base—the part that attaches to the sail—when the top end, the one always fastened to a pivoting, sliding car on a track on the mast, lets loose. I catch it on my thigh, with about three feet to where it's fastened to the deck, the other nineteen feet free in front of me. This point of leverage makes it heavy, so I shimmy forward for a better vantage point so I can tie it off. After resetting the mainsail with the spare halyard, we sail again—which is a lot smoother than pointing to the weather under motor.

The pole came loose because a fifty-cent keeper ring on the pin that holds it in place came off. I can't find another keeper ring—I *know* I have one somewhere—so I put a bolt in with a nut to keep it on the mast until we can get another. We sail without the pole for the rest of this passage.

Greggii says, "I was scared when you were going up the mast. Were you scared too?"

"I didn't like the idea, little buddy, but I was too busy to be scared. I'm glad I didn't have to."

As excitement abates, I begin thinking about not having a tooth where only moments before, I had one. Emily apologizes for laughing when she first saw it. I tell her I'd rather have her laugh than worry about it; I'm doing enough of that.

After sunset, we're sailing through an area populated with flying fish; many land on deck. I collect twenty and take them to the galley, where Greggii cuts off the heads and tails and removes the guts.

After Greggii goes to bed, the fish keep coming. I retrieve two from the floor of our bedroom that found our open hatch. While Lorrie's on watch, three fly into the cockpit, one of them timing its flight to maneuver itself right under her butt as she's sitting down after rising to take a look around—squished fish—much to her annoyance, and my amusement.

While I'm on watch, two fly toward me. They hit the dodger, *thud-thud*, with the quasi-percussion sound of stretched canvas hit by flying objects. Then Amanda, who's all cozy in bed, runs wide-eyed into the saloon and screams, "A fish flew in my hatch and landed on me!" much to *her* annoyance, and my amusement.

In the morning, not wanting to smell like a floating fish market, I go on deck to clear them. I remove sixty-seven carcasses. Add that to the three that flew in through the open hatches and the twenty Greggii cleaned. Ninety flying fish landed in or on *Faith* last night!

We cook Greggii's fish and find a little meat hidden between the bones; maybe enough for survival, should it come to that.

Sri Lanka

We're instructed to drop anchor outside of the inner-harbor to await boarding by the Sri Lankan Navy. Gunboats of the Sri Lankan Navy are twenty-foot, fiberglass fishing boats, powered by forty-horsepower, tiller-steered Yamaha outboards, with a gun mounted on a pole, little more than a broom stick, in the middle. The weight of the barrel tries to point the gun down, so there's a string from the gunstock to the pole to hold the gun somewhat level (28).

Navy personnel remain on *Faith* to pilot us into the inner-harbor, where we pass the first buoy, a large rope, and floats going to the north shore, and then the second buoy, ropes, and boats tied together to make a barrier to the south shore. We steer hard to port, go eighty meters, then hard to starboard into the inner harbor—a security measure.

Anchoring is stern-to to a floating steel pontoon. The officials in Galle won't let you anchor in the harbor as dinghies tending anchored yachts are presumed a security risk.

Our agent comes for our passports and runs to immigration on our behalf. He's followed by a Customs officer who's more interested in a souvenir from us than intercepting contraband.

After Customs, our agent takes us to an ATM to get the Rupees we need to pay him, and we leave his office in tuk-tuks to see the city of Galle. We see cliff divers, diving off a corner of a fort from a height of twenty meters. The Historical Mansion has a collection of artifacts on display that devolves into a pitch for gemstones and gimcracks at the museum store we walk through to exit. We continue our tour to a silk factory for another pitch.

Then comes the time for the dentist to repair the candy-bar damage. Twenty people are waiting to get in, but I'm pulled to the front of the line. The dentist sees me, but needs an x-ray from the lab next door. For the equivalent of US$3.00, I'm x-rayed. The dentist then drills, cleans, and takes an impression for a new tooth. He apologizes when he quotes me the cost of 5500Rs—about US$50.00—and says it'll be ready Monday (today is Friday). As an afterthought, he says I should have something to keep food pieces out of the cave he just excavated. He tears off a small hunk of cardboard, wads it up, and using one of his tools, packs it in the open hole awaiting my new tooth. I'm impressed; a chunk of cardboard and US$50—plus the x-ray—for a new tooth in one business day.

While sitting in *Faith* at night, we hear our first depth-charge. It sounds like a dock line snapped, only louder—a shrill, twisted-metal *bang* that sends me on deck wondering what we hit.

Depth-charges are the Sri Lankan Navy's greeting to Tamil Tiger frogmen who might enter the harbor to create their own special antisocial havoc. The cause of these *terrorists* is the creation of a separate Tamil state in the north of Sri Lanka.

As I understand it (probably wrong, the way I understand a lot of things), the Tamils are Indians, brought to Ceylon under British Colonial Rule as slaves to work tea plantations. When Ceylon gained independence and emerged as Sri Lanka, the indigent population of Sinhalese controlled the island with no voice given to the Tamils. India didn't repatriate them and Sri Lanka doesn't recognize them. As a result, the Tamil Tigers or LTTE, like so many other disenfranchised annoyances, are now an internationally recognized band of terrorists.

Our tour of Sri Lanka starts poorly when our driver, Nelaka, thinks he's coming only to meet us and not to start the tour. First, we must go to the Indian Embassy in Columbo to begin the process of getting visas. Colombo is a vibrant, low-rise city, inhabited by two million people, which would take more time to appreciate than we choose to give it. It fulfills our expectations as a minor hurdle in the start of our tour.

Leaving Colombo, we arrive at Pinniwala Elephant Orphanage in time for the afternoon bath in the river where we join a number of elephants and splash a little water on them. The tickets Nelaka gets for us have a face value of 1,000Rs. per person We heard they should be 500Rs. After twenty minutes in the river, Nelaka quickly corrals us back into the van to exit before park personnel discover our tickets don't have the camera surcharge paid. Later, I call the Sri Lankan Tourist Board and learn the entry has always been 500Rs. The woman I speak to has never heard of the ticket I describe.

After a heated exchange about the 5000Rs we paid for our brief encounter (you can get a new tooth for that kind of money), Nelaka takes us to a place that gives us a better experience, including elephant rides for Emily, Amanda, and Greggii first, then Lorrie and me. The kids mount the elephant to have her dip her trunk into the river, then raise it over her head and spray them.

We drive to the Lion Rock Sigiriya Hotel, from where we'll visit the cave temples of Dambulla in the morning and Sigiriya rock in the afternoon. Sigiriya is a world heritage site, a castle or fortress constructed on the flat top of a sheer-walled, 370-meter-high mountain.

Before leaving the hotel in the morning, I check our dinner bill for last night and find the rice and curry we ordered mysteriously increased from the price in the menu.

We visit the cave temples of Dambulla, but our developing dour attitudes obstruct our enjoyment. After the temples, we ask to be dropped off in town to meet again in a half-hour. We've never been as disappointed in our own ability to find food as we have in Nelaka's ability, and are pleasantly surprised with the result. Our inexpensive lunch is much better than dinner last night. We get take-away and ask Nelaka to stop along the road beneath the canopy of a mango grove for a pleasant picnic lunch.

We go to Sigiriya to be hounded by hawkers and *helpers* who hold your elbow and help you climb the stairs to the top. One helper latches onto Lorrie and she can't shake free, but she concedes that he does actually help. I give him 100Rs for his help. He says for 300Rs total, he'll help her down, so I give him 200 more. Arriving at the bottom, he says he meant 500.

In the morning, I ask for both the dinner and hotel bill. It's another negotiation to arrive at the price we were quoted on arrival. Because there are fewer tourists around, it seems every visitor must be squeezed a bit more.

From the moment we got into his van two days ago, we've been telling Nelaka we want to be with and around the people of his country who give it meaning, not the tourism leeches. Following a brief fit of contrition, he disregards our input.

Sri Lanka seems systematically designed to separate us from the people in whom we find the greatest delight of our voyage. And then it hits me. It isn't Sri Lanka; it's tourism. It's this layer of invented reality meant to inflate perceived value, created not by men engaged in adding real value through a physical attachment, but by parasites working perceptions. It's designed to channel our attention away from the true value of a place and people created by God. We saw it in the Caribbean where the cruise ships called, in Panama where we were told all the restaurants we liked were in dangerous neighborhoods, in Australia where it took us two and a half months to learn how to climb the Sydney Harbour Bridge on a budget, and in Malaysia and Thailand. Tourism's goal is not to let us experience a place, but to shield us from it.

We have stamps in our passports from thirty countries since leaving the United States three years ago, and have never faced this much difficulty scratching through the wall of tourism to get to the culture, sometimes vibrant, often not, of everyday life that defines a place.

I have had enough and tell Nelaka to take us back to *Faith*.

He says he can't because of rules about guides driving at night and that our best bet is to get to Nuwara Eliya for the night, then continue tomorrow.

We get two rooms at Ramboda Falls Hotel for too much. We eat a terrible, over-priced meal and go to bed. They win.

Nelaka takes us to a tea plantation that's not operating on Sunday. All tea factories in Sri Lanka are closed on Sundays. Greggii and I get back into the van, where Greggii cries and I seethe.

We salvage the day in the observation car of the train from Nuwara Eliya to Ella. Facing aft in the last car with windows all around, we witness spectacular mountain views. We sleep at a local guest house. It's cheap and it's bad, but it's reality and reality is always better.

Were we to ever return to Sri Lanka, we would buy a guidebook and throw ourselves into the local transport, local restaurants, and local guest-houses. We have a guidebook now, which works well for other travelers we meet, but Nelaka insists that it is wrong.

When we return to Galle, Nelaka asks about getting paid. Lorrie and I are sure there should be some consideration for the disappointments designed into the trip. We tell him to let us get to the boat, talk it over, and later, we'll meet with him, his partner, and the agent who sold us the tour. Lorrie and I figure out several ways we don't owe as much as he claims.

After a few moments on *Faith*, Lorrie and I pray about it as we walk to the gate to meet them. This is not a brief discussion, and sometime during our talk, I get an inkling this isn't right. I'm not going to feel better about our trip if they give it to us for free.

(That's the trouble with asking God to help you make the right decision: He does.)

They made mistakes, we made mistakes; as a result, we had a rotten time, and there isn't a financial solution to make anything better. I pull Lorrie aside to say our integrity is at stake; we should pay the whole amount. God answers our prayer, and it costs a few bucks. Actually, I think God had a different agenda in our negotiations. The guys involved in our tour are Buddhist, and we are Christian. God uses our negotiations to promote Himself in our solution.

I see more gunboats, more personnel, and hear more depth charges than I remember before our tour of the country. I ponder the depth charges. What self-respecting young man, anywhere in the world, given the job of riding a boat around a harbor setting off harmless hand-held depth charges, wouldn't think that the best job in the world? It would be different if anybody was actually out there, but that's the whole point; nobody will enter the harbor so long as the depth charges continue. I'm not a kid anymore, and don't qualify for anybody's navy, but I think it would be fun.

Surviving another night in the harbor, thanks to the Sri Lankan Navy, we embark with the guys who conspired to ruin our last trip.

They use today's tour as an apology. First, we go to the beach where stilt fishermen ply their trade. Actually, the stilt fishermen ply their trade early in the morning, and by the time we get there, the two guys are, as one bluntly says, "fishing for money." These guys just act as if they're fishing to get money out of tourists with cameras. I see one of our guides slip the cashier (probably one actor's wife) a bill, and I know they're rewarded.

Following the fisheractors, we take a very small road away from shore where we see women in rice paddies harvesting with a sickle. Since I know so little of how rice grows, and have never even looked closely at a plant, I ask to stop. The ladies warn me about the mud, but I'm a guy, and mud is a guy thing. I shake off my sandals and hop down the road embankment into a nice, comfortable, axle-grease-consistency mud that swallows my feet to a couple inches above my ankles. I ask one lady if I can try, and she hands me her sickle. I reach down, grab a handful of the straw supporting the seeds, and cut it off (42). After cutting three or four handfuls, I return the sickle, crawl out of the mud, and wash my feet in a nearby stream.

Then we go to a working tea plantation for a tour. We mingle with a picker who shows us what she's doing and why she's doing it that way.

We eat lunch and return to *Faith*. Our guides won't accept payment for today.

Emily, Amanda, and I board the train to Colombo to retrieve our completed Indian Visas, and travel through areas hit by the Boxing Day Tsunami of 2004. Rebuilding happens slowly. Everybody is quick to point out whose aid has helped in what area. The fruit market in Galle was rebuilt by Americans, the fish market by Germans, one housing-relocation by Chinese, another by Singapore, a large Buddhist memorial and maybe even the railroad bridge itself by Japanese. The train we're on was full the day of the tsunami, and fell into the river when the bridge washed out.

After returning to Galle, Amanda and I help haul in a fish net. This net is looped far out into the harbor from two points on the beach, and there are twenty men on each point pulling it in. As we walk by, they motion us to help, so we grab the net and begin our tug-of-war with the sea. After fifteen minutes, we have the net and several hundred pounds of various shallow-water-type fish on the beach, gasping for water. People stream out from the road to purchase their share.

We need fuel before leaving Galle and pull alongside a tug boat to get it. Our agent makes it happen. We depart after he gives us our clearance documents.

Oman

Our anxietometer spikes again, partly from the stress of Sri Lanka and partly from our inflated perceptions of pirates in these waters. In the Indian Ocean, the farther we move west, the more pirates there are purported to be. While we are sailing thirty miles south of Cape Comorin, India's southernmost point, Lorrie wakes me from an afternoon nap to report an approaching boat. I go above to see a large, wooden fishing boat with eight men aboard. Most fishermen approach tentatively and wait for a signal from us before coming closer. This boat positions itself in our path. Thankfully, the winds are light. I start the engine and hit reverse to avoid a collision. Once they're on our port beam, I holler at them to get away from us, and after a few of their gestures begging for cigarettes and our gestures demonstrating displeasure, they leave. Lorrie's convinced they carried malicious intent; I attribute the incident to bad boat handling.

I hear the fishing reel wailing like a newborn baby. It's Amanda's turn and she's just about ready, fighting pad, life jacket, and tether, by the time I get to the cockpit. The baby keeps screaming. By the time she's situated with the rod in her hands, most of the line is gone. The reel is too hot to touch. Two hours later, after she fights for a while, then I fight for a while, then she again, we see the fish; about as long as I am tall, we can't guess how much it weighs, but we know it's a marlin. After my inept attempt with the gaff hook, it shakes off. Gone. Amanda is upset, but I don't know what we'd have done if we'd landed it.

All the while, Lorrie cautions us to be careful.

Nets in the Arabian Sea are up to ten miles long, suspended by empty five-gallon fuel jugs or other containers. While fighting our fish, we come within fifty meters of one, see the large diameter rope at the surface and, to our relief, Lorrie shifts the focus of her panic. When I see the net, I start the engine and make a seventy-degree turn to starboard to run parallel to it instead of over it. We hope we don't meet more nets as it gets later and darker. They're usually tended, and a fishing boat will give the coordinates of the ends of it when requested.

After being on watch through most of the night, I'm lying in our cabin in a state between awake and asleep; I sense someone sizing me up. Glancing toward my feet, I see Emily, Amanda, and Greggii commenting how the fish actually was about as long as me. They're imagining me with fins and a snout; Amanda's composing an email and I'm the metaphor. I'm glad they aren't holding a fillet knife.

Finally, I admit I'm homesick. After nearly four years, there are people and things I miss. I miss mom and dad and our family; I miss a number of friends and Gun Lake Community Church. I miss standing in Lake Michigan at the mouth of the Platte River watching Aurora Borealis dance past one of the last shorelines without lights anywhere in America. Michigan's Sleeping Bear Dunes National Lakeshore has thirty-five miles of undeveloped waterfront. Privatization might change that, but for now, it's worth missing.

The breeze is light and the seas are calm, so I tackle some jobs I've been saving for Oman. The most important is the bilge pump. I go swimming to clean the barnacles clogging the discharge hose. I spend ten minutes telling Lorrie why I need to do it here in the clean, clear water of the open sea instead of the cloudy waters of a commercial harbor and spend one minute in the water actually doing the work, which is to take a screwdriver to the thru-hull and ream it around. It works, and so do both manual bilge pumps now.

Salalah, Oman, is a welcome sight. We must call the port authority from five miles out, and again at the fairway marker. Their concern is the heavy container traffic and yachts mingling in the waters of this busy commercial port. After we anchor, a small, white, wooden boat motors to *Faith*, and a man who looks like and has the mannerisms of Eddie Murphy boards us. He wears a flowing white robe and a *mesheda*—man's head scarf. Muhammad is our agent, to clear us into Oman and to provide other services.

Our clearance from Sri Lanka is for Cochin, India; we sailed here instead.

Muhammad sees this and says it will cost US$100 extra because our clearance papers are wrong. I bluff and say, "Just never mind, we'll pull up our anchor and keep going." Hearing of another couple days at sea, the joy on Amanda and Lorrie's faces melts. Muhammad says, "Just look at them, they don't want to go back to sea yet. I'll see what I can do, and if it costs money, *I* will pay it."

Muhammad procures a rental car for us to drive into Salalah. We receive a warm welcome from everybody. Greggii and I go into a men's store to get a *dishdash*—the flowing robe—and a masheda (47). The girls find some fashions for themselves. The Omanis we meet appreciate the opportunity to show us their world.

We go to the Frankincense Museum and learn about Omani commerce. Omanis have engaged in maritime trade with the Far East and Africa for as long as anybody. More recently, the Sultan wrote letters to Omani professionals who had left Oman for better lives elsewhere; in the letters, he, the Sultan, clarified a vision for Oman, and invited these professionals—the doctors, engineers, and scientists—to return to work together to fulfill that vision.

We also visit Job's tomb. The Old Testament Job is an Islamic prophet. During our drive through the mountains, we stop to visit a pack of camels (78), laugh at the camel crossing signs on the road, and see the frankincense groves along the way. Frankincense is a large woody shrub or small tree, grown gnarly from arid winds blowing over the area. Frankincense and myrrh are the crystallized sap of these plants, burned as incense.

Getting fuel is an experience. Muhammad needs payment up-front from enough yachts to make it worth the oil company's effort to send a tanker truck to the port. I drive him to the fuel company to make the arrangements.

The man at the fuel company asks, "How many boats need fuel?"

Muhammad replies, "Just three."

"How long must the tanker sit and wait? How fast can the boats take the fuel?"

"I think it will be less than one hour."

When we get back into the car, Muhammad says, "They just want to empty their fuel into a tank in five minutes. If I tell them the truth, they'll never send a truck."

It takes six hours for the eight boats in the anchorage to take fuel. Because of the difficulty regulating the flow from the truck's pump, everybody ends up with spilled fuel on deck.

In the evening, Muhammad hosts a barbeque at the Oasis, a bar and restaurant for expatriates. While there, we meet four other boats planning to leave the same time as us, and form a convoy, an added measure of anti-pirate security, for our passage to Aden.

Yemen

There exists a sensational aspect to reports of yacht piracy, differentiated from commercial piracy, in this area. We depart Oman for Aden on 7 March to sail through an area known as *Pirate Alley*. We name ourselves *The Camel Convoy* for the six-hundred-mile journey. The others are *Aldebaran* from Ireland, *Li* from Sweden, *Windpocke* from Germany (I ask, and *Windpocke* means "barnacle of the wind" in Deutsch), and *Pacific Bliss* from America. We have a good time, maintain minimal radio contact, and never give away our position, having heard that pirates listen to the radio too. When the first fishing boat comes alongside the leading boat, *Pacific Bliss*, we all flex our sphincters and converge on them until they radio to tell us the guys are asking for water and cigarettes in exchange for fresh fish.

Greggii and I wait in *Faith*'s cockpit for a boat to come to us. One finally comes, and Greggii gives them a bottle of water and a pack of cigarettes and receives some fish that were curing in their bilge for several days. We wait until the fishermen are out of sight before releasing their gift. Greggii and I are dressed in our Omani garb for the passage, figuring if anybody with devious intentions approaches, we'll tell them the white guys are on the other boats.

We make contact with, but never see, *Coalition Warship 4-8*, which has an American accent. They ask our position and, not wanting to broadcast our co-ordinates to all the pirates waiting outside the horizon, I give them a bearing and range from their own position. One time, I tell the warship we're two miles off the starboard beam of Motor Tanker *Harmony*. The Coalition monitors all merchant traffic and knows where we are from that.

One project we tackle on this passage is taking inventory of the movies and software we have from Asia. It strikes me: *we* are the pirates.

We survive and arrive in Aden, Yemen, on 12 March, and learn that no reported incident of piracy against a yacht has occurred in over four years. I conclude we're afraid of a fictional concoction of sensational proportions. Cruisers, and especially cruising magazines, are good at turning everything into a harrowing experience, when in fact there isn't much in our life to be harrowed by.

Yemen's government made some decisions that hurt the country on the international scene and caused its economy to suffer. The decisions were first, Yemen's moral support of Iraq during the early nineties Gulf War. This decision caused Saudi Arabia and Kuwait to expel Yemeni workers, whose return caused an economic drain on Yemen's resources. Second was Yemen's alliance with the now obsolete Soviet Union.

It's a toss-up between Yemen and Indonesia for our favorite country. We're approached by no fewer than a hundred people exclaiming, "Welcome to Yemen!" They're especially taken by Greggii walking down the street in his sarong, tee-shirt, and masheda, with his ornamental belt and dagger strapped around his belly. I wear the same, but Greggii is cute. People keep pointing at us, grinning wildly, giving the thumbs-up, saying, "Yes, Yemeni!"

The women of Yemen are covered by the *abaya*—black gown, the *hijab* –head scarf, and the *niqab*—veil over the face. All of these garments predate Islam by over a thousand years, though not in black. They're in the mall or on the street, playing with their children, walking with their husbands, talking, giggling, and acting like women. The spookiness of their attire diminished long ago for our family.

Emily and Amanda wear scarves on their heads to show respect for our host country (79). Later, they too wear the abaya, the hijab, and the niqab. During our last days here, they go out in only these. Our favorite taxi driver calls women dressed like this, including his own wife and daughters, ninjas, and jokes about how he can't tell them apart, but I probably wouldn't get away with it, so I won't mention it. Emily and Amanda are thanked often for the respect they show.

In Malaysia, a non-Muslim wearing the fez or any other such garment is frowned upon because such attire is a display of Muslim faith. In Oman and Yemen, we're told the clothes predate Islam, and while playing a role in the modesty of Islamic life, such attire is not exclusively Muslim. Oman imported the fez from Zambia about 600BC, and has worn it since.

After two days in Aden, a bus takes us to the capital city of Sana'a, a preserved city dating back 2,500 years. We leave on a Friday, Islam's holy day, and don't stop for four and a half hours because the driver wants to get to a certain Mosque for prayers. While milling around between the washrooms, a restaurant, and the Mosque, we note that most of the men, in addition to their traditional attire including the dagger in the belt, carry some sort of firearm, from a sidearm next to the dagger to an automatic rifle slung over the shoulder.

"Why do they take their guns to church, dad?"

"Greggii, when I was a little boy and when we went to the Methodist Church, all the men wore neckties. Even me. They were for dress up, but nobody ever used them. I don't remember anybody ever being hanged by one."

"Okay."

Old Sana'a is a trading center, the streets lined with stalls of vendors selling dates, nuts, knives, guns, frankincense, clothing from around the world, and souvenirs, in addition to money changers, and shops where camels turn mills to produce sesame oil (20, 41 & 48). Many of the buildings are housing units of six to eight floors. We sleep on the fifth floor of one of these on mattresses covering the floor, the Taj Talha Hotel. We never thought to ask about accommodations with real beds because we live on a boat and haven't seen real beds for quite some time.

The tourist industry has not overlaid Yemen with fabrications.

There are one hundred and three mosques inside the walls of Old Sana'a. It's not a big city in area, and when this many mosques begin the muezzin's call, it's either chaotic or beautiful, depending on your perspective. In the late afternoon, after walking and visiting venders in the heat of the day, we sit on the rooftop of the hotel, and watch the sky redden over the ancient city. Then a single crystalline tenor breaks, followed within seconds by all the other muezzins, each independent in their mosque's call, but collectively creating a symphony for us.

Back in Aden, Amanda and I are invited to the Coast Guard station where Colonel al Hammedi, the head of the Marine Security Division of the Yemen Coast Guard asks for a letter of recommendation about security in Yemen.

After returning to *Faith* to compose it, Amanda and I carry the letter to his office across the street from our anchorage. Colonel al Hammadi comments on how much Amanda's attire is appreciated. He presents Amanda with a Qur'an that has English text facing the Arabic, and several booklets explaining what it means to be Muslim. He has a small model ship and gives that to her as well. Before presenting each gift, he asks permission. I tell him we're Christian, and ask permission to present him with a Bible. He consents. I return to *Faith* to get a Bible, several pamphlets for adults and children explaining God's promise through Christ, and a picture of our family. Then we say a prayer that God will use us as He wishes, and return to give him our gifts.

A strange and wonderful event takes place when perceptions collide with reality. I suppose American economic interests must vilify certain peoples, whole nations of peoples, around the globe to justify the treatment of those peoples. How else could we sleep at night? But those perceptions that allow sleep are shattered every time the opportunity of reality is introduced in our journey.

In Yemen, and elsewhere, the result is a portrait of God's created beauty in mankind, and we cannot think of much else this early morning as we pull up anchor.

Halfway out of the harbor, we're reminded by Harbor Control that we need to radio them before moving. Later in the day, another Coalition Warship, this time with an Australian or British accent, contacts us to ask a few questions: ship's name, ship's number, port of registry, number on board, citizenship, last port, etc.

When he asks, "Date and time of departure?" I have the microphone keyed while Emily and I discuss it. She says she thinks it's the twenty-first.

"No," I say, "It's mom's birthday." In my fake-serious radio voice, "two-two March, zero-six-zero-zero."

With several accompanying snickers, he asks, "Next Port?"

I picture four or five bored kids in the radio room of the warship, amused to be talking to some guy who doesn't even know what day it is and reply, "Massawa, Eritrea."

He then asks, "Do you have any information regarding the maritime community in this area that you wish to offer?"

"Do you want information on other cruisers? Or local fishing boats? Or what?"

"Do you have any knowledge of smuggling activity, the Yemen Coast Guard, or other vessel activity since departing Aden?"

I'm relieved he doesn't ask about while *in* Aden, forcing me to relate the story of Colonel al Hammadi, and Amanda, and me, and Qu'rans, and Bibles, and model ships and things.

I feel sorry for him, and want to put him onto something to give them purpose and direction, but without the time to prepare a believable story, I tell the truth:

"No."

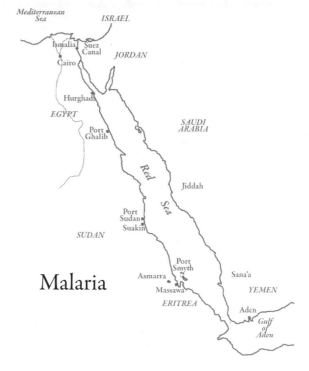

Malaria

The best way to prevent malarial infection is to take measures to avoid being bitten by mosquitos.

International Medical Guide for Ships, World
Health Organization, Geneva, 1988

We steer for the Red Sea, trying to grasp the information in the cruising guides about anchorages and safety in this area. Cruising guides encourage boats to use the main shipping channel of Bab el Mandeb to enter the Red Sea, but we think the Small Strait, east of Perrim Island is better because it *isn't* the main shipping channel. Sailing in shipping lanes is like riding a bicycle on the freeway. We take the road less travelled, close to Yemen's mainland to stay out of the prohibited military area surrounding Perrim Island. We hear stories to inspire fear in travelers—stories like the navy will approach in their patrol boats, just to scare us and shake us down a little, or the navy will fire on yachts in this or that anchorage, to chase them out of sensitive areas rather than to sink them, or my personal favorite, that the whole area is so darn infested with pirates that you must keep diligent watch to not bump into them.

Sailing the Small Strait, we see a patrol boat working the perimeter of the prohibited area. There are several small boats, fifteen to twenty feet long, violently bobbing in the choppy seas where they're anchored. In each, we see two large figures and one small, or one large with two or three small. All but the smallest hold fishing poles or nets. When the face is covered in black, we know that's the mother. The only thing we can think of, confronted with such a threatening sight, is to wave to each other. I hold my hands two feet apart, asking in Universal Fisherman's Signal, how big the fish are. The reply, again in UFS, is them holding their hands about four inches apart.

The next day, we sail on the east side of the shipping lanes, waiting late into the night to cross. Ships in the Red Sea and anywhere in our travels don't just appear. On rare occasions, we'll see a speck on the horizon, but that's the exception. The rule is that an object on the horizon slowly transforms from the nothingness of haze into a hallucination or ghost, followed by reality as a ship is born into focus. A time element exists in the formation of ships on the horizon. When a choice is available, we cross shipping lanes in the dark of night. Navigation lights eliminate guesswork. So does radar.

We complete sixty hours of sailing and would continue to Massawa if we knew we could enter the harbor in daylight. Massawa is another thirty miles—more than four hours away—and it's too late. We enter the narrow pass at the small island of Port Smyth to anchor for the night, and see a friend in the water cleaning his hull. Greggii thinks it looks like a good place to swim, and since I'm not keen on his going alone, we swim over together to bob around and watch Jorgen scrape the last six months growth from his waterline. I'm more tired than I think I should be, so we swim back. I also have this tendency, since Australia, where every creature is marketed as deadly to attract tourists, to get the willies swimming in new waters, thinking Greggii will be the appetizer and I'll be the entrée.

After our swim, we explore the reddish-golden island. I assume what little grows here is dormant because it doesn't contrast with the color of the place. There are signs, including the name Port Smyth, that Port Smyth was occupied at one time; today, the island's population is us.

After dinner, the fever sets in. It doesn't sneak up as fevers do, but grabs me in a powerful way, running up to 104° in the time it takes to light a burner on the stove. There's no time for subtly reflecting on how I feel, none of that *gee, I don't think I feel very well* stuff. I'm sick, overcome with chills, and go to bed with every blanket I can find. I take some ibuprofen to help the fever. Lorrie displays great medical wisdom in suggesting a cold shower, but I like my method better, and think we should give the ibuprofen time. She does steal my blankets—an act in which I find great insult. Two hours later, the fever leaves. Bad food, I think.

In the morning, we leave for Massawa. While dragging up the anchor and navigating out of the reef, I get sick again, but pretend otherwise. This is a neat trick dad taught me when I felt too sick for school as a kid; pretend you're not sick and often you won't be. We get out of the reef, but not out of the fever. Again ibuprofen, again stolen blankets, again a discussion about a cold shower, and again, the fever leaves after a few hours. We enter the harbor.

A responsibility of mine, as captain of the good ship *Faith*, is to clear in with the port authority, immigration, and Customs; I usually take somebody, Emily in this case, with me. We arrive during tea time, or lunch, or a card game, or something, so we have to round up the guys in each office to proceed with our business.

Next, we take a quick walk outside the port facility. Massawa has the same reddish-golden glow as Port Smyth, with no vegetation but a larger population. Following years of civil war and with few natural resources to spark an outside interest in exploiting them, Eritrea is financially strapped. Official payment for anything must be made in US Dollars, but the only source of cash is the Eritrean Nakfa. Massawa is dry and dusty, and no money is available for rebuilding or even cleaning up after the wars. When we enter the harbor, we see a building with a golden dome that has a hole in it. From the anchorage, on the other side of it, we see that the whole back side of the dome is blown out. Massawa frames the story that is unfolding.

When I return to *Faith*, the fever returns to me, lingering longer than before, and Lorrie is again rewarded with a real issue to concern herself with. Two boats, *Snowgoose* and *Legend II*, offer support. Cathy from *Legend II* suggests I go to a local clinic to be tested for malaria. When we get there, I feel better. I'm sure I'm the only person required to pay in US Dollars, but that's the way it goes. In fact, that's the way all of our US Dollars are going. The clinic takes blood and money, and says to return in a half-hour to see if it's malaria. We do and it isn't.

Though I am relieved at not having malaria, the fever returns to torture me through the night. Lorrie and Cathy seek another opinion. They go to the wharf where a cruise ship is berthed and return to *Faith* with the captain and medical officer of *Topaz*. After much hemming and hawing, and since all their medical doohickeys are on *Topaz*, and since they don't have much to do—all their clients are on an excursion to the capital city of Asmarra—they invite us to the ship's hospital. The doctor makes a fine project out of me, and I know I'm in the best place I can be, lying there on the gurney with needles in my arms and bottles of libations hanging from cold little trees on wheels, surrounded by stainless steel cabinets and odors and echoes of sterilization.

Believing last night's test, the doctor doesn't think I have malaria so he doesn't test me, though he does give me one or two of just about everything else in his arsenal. A shot of this, a pill of that, and all the while, the back of my hand drinks bags of fluid. He sends me home with Lorrie, Cathy, and Greggii, who's had the captain's permission to raid the ship's kitchen for whatever he wants all afternoon.

They get me home and put me to bed in time for the fever. This time it doesn't depart, and in the morning, Lorrie and Cathy talk again to *Topaz's* doctor, who tells them to get me to a hospital. He's done all he knows how with the resources he has.

While they're on shore, all the vans are returning with *Topaz's* cruisers from Asmarra. Lorrie and Cathy, with help from the U.S. Consulate in Eritrea, decide the best place for me is the UN Hospital in Asmarra. All the vans are heading back there anyway, so they hire one to take us. They come to retrieve me and the rest of the family for our own excursion to that wonderful city. I try to get comfortable lying down in the back, which is bad, then sitting in front, which is no improvement, then near the middle before I realize how sick I am.

UN Hospitals are strategically located where peacekeeping missions occur, and it's a tribute to either the effectiveness of the peacekeeping mission in Eritrea or the fighting factions' ability to shoot straight that during my visit the UN Hospital has one patient. The hospital is run by competent medical officers of Jordan's military. This time, the test for malaria is positive. They begin a regimen of sleep with brief periods of wakedness to change the IV bag, or give me some pills, or poke me with something. Lorrie gets a room at a hotel for the family, and Amanda stays with me the first night. After the family leaves, it's just Amanda and me. She pulls out a can of sour cream and onion potato chips and offers me some. Since I haven't eaten anything for three days, I try two. Bad move. I grab hold of a wastebasket just in time.

Asmarra is at an elevation of over 7,000 feet, and is cold at night. I am not affected much because my room is in an enclosed part of the building. There are times, however, that I need a trip to the bathroom. My greatest periods of physical activity occur when I grab the IV tree, wheel it to the door, over the threshold, down a step, down the cold, outdoor alleyway, then up a step, and over the threshold into the bathroom and back again. After a couple times of my doing this, always late at night, one of the nurses catches me and says that if I just turn this little knob and unhook this thingamajig, I don't have to take the tree with me. He also says—I think, because my Arabic is as limited as his English—to call when I need to go, and somebody will help me. He probably figures I just didn't understand what he said, but pride forces me to go to the bathroom alone. Cold to be sure, but alone.

Lorrie, Greggii, and Emily come back in the morning, and after Lorrie and Dr. Ahmad Shono, the hospital's director, grumble in low tones in the corner for a few moments, we visit. I don't remember much, except that it's Emily's turn to stay with me. I change beds because the bed I had last night has a broken brace and my right shoulder was about two inches lower than my left.

Everybody on staff and in my family tells me I must eat something. The staff sows seeds of guilt, asking, "Don't you like the food we serve you?" and, "You must eat this, I made it special for you." I don't want to eat anything. Nothing.

On the morning of my third day here, two of Dr. Shono's assistants enter and say they finally found the right medicine at the Indian Pharmacy on the other side of the city. One of them holds a giant syringe, and both of them grin with sly satisfaction, knowing this stuff is magic. They tell me to turn over. I do. We wait for the magic. It doesn't happen.

Early in the evening, Dr. Shono takes Lorrie aside for another round of grumbling. When they return, he tells me they've done all they can and I should go to Cairo, where better medications are available. (Lorrie shares with me later that the reason for Cairo is that I have a type of malaria that will be fatal, should it go to my brain, and no life-support equipment exists in Eritrea.) They prepare me to board the 3:00 AM flight to Cairo. We must pay our hospital bill first, which is US $125 per day. When I ask about the drugs, the x-rays, and the tests, Dr. Shono says the price is for the room, the treatment, the doctors, everything(21).

Our supply of US Dollars dwindles, even with *Snowgoose* and *Legend II* helping as they are able. We leave the hospital, and I notice for the first time the security surrounding it. The ambulance exits through an armed checkpoint.

Amanda plans to go to Cairo with me, but we don't have enough money for two tickets. The cost is US$400 per ticket, payable at the counter. They won't accept payment in Nakfa nor will they let us pay for our passage, on Egypt Air, when we arrive in Cairo. The airport manager, who on first impression is stern and unfriendly, tries to help, but cannot get both of us on the plane with the cash we have. I say goodbye to a crying family and leave alone.

While we are sorting out the details, the three o'clock departure is delayed. By the time I board, it's 4:00 AM. There's a man sitting in a seat next to me, but he moves one row back because the plane is less than half-full and he wants to stretch out.

Then, I learn the pilots aren't comfortable with my medical evacuation.

After several minutes, the airport manager asks a man across the aisle from me to join him in the cockpit. Five minutes later, he returns and the manager asks the man who moved behind me to join them. After ten minutes, the manager returns my medical evacuation letter and tells me to relax. The man behind me tells me he's from Guyana, working for the UN as a specialist in sub-Saharan infectious diseases.

Somewhere outside the gate, my family is praying for me, and God plants a man next to me with the credentials to convince the pilots I'm not a threat. How cool is that?

The plane takes off at five, still well before the predawn grey, and my status as someone important enough to keep the plane grounded, like any other terrorist, diminishes.

Immigration goes quickly and I walk toward the exit. Two guys in white coats hold a *Mr. Gregg* sign. They escort me to an ambulance, where a third guy waits so it won't get towed. Their English isn't much better than the staff at the UN Hospital, and since my Arabic hasn't improved, we don't talk much. One guy asks if I want a drink, and I say yes. We pull up to a roadside stand, and enjoy smoking cigarettes and drinking Cokes. Then, the guy who offered the drink motions for me to pay. Several miles later, with the drinks scenario still fresh in my mind, I'm asked and decline their offer of breakfast.

Cairo must be big because it takes forever to get to the hospital and we're all good friends by the time we arrive. Their English shows a dramatic improvement when they tell me a tip for their services isn't out of line, if I'm so inclined. Then, they place me in the care of the emergency room at the Arab Contractors Medical Center. I'm escorted to one of a half-dozen beds, and the curtain is closed around my loneliness. I hear medical professionals talking in Arabic, or medical-speak, or some other foreign language.

No sleep, fever, crying family, travel, ambulance—it's all a dream. A woman enters for information: age, marital status, weight, temperature, etc., and makes notes inside a folder. She then hands me the folder. A man escorts me to the lab, and then to radiology. The lab takes blood and puts the results on a piece of paper, slips it into my folder and hands it back to me. Radiology takes a chest x-ray, prepares a report, and puts the x-ray and the report in my folder and hands it back to me. I'm escorted back to the emergency room for an abdominal ultrasound.

None of these tests or results requires being flung around the hospital's duct-work in vacuum tubes or electronic cables while elite white coats guard the contents.

Within an hour, my file is filled with an x-ray and report, a lab report, an ultrasound and report, and other pieces of the diagnostic puzzle. A doctor enters and asks permission to see my file. He says they don't have any difficulty with the UN Hospital in Eritrea, whose notes are also in my file, but by policy, they must start fresh. He tells me I have malaria and that I'll be spending time with them. Then I'm led to the financial office to get a room.

At first, I have difficulty with the room charges quoted in pounds. I know a British Pound is worth a couple dollars, and get nervous about the cost. I ask what Egyptian Pounds are worth, and am relieved when I'm told a dollar will buy about five of them. I agree to pay an extra thirty pounds per day for a private room. After we walk back to the emergency room, they place me in a wheelchair to take me to my room. The elevator takes longer to arrive than my wheelchair pusher and I think it should, so we carry the wheelchair up the stairs where he finishes wheeling me to my room.

Dr. Ghonemy Abdelazeem comes to say he's my doctor. He trained in the United Kingdom and is the director of the infectious disease department here at Arab Contractors Medical Center. He reviews my file, hands it back to me, and says he doesn't think I have pneumonia as Dr. Shono thought, but concurs with everything else from Eritrea. He starts me on a diet of pills: Vibramycin twice a day and Fansidar once a week. I don't have much medical knowledge, but I think the antibiotic Vibramycin is supposed to beat up any bugs that would take advantage of my weakened state, and Fansidar is the pesticide to attack malaria parasites.

In the afternoon, a woman from the United States Embassy visits. She works with Citizen's Services and asks if there's anything I need. I give her my ATM card, and ask her to get some money for me and a SIM card for my phone.

Brian, from the US consulate in Eritrea helps make my first contact with Lorrie happen. He calls a restaurant near where *Faith* is anchored and sets up a time when Lorrie will be there so I can call her. We arrange for me to call at 10:00 AM daily.

I still can't eat, so Dr. Ghonemy sends the hospital chef to me to see how she can make the food more appealing. Either I'm feeling better, or her performance is better than the Jordanians because she makes me feel lowdown and ashamed for not eating her food. She's matronly, dressed in the brown headscarf and yellow uniform of all the women in the hospital, and it pierces me as if from my own mother when she asks if her cooking isn't any good. I start nibbling pitas and eating tomato wedges and jellos, so we both win. I try to make her feel as if she's winning more by taking a bit of chicken here and half of the beans or rice there, wrapping them in a napkin and disposing of them so she thinks I ate them.

Through the first day and a half at the Arab Contractors Hospital, my fever hovers, not always at 104°, but never below 102°. Actually, it hovers between 38.8° and 40.2° centigrade because the rest of the world is yet to adopt America's superior system of weights and measures.

Meanwhile, back in Eritrea, Werner from *Legend II* helps Emily ready *Faith* for the move up the Red Sea. I've been in charge of *Faith's* maintenance since our journey began, and have my own *bandaids* on things to keep them running without the original parts. While I'm in Cairo, and Werner is working on *Faith* with Emily, I'm not all that comfortable with him seeing my fixes. Werner nicknames Emily *Grease Monkey* while she repairs the water-maker and changes the engine and generator oils (18).

The longer I'm in Cairo, the more difficult things become in Eritrea, but the more blessings are provided at the same time. Lorrie's money is running out. On hearing this, a French man sailing to Asia, who could never expect repayment, hands Lorrie $200 and says, "With what you've got going on, anybody would do that."

A boat in the anchorage is broken-into while the owners are sleeping. They lose a camera and a laptop. This *is* the definition of piracy. The officials, with exception, make life uncomfortable, and Lorrie finds difficulty with everything. Food is scarce; the main staple is cabbage. Cabbage soup, cabbage casserole, cabbage stews. They can't buy eggs, or even a chicken.

They experience a scary time in a scary place, and do the best they can. They don't eat because there's nothing to eat. I don't eat because I'm sick.

After two nights, I know I'm getting better and will be released someday. I ask Dr. Ghonemy if I can taxi downtown to buy a guidebook from which to arrange for a room when he does release me. In the afternoon, I walk around one city block, and buy the book. Following my brief tour, I go to McDonald's and eat a small hamburger and fries, a feast after not eating for over a week. I'm so worn out that I ask the manager of McDonalds's to help me into a taxi for my return to the hospital.

Dr. Ghonemy holds out hope of my being released, but has reservations about my ability to rest. He needs assurance I won't be touring the pyramids or museum. I have no interest in seeing the pyramids without my family, and no interest in the museum even with my family, and tell him so. When Dr. Ghonemy releases me, all I have left to do is pay the bill.

I go to the financial office and I'm handed the bill. Three days hospitalization in a private room, doctors' fees, drugs, lab, x-ray, ultrasound, even the ambulance from the airport—it's all there. This hospital is privately owned and for-profit, and I don't qualify for subsidies as I'm not Egyptian. I'm billed the equivalent of US$475.00 and they make money on me.

When I return to my room to pack the few items I have, there's a man delivering flowers, a huge bouquet from Mama Maggie. I don't know who or what Mama Maggie is, but the driver explains she founded a mission of Egyptian Christians in Cairo called Stephen's Children. I tell him I'm being discharged, and he drives me downtown to the hostel where I have a room reserved.

My second floor room faces a traffic circle. The balcony door doesn't close enough to keep out the mosquitoes or the sounds of the street below. Egyptian cars have horns that go *beep-beep* rather than *honk*, and get plenty of use. I don't sleep well and change accommodations in the morning.

I have medications to continue, and I'm supposed to be resting. I'm in contact with Lorrie on a daily basis and with Mom and Dad on a daily basis and with my brother Gary more than once daily. Everybody's worried about Lorrie. Our plan, contrived by Lorrie and Cathy, is to have a German man who's in Langkawi join Lorrie and the kids in Massawa, and sail *Faith* up the Red Sea to Egypt, where I can resume being captain and father.

One afternoon, Dad says he's amazed how fast God provides healing once the corner's been turned from being sick to getting well. I think his intentions are to inspire, and within an hour, I decide to return to Eritrea and sail my family up the Red Sea myself.

Knowing there are two flights to Asmarra each week, one on Wednesday and one on Sunday, each at 1:00 AM, I'm determined to make this Easter Sunday's flight. Being determined doesn't make it happen. When I go to the Eritrean Embassy to apply for a visa on Good Friday, I'm told they write visas on Tuesdays and I'm invited back then. I'm also told there's no guarantee.

Between the US Embassy in Cairo and Brian from the US Consulate in Asmarra, nobody holds much hope of a visa by Easter, or ever for that matter.

I learn a little about US diplomacy during this time. Brian tells us that US relations with Eritrea are strained because Eritrea won't allow the US to carry what is called diplomatic pouch in Eritrea. I don't know much about it, but understand, from the Tom Clancy novels I've read, that diplomatic pouch provides a corridor to the diplomat's embassy or consulate in the host country, so documents and other things can be moved in and out of foreign offices without scrutiny.

One element of foreign policy is that it's a sign of weakness for one country to overlook an insult from the other, so the US Consulate in Eritrea stopped writing visas. This adolescent diplomacy fuels my difficulties in returning home to my family.

I tour parts of Cairo with Emad from Stephen's Children. While I was in the hospital, my brother shared his concern about me with others in West Michigan. One of those others is a Christian, a successful businessman affiliated with the ministry of Stephen's Children, founded by Mama Maggie Gobran, a member of an Egyptian family in Cairo's Coptic community. It's his call to Stephen's Children that causes the flowers to be delivered, which turn into a ride to the hostel and into this tour. Emad picks me up and takes me to a facility where boys are taught to make shoes, and girls, sweaters. The mission provides a skill and a Christian education. School isn't available to these children, so this mission provides them with hope for salvation and hope for the future. As a gift, they give me a knitted scarf, which makes me feel guilty, as I bear no gifts. All I did to get here was get sick, which doesn't warrant such a treasure. The next place we go is an orphanage for young girls, whose physical needs of food and shelter are provided, but more importantly, they're given a loving, caring, Christian home.

Lorrie says they can't buy food and wants me to bring back protein, so Emad takes me to a store where I buy twenty kilograms of beans, lentils, and nuts. I know Lorrie wants meat, but I can't figure out how to travel with it. Then, Emad takes me to the most fascinating part not only of Cairo but of our tour of the world. The Garbage.

In Cairo, communities exist where the economy is built on garbage. Literally. A neighborhood might be a quarter of a mile square or a mile square, with streets wide enough for two cars to pass in some spots, but mostly narrower, lined with three- or four-storey brick, multifamily townhouses stained dark from years of fires or smog or cooking fumes with garbage and children and donkeys and men and women and trucks and cars and bicycles and animals and noise and an overpowering stench. The neighborhood is populated with families comprising a dad, a mom, a bunch of children, and a donkey. The way it's told to me is if they occupy a two-room flat, dad, mom, and the kids will occupy one room and the donkey lives in the other. The family depends on the donkey because at night, dad harnesses it to a cart and takes it to the city where garbage awaits removal. He loads it up, takes it home, and dumps it into any area available, up to and including the stoop of his townhouse. During the day, mom and the able children, mostly barefooted and under-clothed (note the shoes and sweaters earlier), will sort the garbage into donkey fodder, saleable plastic, metals, paper, glass, and whatever else they can salvage. These items, except for the donkey fodder, are baled for sale, and this is life in the garbage of Cairo (39).

School is not part of this life. On first appearance, it illustrates Cairo's need for a modern solid waste plan, but if they introduce one, hundreds of thousands of people will be left without livelihood. It's too easy to look at places and know in my superior western mind how to fix things. The garbage only reinforces how dumb my superior western mind is.

Stephen's Children also provides medical clinics in the garbage areas. They treat many needs, but the most common are foot infections and viruses from the garbage.

When I return to the hotel, the odor is etched on my body, in my nose, my hair, and my clothes; but the scene is etched in my being. Jesus talks about ministering to people, in their homes and livelihoods. Stephen's Children meets them here.

I talk to Lorrie and wish everybody a happy Easter. She tells me the girls are going to church with some friends they made, girls that work at the restaurant where Lorrie takes my calls. She also tells me a young man from the port authority, Mulgiha, is working to facilitate my return to Eritrea.

Lorrie and Brian tell me to go to the Eritrean Embassy on Tuesday, and a visa will be granted. Brian mentions there are no guarantees until I actually have it. When I arrive, the man who greets me looks in a notebook and confirms my name is there from the weekend's telephone messages, and ushers me to a window where my visa will be processed. I give them my passport, fill out a number of forms, and I'm told to return later. I do, and walk out with my visa.

The embassy in Cairo didn't do it. The consulate in Eritrea didn't do it. The congressman in Washington whose office my brother has been calling didn't do it. It took a young man at the dock in Massawa to get me home.

I book the 1:00 AM flight to Asmarra that night or the following morning, depending on how you see things.

Emad takes me to the airport. I'm in Asmarra at 2:30 and am met by Brian and his Eritrean driver, who drives me to the bus station for transfer to Massawa, to Lorrie, Emily, Amanda and Greggii.

Brian's driver gets me the last seat on the bus, and causes no small degree of contempt in a woman sitting by the window with a bushel of tomatoes next to her. She has to put her tomatoes on top of the bus and changes her seat to a row forward. The best reason I can make out for her distress is that maybe she's Muslim and isn't supposed to sit next to an unknown man, or maybe she thinks I should be on top of the bus instead of her tomatoes. I don't know. I do know that every time the bus stops and she can find an ear outside her window, she cackles a bunch of foreign-type language in a high-pitched voice and points at me so her audience can know the object of her distress. I start feeling not only tired, but sick, and it warms me to know someone pays such attention to me.

There's one other white-guy on the bus. Lorrie told me he might be here. He's the French stranger who gave her money last week. We talk only long enough for him to realize I'm not feeling well, and we share a taxi to the restaurant from the bus station in Massawa. In addition to the nuts and legumes, I have enough US currency to repay the friends Lorrie made in my absence, including him.

When I arrive at the restaurant, Lorrie, the girls, Greggii, and I have a good reunion cry and our emotions spill. Emily and Amanda spent Easter night with girls from the restaurant and want to tell me about it (80). Everybody wants me to sit in the restaurant to visit and have some of the special Eritrean coffee and talk, but after only a few minutes, I must go to *Faith* and lie down.

The fever doesn't return, but I'm whipped from the past week-and-a-half. I lost thirty pounds, and gained twenty years. I know Lorrie, the girls, and Greggii are whipped too, having held up the boat in my absence. My experience pales next to what they faced.

The worst thought is that our hardship over the past weeks in Eritrea is normal for Eritreans without access to medicine or protein.

Lorrie, Emily, Amanda, and Greggii sail; I offer moral support between naps.

The Red Sea

Suakin, Sudan, doesn't offer much more than Massawa, so Lorrie and the girls take the half-hour bus to Port Sudan, and purchase ground beef, breakfast sausage, and fresh veggies (43).

I don't want to go ashore in Suakin, which is a good thing because our agent here, Muhammad, has trouble keeping commitments, and I must wait on *Faith* for him anyway. The fuel he commits to bring early is delivered at sundown, sufficiently dirty to occupy us late into the night as it trickles through our *Baja Filter*—a special triple filter for coarse sediments, fine sediments, and water. Laundry arrives a day late, dirtier than when we sent it, and rinsed with saltwater, providing a texture and a taste different than we're accustomed to.

To be fair, I'm coming back from malaria, thirty pounds lighter, and I use orneriness to make up for my diminished stature. No place would be nice for me, and there's no place I would be very nice. Lorrie and the kids tell me of Suakin, of how it feels like a thousand years ago with donkeys, camels, and men in flowing robes in the dusty streets (81).

Customs and immigration are handled by the marina at Port Ghalib, Egypt. Port Ghalib is a large development in the early stages. When finished, it will be a high-end, marina-resort complex. Today, we occupy what can best be described as almost a marina with a restaurant, small hotel, and dive shop. We berth alongside a wall next to the construction area where underground utilities are being installed. The landscaping outside *Faith* is reddish-golden dirt for several miles until it meets the sky.

From Port Ghalib, Lorrie and the kids take a trip to Luxor and the Valley of the Kings. They return excited about Egyptian history and relics, but annoyed with overbearing touts.

Our next port is Hurghada, Egypt.

Emily washes *Faith*'s deck and steps on the slope between the cabin and the aft deck. Her ankle gives way and she hears something crack. We ask where it hurts and she points to the center of the top of her left foot. I think she broke one of those bones that splay from the ankle to the toes, but remembering my self-diagnosis in Malaysia when I thought my shoulder was dislocated, I think a trained opinion is needed. Lorrie is beside herself with concern.

We ask the marina office for help, and the manager fetches us for a trip to the tourist hospital. Emily is wheeled in, x-rayed, and diagnosed. Nothing's broken, but there's a strain or a tear on a ligament. We're given an order to pick up some stuff at the hospital's pharmacy, and she's told to rest and use crutches for a few days.

Whew!

When we get the bill, I find we owe considerably more because we're American, nearly double. I take the meds, ankle brace, and crutches back to the pharmacy, and after a bit of futile griping with the staff, we pay it, still a fraction of what we would have been charged in America. We find the meds, ankle brace, and crutches at a pharmacy on the way back to the marina.

Greggii and I go to a water park. In the two weeks since leaving Massawa, I feel stronger every day, but in the locker room of the water park, I see a scary figure in the full-length mirrors surrounding us. The face resembles mine, but the body is bulimic. I wear my shirt for the day.

Greggii and I get haircuts. Greggii's is forty pounds—roughly eight bucks, but because I also get a shave, mine is seventy. Lorrie has some hairs or eyebrows or something plucked for twenty-five. In the middle of my haircut, one of the guys asks if I want some potion he has in a little jar put on my face after my shave. Sure. When it comes time to pay, they say I owe three hundred and fifty pounds. I don't know where they learned their math, but I am guessing some Sri Lankans were in the class.

After several days, a boat returns to a slip where I noticed several dock lines had been left. *Caribbean Soul.* Kobe, the dog, lounges lazily, but shows spasms of energy when we walk past. We introduce ourselves to Steve and Kim, who invite us aboard for a visit. They're from San Diego, purchased *Caribbean Soul* new in France last year, sailed the Mediterranean last summer, and came south to Hurghada for the winter. They're preparing to sail into the Mediterranean again and make the Atlantic crossing about the same time as we do.

We leave Hurghada and go to a reef where *Caribbean Soul* tells us dolphins might join us for a swim. We think the kids will like that, but while we're here, the dolphins aren't. The kids say the snorkeling is good, though.

On our way to Port Suez, we motor into the twenty-knot breeze and two-meter seas, while staying on the edge of the shipping lane and watching the traffic barrel down on us and pass on our port side: big ships, fast ships, and close enough to smell the fumes as they pass. I photograph the sun, red and rising, framed between the booms of cranes on an oil platform.

The Suez Canal is eighty miles long, with southbound and northbound traffic separated by a long island in the middle fifteen miles of the canal. It's a daytime operation. Ships enter each end of the canal early in the morning, pass each other at midday where the island separates traffic, and exit by evening. Yachts, being slower, must stop at Ismalia, the halfway point.

We anchor until the northbound ships move into the canal, and then follow them until we arrive at the Suez Canal Yacht Club, a mile into the canal. We're boarded by Captain Hebi of Prince of the Red Sea Yacht Agency. He's our agent for the transit.

The Suez Canal Authority doesn't compute a fee for the canal based on length, or beam, or displacement, or any rational combination of these values. The best I can tell is that between our agent and the Canal Authority, they arrive at a fee based on our apparent ability to pay.

We pay it, and are scheduled to transit the first half of the canal tomorrow.

Captain Hebi tells us we're allowed to carry only two jerry cans of fuel aboard in Ismalia, so we need to get fuel from him in Suez at US75¢ per liter. This is not true. Cheaper fuel, at 15¢ per liter, is available in Ismalia and they do let you carry it in. A lot of things aren't true in Egypt.

Cruising guides say the pilot for our trip through the canal will demand *baksheesh*—something between a gratuity and the lubrication that gets things done in Egypt. We agree on twenty dollars for *baksheesh* before entering the canal.

Prayers happen twice during our time in the canal, and our pilot asks for a towel to take to *Faith's* bow and kneel on to honor this aspect of his religion. Lorrie uses our time with him to witness Christ, but his grasp of English falters during these discussions.

When we arrive in Ismalia, we pay him twenty dollars. He asks for bus fare, and I give him another five-dollar bill. Then, he asks for money for food. I tell him he can use that twenty-five dollars for whatever he likes, but that's all he's getting. Once the game's over, he's fine.

The next day, that same pilot steers the boat he's on into a channel marker. Those owners don't feel as compelled to play the *baksheesh* game.

We board the train for Cairo and we begin our time there with the Egyptian Museum. There aren't many things I don't like to do, but museums are one of them. Not all museums, certainly not the Devil's Rope Museum of Barbed Wire on the corner of US Route 66 and the state of Texas. But generally, museums are places I distance myself from, and the Egyptian Museum in Cairo fits well into this generalization. For one thing, it's too big. For another, it has too much stuff, unsorted and just there without much description, unlike the Devil's Rope Museum where every wire, tool, and picture comes with a full explanation of what it's for, where it comes from, and how it's used. And, there's no barbed wire at the Egyptian Museum in Cairo.

Greggii thinks the mummies are cool, Amanda enjoys the intricate carving of Tut's gold, Emily likes the whole thing, and Lorrie always likes museums.

After absorbing our share of museum excitement, Emily, Greggii, and I go wait in a coffee shop where we can have a cup of tea and tug on a *shisha*, or *hookah*, or waterpipe, while Lorrie and Amanda continue to nourish their amusement at the museum.

Then, following a good night's rest, we head to Giza to see the Great Pyramids and the Sphinx. In Egypt, you can't simply hire a taxi and expect the driver to take you where you want to go and let you off and you pay him. Instead, he must get involved with the camel venders to fix you up with camels and a camel driver to show you around. We choose to use our own feet, and enter the gate to walk around. As far as being shown around, there are pyramids and there's the Sphinx, and they sit in the middle of a subdivision that used to be desert. It doesn't take a whole lot to figure out.

Either Greggii or Amanda want to ride camels, or Lorrie wants to get a picture of them on camels, so we hire two from a guy to walk Greggii and Amanda around one of the pyramids. While they're on the far side of the pyramid, two very nice boys come up to us and say, "We want to give you a gift." Their gift turns out to be a pre-cut and pre-stitched *mesheda*, with an elastic band stitched into it to keep it on your head.

"Thank you. That's very nice of you."

"Now, you give us gift?"

Lorrie reaches in her purse and hands them a fresh pastry wrapped in a napkin and says, "Here you are. It's very good."

That catches them off-guard, and they quickly snatch back their gift, return Lorrie's pastry, and leave as the camels return with Amanda and Greggii.

We walk to one pyramid where you can pay extra to walk down a set of stairs and inside. It doesn't generate too much excitement in Lorrie, who's claustrophobic and has an aversion to tight places, or me, who's tight and has an aversion to expensive places; but we get *student* tickets for the kids, after a discussion with the ticket vender about what constitutes a student—home-schooling is an obstacle. Emily enters, but returns shortly to get her camera. The signs all say *No Cameras*, but everybody has them. She's almost back inside when a security guard begins chase. When he finally catches her and points to it, she motions to the other people with cameras and refuses to give up. Once back at his perch outside, he looks at me, smiles, and in the manner of one father of a devious child to another, gives me a thumbs-up. We understand each other.

When I was in Cairo with malaria, I asked Emad if he would give a tour of Cairo to my family when we return (22). He spends a day with us, showing us the garbage, the orphanages, the manufacturing, and a summer camp that coincides with our time in Cairo. The camp, on the small campus of a Catholic Church and school, is an opportunity to reach large numbers of children. We meet Maggie Gobran, fondly called Mama Maggie, the founder of Stephen's Children, after she delivers a message to the congregation of children at the camp before Emad helps hire a car and driver for our return to Ismalia.

We request a pilot for the second half of the Suez Canal. A knock on the boat at 10:30 PM by the marina operator, Ahmad, informs us that a warship will be transiting tomorrow, so we can't leave. International treaties allow warships passage without small boats like *Faith* around. During our eight days in the canal, we hear of three canal closings for warships, but have yet to see one. Even in Port Suez, when a warship was scheduled at 4:00 PM, and other boats were held at the yacht club on that account, and we were watching for it to point it out to Greggii, we failed to see it, which speaks wonders for modern camouflage. I think the *warship is transiting so you can't go today* is used as a convenience.

George and Mirema arrive on *Moonshadow*—I presume they possess a higher security clearance than we do—on the day the canal is closed for a warship. They want to move tomorrow, just as we do, and he and I visit Ahmad to confirm the timing of the morning's pilots. We're told to wait until the football game between Ismalia and Cairo is finished. At 11:30 PM, we learn the pilots will be here at 5:30 AM. The scheduling issues are compounded in the morning when four pilots arrive for the seven boats. *Monte Cristo* is paired with the Russian Catamaran, whose pilot is to guide both boats through the canal. Our pilot forgot to show up.

I ask about this while watching the first five boats depart, and I'm told our pilot will be here in five minutes. Five minutes in Egypt means sometime. Fifteen minutes later, *Moonshadow*'s pilot arrives. I ask him where our pilot is; he says he'll be here in five minutes.

I untie *Faith* and radio *Moonshadow* to ask George, "If our pilot doesn't show, can we piggyback on *Moonshadow* and have your pilot make the calls for us?"

George radios back, "He says to wait a little longer."

"George, I'm asking *you* if it's okay. If you're okay with it, maybe you can tell your pilot we aren't asking for permission."

"I'm fine with that. Let's just go and see how it works out," is George's reply.

The transit goes fine, and George tells me this pilot is helpful and a great guy, far better than his pilot yesterday. Every now and then, George radios and tells me his pilot wants me to move *Faith* this way, or that way, or something, to earn his keep on two boats.

Approaching Port Said, George tells me his pilot thinks I should bring *Faith* alongside with *baksheesh* before we reach the end. That sounds fair to me. His presence on *Moonshadow* makes him the best pilot we could have hoped for. We ask George to determine his own gift, and we'll match it, so neither of us appears too cheap or too rich. One hundred pounds each.

Part VI. The Mediterranean Sea

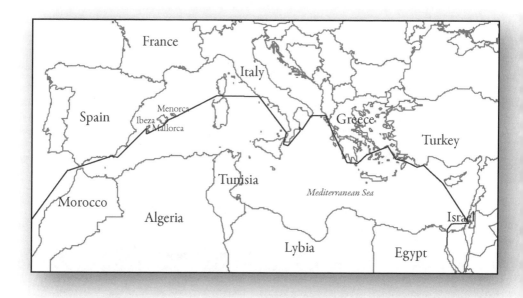

The Mediterranean Sea
4 June to 11 November 2007

Less than Holy in The Holy Lands

Blessed are the poor in spirit, for theirs is the kingdom of heaven.
Blessed are those who mourn, for they will be comforted.
Blessed are the meek, for they will inherit the earth.
Blessed are those who hunger and thirst for righteousness, for they will be filled.
Blessed are the merciful, for they will be shown mercy.
Blessed are the pure in heart, for they will see God.
Blessed are the peacemakers, for they will be called sons of God.
Blessed are those who are persecuted because of righteousness, for theirs is the kingdom of heaven.

The Beatitudes, Matthew 5:3-10

We don't stop at Port Said. *Moonshadow's* pilot leaves when a Canal Authority boat comes alongside, and we slide silently into the Mediterranean evening, them heading north to Cyprus and us heading east to Tel Aviv.

As *Faith* points toward Tel Aviv, the breeze and sloppy seas originating there shatter our comfort. We point north again to follow *Moonshadow* to Cyprus.

After six hours, the wind tosses about as if it's lost its way. There's no point sailing at all in this condition, as my amateur adjustments at the mast to quiet the rigging are obsolete by the time I return to the cockpit.

Then, the breeze settles into slumber, but the sea neglects to do the same. We're

205

motoring, and since no direction will ease our discomfort, we opt for our original plan, and resume a course for Tel Aviv.

Israel has a security thing going on that resembles paranoia. I can't understand why, except for the apartheid.

Our first contact with the Israeli Navy is thirty miles out. We're supposed to initiate contact as soon as we come within radio range. The Navy tells us to contact Haifa Radio, and answer questions about our ship's documentation, passport information, cruising speed, and currents so they can determine our arrival time.

A patrol boat enters the haze from out of nowhere, circles us twice, and disappears without contact. This is our first experience with this level of security. I sometimes wonder if the security some people pretend provides freedom doesn't effect the opposite. In the United States, our freedoms have disappeared not because of airplanes flying into buildings, but in our response to it. We applaud our leaders for doing to us what terrorists failed to do to us.

Greggii is nervous about our BB gun. I don't know why he gets nervous now. I never declared it at any previous port, but he keeps asking, "what if they find it?'

We arrive at Tel Aviv after waiting at sea for an hour. They don't want us in the harbor until security personnel can give us a proper welcome. When we are allowed to enter, a man comes aboard. A few minutes later, a woman carrying an electronic sniffer boards *Faith*. She wipes several surfaces with special paper, and runs the paper through the sniffer to tell if explosives have been tinkered with on *Faith*.

When she asks about firearms, I tell her about the BB gun. She impounds it, saying, "If you ran through the mall, or anywhere in public with this, it might cause too much alarm."

We've had that gun on board for almost four years and never even thought of all the fun we could have had if we ran around in public with it.

After we clear in, we motor five miles north to Hurzliya Marina.

Five times a day while in Hurzilya, we witness groups of a half-dozen military helicopters fly overhead. They are all southbound, toward the Gaza Strip, intended to maintain a reign of peace and terror over those annoying Palestinians.

I buy a guidebook to plan our tour of the Holy Lands.

We rent a compact car and by Monday at 9:15 AM, we're on our way north toward Haifa. We aren't going to Haifa, but head that direction to get to Mt. Carmel, where Elijah and his God, the God of Abraham, challenged Ahab and his gods, Baal and Asherah, to a contest. The God of Abraham won that one, in case you're wondering.

Then we continue toward Nazareth. While Lorrie is getting up to speed on the highway, the hood opens with enough force to smash the windshield. She hits the brakes with her vision completely blocked. The mirror, dangling from the broken windshield, is now adjusted for me in the passenger seat, and I see we're going to be hit from behind. After the Volkswagon van hits us, another car hits the van.

Amanda's neck aches a little, but other than that, we're okay. The guy who hit us seems shook up, and the woman who hit him is sore, but neither is serious from what I can tell. But remember, I'm the guy who thought my shoulder was dislocated and Emily's foot was broken.

The police and two ambulances come after what seems a long time, but probably isn't. Then the rental company brings us a new car. After three hours of standing on a busy, high-speed freeway talking to the police, the other crashers, and the ambulance drivers, we're on our way to Nazareth in a different rental car.

We go to The Basilica of the Annunciation. In the basilica is a grotto, where a marker is placed on an altar to mark the spot where the angel told Mary of God's plans for her. How they came up with this exact spot remains a mystery, but we're flooded with emotion and tears well up in our eyes. We're also told the gate to the grotto is normally closed, but the monks opened it today for Eucharist. Each of us touches the spot where Jesus was conceived, and Emily, following the lead of some nuns, kneels to kiss the spot.

Then, we go back to *Faith* for the night to bask in the delightful *whump-whump-whumping* of helicopters.

On Wednesday, we drive to the Sea of Galilee—Lake Kinneret on the road map. We visit a number of places where Jesus lived, taught, and performed miracles.

Without explanation, a mood more foul than usual descends on us. At lunchtime, the attractions close, so we drive to Tiberius looking for take-away. We drive to a stony beach on the Sea of Galilee to eat.

The first thing Lorrie says when we sit down is, "Here we are at the Sea of Galilee and you guys don't even *pray* before you start eating!" She's right, but neither her tone nor the way any of us receives it fosters the fellowship we hoped to share. Lorrie gets up to find a different rock to sit on, away from us, and we manage to ruin another day of our journey.

We continue to the Mount of the Beatitudes, where Jesus' sermon included the preface to this chapter, soaking up all the holiness our rotten attitudes have room for, and then drive through Cana, or Kfar Kana, where Jesus performed His first miracle of changing water into wine.

One thing that makes touring more enjoyable—just think of how miserable we'd have been otherwise—is to tour for a day, then take a day off to watch the helicopters, then tour again. We rented the car for a week, beginning Monday morning. We tour Mt. Carmel and Nazareth on Monday, Galilee on Wednesday, Jerusalem on Friday, and Bethlehem and the Dead Sea on Sunday.

Because of its history as a crossroads of trade, culture, and religion, Old Jerusalem thrills with its flavor of humanity. It's crowded with people and noisy with different languages wafting through the narrow streets. The smells of trade—cooking fats, nuts, dates, spices, and burning incense—echo from the stalls and follow the languages.

We walk up the Mount of Olives to the Garden of Gethsemane. We see the heavily guarded Western Wall. We try to enter Al-Aqsa Mosque, but because it's Friday, Islam's holy day, we're turned away by an ethnic Jewish policeman of Christian faith who's cheerfully assuring a safe haven for Muslims to worship. In spite of everything we think we know about the world, it's the man on the street, in this case the policeman guarding the mosque, who shines a ray of hope.

The signs to Bethlehem bring us to an armed checkpoint. The woman here tells us to park and enter a large concrete and metal building with an abundance of security equipment inside. The wall, eight meters high, runs north and south from this building (82). The army personnel staffing the checkpoint check us and check our passports before letting us through. We exit the building on the Palestinian side to take a taxi to what was, until recently, a suburb of Jerusalem with a vibrant trade of manpower, goods, and services, travelling the main road between the two cities. The taxi driver tells us we can't use the main road on the West Bank side of the checkpoint because the wall wraps around Rachel's Tomb.

A straight wall would be enough of a symbol of apartheid, but the fact that our taxi can't drive the main road from the checkpoint to Bethlehem is bizarre. I guess this inconvenience is okay though, because it's only Palestinians housed in this prison behind the wall.

Our visit is a year and a half after the elections in Palestine. The United States supported these elections as part of our stated intention of spreading democracy. Palestinians elected Hamas against Israel's and the United States' wishes. To reward their newly acquired democratic principles, the United States helped Israel freeze the flow of goods, services, tourism, and especially money into Palestinian territory. It worked, and Bethlehem is sad. We visit the shepherd's fields and the nativity, and purchase postcards from the one shop not boarded up on the day we visit.

Over 95% of the United States' foreign aid to Israel is for military security. Aid to Palestinians through the Palestinian Authority is for security only, and intended to prevent uprisings against Israel. The ratio of aid is slightly under ten dollars for every Israeli to under one dollar for a Palestinian.

Israel's 1948 borders were drawn by the French and the British when they became fatigued with their colonization of this region. In 1967, Israel captured Jordan's West Bank, Egypt's Gaza Strip, and Syria's Golan Heights, and have occupied these territories since, in the manner that Rome occupied Israel when Jesus walked these lands.

You know, a lot of the places you're going don't value human life like we do.

The place that devalues human life is the place responsible for the conditions we witness in Bethlehem. The people of Bethlehem are hiding. Somewhere on the other side of the wall, in Tel Aviv, and on the other side of the Atlantic, their captors hide.

Our voyage, until we arrived in Bethlehem, created a discomfort we couldn't identify about our role in the world. It is here we realize the unintended truth of that statement:

You're going to a lot of places where they don't value human life like WE do.

After Bethlehem, we go to the Dead Sea. The girls and Greggii take mud baths and bottle up some mud to take home. It's a different sensation to float so high in the water, to hold our hands in the air and not sink.

Finding our Family in Turkiye

We're bored and I'm worried. Worried we will carry our sorry disposition through the Med, across the Atlantic, into the Caribbean, and home with us, and that is how we'll remember this part of our lives. What a terrible waste. I can't blame malaria forever.

About forty miles out, as we approach Turkey, it hits me. I have to take my sweatshirt off. Israel was chilly at night and so was most of our passage to Turkey. The closer we get to land, the warmer it becomes. Even toward dawn, that coolest part of the day, the temperature continues to rise.

We enter the bay that is home to Finike as the sun rises (map, page 217).

I cook breakfast for the crew: potatoes with onions and garlic, bacon, scrambled eggs, and toast. Everybody is awake by 6:00 AM, and I inform the crew that breakfast will be served as soon as the mainsail is down. It's easier to cook breakfast than to take *Faith*'s sails down alone.

We dock *med-style*—stern-to to the dock with a mooring line tied to the bow.

Pat, from *Aldebaron*, comes with two men from the marina to help us dock *Faith* tight to an adjacent boat. I suggest we move away from the other boat in case a swell comes in. Pat sees my dander rise in spite of my efforts of concealment. He says that's the way it's done in the Med and sometimes, when there isn't any room at all, you just force yourself between boats, using fenders and wedging yourself in. I heed his advice and let it go.

We enjoy Finike. It's a low-key touristy place serving Turkish tourists who don't need to be won over with exaggerated perceptions, as opposed to foreigners who must have it laid on a little thicker. Little, but enough, English is spoken, and nobody hassles us (46).

The town is built on the side of the mountain. Not old-city stuff—everything I see has been built in the last thirty years or so.

I walk to town alone, and through an area of workshops, where not much work is getting done, maybe because it's Friday or maybe because in Mediterranean Turkey not much work gets done; I don't know. One fellow invites me into his carpentry shop and orders *chai*—tea—from a neighboring shop. We sit and sip and stare and smile at each other, neither knowing the other's language.

A bit further, an assortment of men sit outside their shops playing dominos and invite me to sit with them. They order *chai* and we also have a good time staring at each other—better than at the carpenter shop because here they have their game as a diversion.

We leave Finike. The last time we anchored was on the reef outside Hurghada, Egypt, a month and a half ago. It's good here at Kekova Roads, where we can swim and clean the hull.

We're anchored beneath a castle from the Middle Ages, built over ruins of another community from 4th century BC. There are more ruins to be seen along the Turkish coast than anywhere else (83).

The world of tourism wears a number of faces as we move through it, and Mediterranean Turkey's is among the best. The only time tourism is better is when it's a non-entity like in Indonesia and Yemen, for example, where people take us at face value. But this part of Turkey is close. We feel accepted for who we are rather than what we can contribute to the local economy, and after the hassles of Egypt, the fast pace of Israel, and the sadness of the Palestinian Territories, Turkey is a delight.

The personalities on *Faith* have changed since we moved on board. Our voyage provides each of us with growth: growth in our outlook, growth in our ability to see God's created world rather than the intentionally false world presented to us as Americans, and growth in our ability to relate to each other in our family and to each other in the world.

These are big changes achieved in baby steps. They're the result of the journey, of experiencing worlds concealed from us inside the United States: worlds of religion, worlds of politics, nationalism, socialism and values, worlds where human rights are not standards to impose on others, but genuine reflections of a culture, and worlds where human rights don't exist at all, worlds where the family is esteemed society-wide more than career or social status. Worlds foreign to Americans.

These changes are also the result of the lifestyle we have chosen, of living in close quarters with each other, where we must address issues as they arise in our family, rather than ignore them in the hope that these issues will magically disappear.

Each of us has a system for receiving and holding our experiences, but we all have similar frames of reference. We're all Christian, all American, and all from the same socio-economic class. God gives us individualism that, while holding to the hub of our family, allows us each different reactions to and memories of an experience. Then, when we process events as a family, the richness grows.

My approach to maintaining the information I receive is not unlike making sausage, with all the scraps ground up and not much sorting occurring. All the bits and pieces are added to the mass of bits and pieces already there and packed into the casing of my frame of reference. Existence becomes a cloudy conglomeration of the information I store, almost all of it accessed easily because it just lies there on top of my messy mental desk.

Lorrie's approach differs from mine in her remarkable ability to dump massive quantities of information without processing it. She clings only to the data she deems relevant to the future, especially as it relates to safety. She is selective in the information she chooses to process and retain, and can listen to somebody talk about how beautiful a place might be, how fantastic the people are, how good the food is, how the anchorage is a bit rolly when the wind turns to such and such a direction, and all of a sudden her ears perk up. "How hard does the wind blow? From *what* direction?" She doesn't process as much information as I, but her filing system is worlds better for the information she does process. Where my mind keeps me confused with unrelated bits and pieces, hers is focused on the task at hand.

Emily is the most compartmentalized thinker on *Faith*. She has a bank of tiny file cabinets between her ears, where all the information she receives is neatly categorized, sorted, and filed in its own special place, to be easily accessed when she needs it. What is really special about this way of thinking is that when she doesn't need it, it isn't out there cluttering things up. Her way of thinking reminds me of the personal computer before Windows. DOS would let you do only one thing at a time, but it was fast *because* it processed only one thing at a time.

Amanda doesn't spend much energy raking things over the intellectual coals.

She is, and she does, and she processes her experiences through an emotional filter she has rigged up. Where the rest of us, told that 100 minus 28 equals 72, will process it logically and say something like *that's right*, Amanda personalizes the problem and says something like, "Well, I'm happy about that because it means I got the correct change back when I bought those eggs last week," or worse, "You know, that really makes me mad, because remember when we were in Egypt and that guy was selling those belts, he told me I get 18 back."

Then there's Greggii, the inventor, the one who knows in his heart there's more to every experience than the experience itself. He and I can be looking at clouds, and I'll say, "Look at that one, do you see the whale?"

He'll look up and say, "Yeah, I see the whale, but if you look at it this way you can see two of those old ships, with the cannons shooting each other, and men jumping off the sides into the water near the lifeboats." And I'll tilt my head a couple degrees to the left and by gosh if I can't see it too.

Lorrie takes the kids to Myra and Demre with a man we meet in Üçağiz—pronounced OOWLcharles—the town-center of Kekova Roads. They enjoy Myra, the village where Saint Nicholas lived his life and was martyred. While they're gone, I ask the guy whose dock we're tied to if the water will be turned back on anytime soon. It seems there's a broken pipe somewhere in the mountains, maybe fifty kilometers away, and the village is without water. He says maybe in a few days. I want to go out to anchor in the bay because the wind is picking up, and ask him to help me untie. He says he'll help, but first I must join him and his friends for *chai*.

The next day, we move *Faith* to the west end of Kekova Roads where we walk across an isthmus to Aperlae, a part of ancient Lycea, to snorkel the underwater ruins there. We were told these ruins are among the best anywhere if you like snorkeling ruins. When we're done, we decide we're not that excited about snorkeling over ruins.

Emily and I hike through more ruins up the mountain, amazed that we can climb on anything we want and there isn't another soul around, or even anybody to tell us we can't do this or that. We have this place to ourselves, which speaks to our mode of travel.

In the morning, Emily, Amanda, and I go to Theimussa, the ruins of the old city surrounding the existing town of Üçağiz.

A dinghy raft-up is organized to celebrate America's Independence Day, where we join another American couple, a Canadian couple, some Brits, Germans, French, and a couple from Cairo. Greggii has the evening's fireworks, one rocket and some sparklers.

We stay in Kekova Roads for ten days.

We leave Üçağiz for Fethiye (FET-ee-yay) at night. The moon hasn't yet risen, and the stars are magnificent. Greggii sees it while he's forward raising the anchor. He asks if that's the Milky Way or a cloud. It's the brightest Milky Way I've ever seen.

A man introduces himself to us at the park in Fethiye. Amanda and Greggii are doing homework, and the rest of us are hanging out.

Mehsen approaches around 2:30 and starts telling us all about himself. I don't get the feeling we're being hustled or anything. He's just a nice, lonely, thirty-seven-year-old man here by himself on vacation. His home is Antalya, and he tells us of the oldest church in the world there. Antalya is the modern name of Antioch; the church is St. Peter's.

He tells us many other things about himself too, sometimes more than once, and even more than twice. He's Muslim, but a modern Muslim who prays at home before meals and bed. He enjoys being around Christians, Muslims, and everybody, with the exception of Muslim traditionalists whom he doesn't understand. I take an hour-long nap there in the park during his visit, because, as sometimes happens, I tire of being sociable.

Lorrie witnesses for Christ, knowing the outcome will be that he'll become a Christian, which would be great, or that he'll leave, which we're thinking by now wouldn't be all that bad. Neither happens. He stays with us for four hours this afternoon. I can't think of a reason why that should bother me, but it does.

Next, we sail to Marmaris, where it's hot. Heat is part of the reason we don't care much for marinas, but the heat in Marmaris isn't because of the marina. This part of the world is in the middle of its hottest summer on record.

While here, we prepare *Faith* for our Atlantic crossing. The biggest job I must perform is to rebuild the *bonding* system where it needs it. Bonding is the hooking-together of all the major metal fittings to the zinc anodes that are sacrificed, instead of having corrosion eat the fittings. It's an education and a big job, and I notice it only because some of the deck fittings we took off and remounted at Wavemaster show stains of corrosion faster than before.

We purchase a new computer because the one we have from Panama is acting up. The motherboard gets too hot and locks up and needs rebooting every two hours. Corrosion takes a toll on the guts. Getting all the programs running again and saving all our important files is a hassle, but I am again provided with a fresh round of education.

From Marmaris, we go by bus to Istanbul to find it ruined by tourism and not nearly as enjoyable as Mediterranean Turkey. We see a lot of major sights, but are hassled by people who think we're here only for their benefit. The best part of Istanbul is when Greggii and I take the train away from the old city center, to again be accepted as people.

Our twelve-hour return to Marmaris is less enjoyable. No food, no water, and they even forget to stop at the restroom on the way back. Lorrie has to go, so we make a scene and they finally stop the bus.

It's hot, we're tired, and both the marina personnel and many other yachties act intentionally unfriendly. We're grumpy ourselves. According to one friend, it's 104° and above, and it hovers within one or two degrees of that since our return from Istanbul; it cools only slightly at night.

Lorrie, Emily, Amanda, and Greggii visit Ephesus, one of the most well-preserved and restored old-city ruins anywhere. I'm toured-out and don't go.

It's interesting how my opinion of Turkey changes with our westward movement. Finike and Kekova Roads were great, but the farther west we move, the more the culture is influenced by tourism.

I ship the main and Yankee sails to Moby Sails (actually, I don't do anything; they pick them up) to have new ultra-violet protection sewn on the Yankee, and the leach and luff shortened on the main. It stretched during our time in the Indian Ocean.

I work on the SSB radio, mostly as it relates to grounding, but also some other electrical stuff, trying to isolate the reason it affects the ship's ammeter when transmitting. I don't fix anything, but start to believe it's affecting only the gauge, and not the whole electrical system.

In addition to the other chores, I rebuild the pump for the aft head. The term head comes from the timber on old ships called a cat head. The cat head was a large timber going out both starboard and port of the bow for the purpose of what we now have a bow roller—a structural member to take the load of the anchor chain.

It was large, structurally sound, and horizontal over the water, making it an ideal place to serve another function before indoor plumbing was installed on ocean-going vessels. In his journals, Captain Cook mentions an able-bodied seaman who didn't return from his trip to the head, which sounds like a crappy way to die.

Speaking of toilets, traveling around the world offers some surprises. In Saumlaki, Indonesia, the houses built on stilts over the water don't have to worry about the plumbing getting stopped up. The hotel that acted like a yacht club and played host to us there had real toilets, sit down style, where a poop would splash twice, once in the bowl and again when it hit the bay, ten to twelve feet below. Asia as a whole made use of the squatter—a simple porcelain hole with foot pads on the sides. I avoided these when I could.

In Muslim countries, a source of water is always provided, sometimes in addition to tissue, sometimes not, but the best toilet I ever had the opportunity to relieve myself in is here at Marmaris Yacht Marine in Turkey. These have built in butt-squirters, where, by simply opening a valve next to the toilet, a squirt of water from the rim, centered between the seat hinges and aimed at just the right spot, does the job. We spend a month at the marina in Marmaris, two weeks straight with the temperature over 104°, and I never have an itch in the wrong place.

Perspectives in Greece

Leaving Marmaris, we move between Greek islands and Turkish mainland. Our attitude about formalities—clearing in or out of a place—grows relaxed, and officials don't seem to want to be bothered with it any more than we do. We sail to the Greek island of Symi for a couple days, and then back to Turkey for a day. Then back to Symi to get fuel and pork. We're heading to Greek Kos when the wind picks up, forcing us to anchor in Turkish Knidos.

At Knidos, we're in a small bay with a lonely mountain south of us, connected to the mountains of the mainland to our north by a low, narrow isthmus to our west. Emily and I are walking on the isthmus and see the Turkish flag, red with a white crescent and star, on the summit of the lonely mountain.

Emily asks, "Do you want to climb to the flag?"

While my mind is saying *not really,* my mouth interrupts with "Sure."

The slope is covered with bits of red pottery from people who were here in a different time. It's dry and porous so any rain that does fall doesn't stay long enough to nourish the straw-colored grasses and gangly grey shrubs.

It feels as if we've climbed a long way. We're not far from the flag, and we have a great view of *Faith* in the bay below and ruins on the mountain across the bay. I'm breathing heavily and ask her, "Do you think we've climbed high enough?"

"Dad, we didn't set out to climb within 200 meters of the flag!! We need to finish it."

On the motorcycle trip of my youth, I went to Maine and then to California.

On the way home, I called mom and dad from Amarillo, Texas, to say I was tired and wanted to come home, though completing the trip was my only option. It's the last quarter that makes a difference in football, basketball, sailing, motorcycling, and climbing hills in Turkey. Nobody ever wins a game in the first three quarters. As Emily said, "Dad...We need to finish it."

When we get there, about fifteen meters beyond the flag is a sheer cliff to the windward sea. We see one of those spectacular sights that come only from crossing the finish line.

Kos is our port of entry for the European Union. The EU requires insurance on *Faith* after three years of being self-insured. It takes two days, but after paying €140, we have three months of liability coverage good only in Greek waters. The benefit is, because our policy is in Greek, I have to translate the spelling of the company and read the policy number for any other countries where it's requested, and nobody ever asks about the coverage, except of course, in Greece, where it's valid.

Our next stop is Kalymnos.

I apologize for being an ass to my neighbor on a charter boat who forces himself into a berth between *Faith* and another boat where there isn't enough room. It seems I should know by now it's the Mediterranean and that's how it's done here. The harbor floor is covered with anchor chains woven together, and we spend a good part of every morning sorting out anchors, which aren't as bad as I think they should be, but it takes time nonetheless.

Our opinions and levels of patience change, and Mediterranean mooring becomes an entertaining delight. The last boat in should be the first to leave, but never is. The tolerance and lack of it (including my own) are amusements in themselves.

Kalymnos is where the sponge divers are from. We learn that most of the Greek sponge diving community in Tarpon Springs, Florida, trace their roots to Kalymnos. It's a dangerous job, so dangerous in fact that Lorrie and the kids go to a night of traditional dancing where the dance is a tribute to injured and killed divers. Most sponge shops are cheesy souvenir stores staffed by hired help and have more non-sponge inventory than sponges, but one shop is different. A woman, with her baby in a diaper and tee-shirt resting on her hip and cradled in her arm, greets us. Her husband is a sponge diver; he personally acquired most of the sponges in their store. His claim to the inventory is dwindling though, because she doesn't let him dive anymore since the baby was born. The best sponges come from depths of seventy meters. We visit her shop several times and purchase a number of sponges from her.

We're moored against the quay. Five meters from our transom is Kalymnos' main waterfront road, and across that is a small information kiosk on the sidewalk with bars, internet cafés, and restaurants surrounding it. Young Greek men like loud motorcycles, trucks service the restaurants and bars, and a small ferry next to us is cleaning their hull, using a noisy compressor to pump air to the diver. Something in the road is covered by a steel plate that goes *chrah-lunk-lunk* every time a car drives over it. The buildings are all three floors by European standards, four by American; being situated facing the harbor, they reflect the noise and fumes of the traffic and the aromas from the restaurants our way. Our berth could evolve into a complaint in an area where people are rude, but here everyone is genuine, hard-working, and honest enough, and the noise is the salt that brings out the flavor of the place.

Emily, Amanda, Greggii, and Lorrie meet Nick at the internet café across the noisy road. He's Canadian by nationality, born and raised in Montreal, schooled in Calgary, and Kalymnian by heritage. He eats dinner with us on *Faith* and we talk about cruising, music, Christ, Kalymnos, and many other subjects. In typical Greek fashion, he wears his emotions outside, and shares with us his excitement about our trip, *Faith*, and God.

Nick's grandfather died two years ago, leaving him his house on Kalymnos. He takes two months every year to fix up the house, visit his relatives, and kick back.

After Kalymnos, we find ourselves swinging on the anchor again. The world seems better when *Faith* swings. To swing usually means the bow points to the wind, providing the best ventilation, and to the waves, offering a comfortable night's rest. There are times when currents hold *Faith*'s beam to both the wind and the swell, dishing a dose of discomfort, but most of the time, swinging is best.

The anchorage where we're swinging at is Archangelos, twenty-three miles from Kalymnos. The breeze is twenty-five knots from the northwest. Our destination is Patmos, straight into the wind and seas. We are here because of those angry seas.

I think about the Apostle Paul's travels. So far, the Mediterranean is not a place I would choose to travel too far in. It's choppy, gusty, and all the winds are contrary, blowing in every direction like farts from a football huddle. Mediterranean sailing has more in common with work than the downwind sailing we're accustomed to. It's certainly not the trade winds, those reliable easterlies in the tropics, blowing twenty-four hours a day for at least five days out of the week with the remaining time reserved for a passing weather system.

Our next destination is Serifos.

When we sail into the wind, tensions build in the shrouds, the stays, and the sheets. More importantly, tensions build in the crew. Work is now involved to trim the sails all the time: reefing, furling, unreefing, and easing. We made it three-quarters around the world and now we must learn to sail. It was much easier when we were racing coconuts.

After five hours beating into thirty-five knots, I take Lorrie's suggestion to bear-off and head to the island of Dhonoussa to hide from it overnight before continuing to Serifos (84). From Serifos, Emily, Greggii, and Lorrie take the ferry to Mylos to see the Christian Catacombs. Amanda and I stay with *Faith*.

We leave Serifos to experience medium, poor, great, and sloppy sailing, and arrive in Parga after three hundred miles. We sail from the middle Cyclades in the Aegean to round Peloponnesus—the southern peninsulas of mainland Greece which, according to the scary accounts Lorrie reads, will give us trouble at each of the three headlands jutting south from the peninsula, then through the strait between Ithaca and Cephalonia. The weather calls for southeast wind, but we get the opposite on our way to Corfu.

Faith is now anchored in the fluid shadows beneath the lighted Old Fortress in Corfu town. The only drawback is the occasional wash from a ferry or cruise ship that hits us on the beam, creating an aggressive roll on *Faith*.

The museums here are small enough to not overwhelm, and I get away with poking my head in and out and sitting in the square watching people. We eat moussaka and several roast beef and chicken dishes along with what might be my favorite compliment to Greek food, tzatziki—a mixture of yogurt, garlic, salt, and cucumbers.

I run the portable space-heater several nights and mornings while we're here to ease the impact of a recent cold front. We're feeling it's time to move to Italy, so without much effort, Emily and I walk to Customs and Immigration and the port police for clearance to leave Greece. All that's required of us is to hand over our cruising log and permit from Kos.

Italy

We stay two nights in a marina on the heel of Italy at Cabo Santa Maria De Leuca. Greggii and I walk up a big staircase on the cape, a monument built by Mussolini to mark the gateway to Italy. At the top is a basilica commemorating St. Peter's arrival here.

An afternoon walk through town finds everything closed, with the exception of two cafés. Some places are closed because the tourists are gone—school started in Europe last week—but most, including the two supermarkets, are closed because that's what folks in these parts do in the middle of the day. Family-type noises resonate from open windows.

At our next stop, we dock with help of a woman and her sixteen-year-old son. I can't say her name, Tørøl (she says that Torill is close), but her husband's is Hans, and her son's is Østeyn—say Oisten. They hail from Norway. We have pizza with them in town on the night we arrive, and become friends. The name of their boat is *Lunna*, and they just began their adventure two months ago.

Greggii and Østeyn have a busy day snorkeling, playing on the beach, fishing, and eating. At the dinner table, Østeyn is tired and comments to his mom he's glad he doesn't have a little brother because of the energy it takes for that kind of activity every day.

In evaluating new friends, since we can't erase our reference points, we always put Thomas and Helén of *Smilla* in a position of comparison. I suppose it's natural, but it's also unfair. Every relationship holds its own dynamics, and reflecting on the friends, associates, and even people I don't like, the constant of each encounter is its uniqueness.

We continue travelling with *Lunna* around the south of Italy, and are entering a marina with them when Cathy from *Legend II* overhears us on the radio and calls. We weren't sure we'd see them again after they departed Massawa, where they offered so much help to us during our bout with my malaria. We dine together to celebrate our time, probably the last together; they are eastbound and we are west. From here, we also say goodbye to Hans, Tørøl, and Østeyn, whose plans take them on a different route than ours.

Rome, with its wealth of Western history and art, is our next stop.

On our first trip into the city, less than ten minutes after I warn everybody about pickpockets and crime, I have my pocket picked. The naked feeling of an empty pocket that moments before was full creates a wave of nausea. Moments later, I see my wallet on the floor of the crowded subway. Everything's there, except €250 and US$100.

Some stranger has just taken a bunch of our money, and an internal struggle erupts to not let him steal the joy of our family's exploration of Rome. We go to the ATM, and I use the debit card still in my wallet to get more money on our way to the Vatican.

St. Peter's Square is packed with people from here to eternity, waiting to get past the pearly gates of military security and into the Basilica. We leave the Vatican, promising to return when it's less crowded, and walk to the nearest of the *Top Twelve Things to See in Rome*, listed on the map the marina gave us—St. Angelo's Castle.

At the castle, I go to the ticket window and see a notice about the *Roma Pass*. The cashier tells me it costs €20, is good for free admission to the first two sights we visit, and includes a three-day pass for the Metro. I buy them for our family only to expose myself to a fresh round of Lorrie's irritation. The entrance fee at St. Angelo's Castle is €6, so Lorrie, who hasn't yet found it within herself to let go of me having my pocket picked, finds new ammo. She lets me know on several occasions we'll never get the value out of those passes. I accept her commentary as a challenge to make sure we do. The best thing about St. Angelo's Castle is that, from the top wall, we see the mob in St. Peter's square dwindling to a crowd.

We return to the shorter line at St. Peter's Square and enter the basilica. One of the Vatican's first marvels is Michelangelo's Pieta. Continuing our exploration, we mosey to a spot near the center. I show the kids where Lorrie and I stood twenty-two years ago when Lorrie looked up and exclaimed, "There's the pope!" Further inspection by us and by the thirty-five people within earshot revealed that her Pope, waving some sort of holy icon, was in fact a cleaning lady waving a feather duster. Sometimes you see what you want, and Lorrie wanted to see the Pope. The kids, even though they've heard this story many times, still pretend it's funny.

A large part of the front of St. Peter's is blocked off from visitors, but security allows a few people in. Greggii learns that mass will be held shortly. He wants to go, so I tell him to ask Lorrie, who used to be Catholic. As he and she walk through the open area to the forward-most chapel, Emily and Amanda say they'd like to go too. I drop my reservations about not being Catholic, and the three of us join Lorrie and Greggii.

Though Mass isn't in English, we stand up and sit down and kneel and pray when everybody else does, and get to where we can mimic the piety around us fairly well. Then, in time for communion, I'm overcome with another bout of not being Catholic, but I shake it long enough to celebrate the few moments with Christ.

Amanda comments that if she were exploring faiths, the unfriendliness of the Vatican's security would encourage her to look elsewhere. I agree; security is high, much higher than when Lorrie and I made our first visit. Maybe it's because Pope Benedict recently said some things to raise the ire of some Muslims, and the security industry does a wonderful job of keeping us afraid of *them*, or maybe it's because of the higher number of people, much higher than during our last visit, or maybe it's many things working together; whatever it is, the Vatican is not a warm place during our current visit.

My job now is to make our Roma Passes come close to paying for themselves. On closer inspection, they don't look like a great bargain to me either. The next day provides an added challenge to getting that value because the museums are closed on Mondays.

We visit some cathedrals. Every time we walk past a cathedral we haven't yet visited, we enter for a look. Some cathedrals have candles you can light for someone for a donation, and stick in a trough of sand to hold it upright and burning alongside others. Other cathedrals have a row of arcade-quality, electric light bulbs that take a fixed fee in a slot in the wall to get one to light. I'm partial to the wax.

Between the transportation value of the Roma Pass and St. Angelos Castle, we need to use another nine Euros per pass. The €9 entry fee for the Coliseum works for me. That's not the best of it though. Once we arrive, there are two lines—one for the *Roma Pass* holders that has no queue and another, about 150 meters long, for those silly people who didn't get the *Roma Pass* and have to buy their tickets. My status goes from chump to genius in seconds.

The visit to the Coliseum, while getting me off the hook for purchasing those stupid *Roma Passes*, is less than thrilling. Lorrie and I gave it a pass twenty-two years ago, having been told it wasn't that great; nothing happened since then to change it. The fact that its image adorns every placemat, menu, and the walls of every Italian restaurant in the world, not to mention its prominent position on pizza boxes, doesn't change the fact that it's a stadium, fallen to ruin over the years. However, that it held over 70,000 spectators and was built in five years *is* impressive.

Before leaving Rome, we go to the Vatican Museums and Sistine Chapel. On the last Sunday of every month, they are open to the public for free. The regular fee is €13 per person, and being free creates today's mob.

We start by waiting in a kilometer-long line. A line that long, eight people abreast, holds many people, and while the museums occupy a lot of space, they don't have *that* much space. The line is wall to curb, and the museum and chapel are wall-to-wall humanity. Every anticipation of open space beyond the next bottleneck is crushed on arrival.

There are two rules in the Sistine Chapel that elevate the chaos: no photography and remain quiet. The no photography rule is odd. Many places have a no flash rule as the flash, or thousands of flashes, can damage the art, but no photography is an unenforceable rule that breeds a silliness compounded by the loudest noises in the chapel—the security guards hollering "quiet!" One guard even clap-clap-clap-clap-claps his hands in noisy staccato and yells "QUIET!!!" to restore holiness to the room.

The scene turns serious when a guard puts his hand over Emily's hand and the camera she's taking pictures with. Lorrie's motherhood tunes her in. The guard senses Lorrie's ire, and fears becoming an actor in a scene with the potential to erode the holiness that the clapping guard just established. He releases the camera and moves out of range.

Exiting the Vatican Museums is akin to disembarking a Disney ride without the finesse of Disney's security personnel. I'm not sure whether it was Disney or the Vatican that perfected the concept of walking everybody through a gift shop on the way out, but each has mastered this marketing technique. Plenty of photographs are available to purchase for those who followed the rules.

In the middle of the night we leave Rome, the moon rises above *Faith*'s stern, a good sign we're heading in the right direction. West. Out of Greece, out of Rome, and into the embrace of *real* Western civilization.

A Storm in Spanish Waters

We experience life: spiritual life, community life, family life, and individual life, with the peaks and valleys that experience entails. The trade in surroundings and cares and concerns doesn't mean they're no longer a part of our life, only different, and in some respects, more basic. One concern is with refilling our cooking gas bottles. Another is with refilling the water tanks, and still another is to find a place to make a high-pressure hose to repair the water-maker.

Life, and life's changes after the initial excitement cools, seems always accompanied by an element of unsatisfied expectations. The solution is to not have expectations, but this is impossible. Our journey's highlights occur when little information exists to foster expectations, or when the information is negative. Indonesia, Yemen, and Vanuatu were such places, and we were captivated by their charms.

We sail from Rome to Menorca, the easternmost of the Balearics in the Spanish Mediterranean Sea, a tourist destination. Restaurants are expensive and lacking in quality. Perhaps we are experiencing another element of our expectations. Since we feel deserving of something special for premium prices and don't get it, we blame the food.

We're out of gas for cooking, so we heat water for coffee and tea on the gas grill with charcoal from the local supermarket. It makes a mess, but gets the water hot. When businesses reopen on Monday, we fill our bottles with gas and move to Cala

Ratjada on Mallorca. We're surprised to be greeted by Hans, Tøról, and Østeyn at the wharf. We visit there for two days, then sail together to Porto Colom where we again swing on the anchor.

This voyage witnessed my life changing from a young man to a not-so-young man. Some people say wisdom comes with age, but I'm pretty sure the people saying that are old people with egos. I don't think my wisdom has been affected a great deal and I'm sure Lorrie agrees.

Our souls, individually, and the collective soul of our family are filled and drained, only to be filled again during this endeavor.

We've been away from home four years. We said goodbye to Ardi seven months ago. We said goodbye to Thomas and Helén over two years ago.

We're incredibly lonely, and that loneliness breeds homesickness.

Our friends in this life have moved or we've moved in different directions, and our friends and family at home never understood, calling it a *Pleasure Excursion,* a *trip,* an *incredible experience for our kids,* a *dream* and many other phrases. Only after we left the dock did reality sneak back into focus. While these descriptions hold some truth, none of them capture the totality of life on *Faith.* Reality is that this is a life Lorrie and I chose to raise our children into, with all of life's ups and downs, and for every benefit to this lifestyle, there's a cost. From its conception, our voyage on *Faith* is a gift from God—for Lorrie and me to give ourselves to our children instead of giving them stuff generated from our productive capabilities.

Risk and profit are related. We've taken a risk, to the point where I don't know if we'll ever have our financial head above water again. But we've profited. Emily, at nineteen years old, asked me if it was wrong of her to let Ardi kiss her on the cheek. How many parents experience that relationship with their children? We just celebrated Amanda's *sweet sixteen and never been kissed* birthday with conviction, and Greggii has an appreciation for others and otherness that could never have been nurtured at home.

We come to the table in the casino of life, and lay down everything not only Lorrie and I have, but the kids' inheritance too. That's the source of the shame and guilt—my baggage—that accompanies me. I can speak volumes of logic to justify using those funds, but the fact I carry that baggage at all suggests logic is a poor determinant of right and wrong.

My baggage doesn't change God or His plan for our lives. It means only that I'm a sinner. Everything I know about God tells me He doesn't want me carrying it, but I've become so comfortably burdened that I can't let go of it now. I'm lonely, guilty, ashamed, proud of my kids, and happy for the opportunity God presented us with, and this is how I feel in the Balearics.

In an exercise designed to make me feel 'not so evil' when I enter this frame of mind, I catch myself finding flaws in others, flaws from which to evaluate my own stature among men and among those others from God's perspective. This exercise doesn't make me any less a sinner, but provides comfort in the comparisons. "Sure, I borrowed from the kids, but look at the growth they've experienced. It's not like the thousands who have lost their pensions and life savings to raiders using questionable accounting practices. Heck, the whole American economy rests on the premise of borrowing from our kids."

From this perspective, having now identified the real sinners, I become no longer able to accept others as flawed and broken individuals just like me; they're worse.

Taking this exercise public is the next trap. And this, my friend, is the story of how *my* sin justifies my use of Christ's name to rally against *your* sin, whatever that might be.

Too often, I make it my Christian mission to work to legislate a bunch of sinners through heaven's gate. The futility of this is already proved. God wrote the legislation and gave it to Moses, and the only guy who ever lived it was Jesus, who knew if he messed up, he'd have hell to pay when he got home. But wait, he *did* have hell to pay. Not for his screw ups—he didn't have any—but for me, and you, and all the other sinners who think a few more restrictions on somebody else's special sin are going to make the world a better place.

We say our goodbyes to Hans, Tørøl, and Østeyn, they bound for Palma de Mallorca, and we for beyond. The morning weather report sounds fair, but we know we're in for a rocky, downwind sail with insufficient wind and choppy seas. Not the nicest outlook, but no storms out there.

I don't think anyone sees this one coming. The sun sets early behind a wall of clouds which appear to be very slow moving. Squalls. I slow down *Faith*, to let them move ahead of us. It makes good sense, but it's wrong. The system *is* moving slowly, but toward us.

As the sun settles further and the system nears, the lightning appears.

I never learned to like rain much and I like high winds even less, but lightning scares me. We do the only thing we can think of as this system engulfs us. We pray, "Dear God, save us, save our boat, and don't let us get hit by lightning." He handles it on all three accounts.

What arrives is an interesting storm that wraps its arms around us, leaving a patch of blue sky that diminishes as the rain and lightning close in from all sides. We reduce sails on its approach and try, under motor, to stay inside this blue patch of sky, away from the lightning. I'm hand-steering from the helm in gusts up to fifty knots, with *Faith* taking a beating from the confused seas, when I feel something in the steering snap; the wheel spins freely (we didn't think about praying for the steering system). The ability to steer is something we've grown to appreciate, and I miss it instantly.

I tell Emily and Amanda to get the emergency tiller, while I figure out what to do next. After playing around with the autopilot a few minutes, I'm able to coax it into steering *Faith*.

Emily looks out of the cockpit to see a bolt of lightning, very close, and says she's never seen flames linger in the air after the flash. I didn't see it, and still have never seen flames linger. I don't know much about lightning, but I'm guessing she saw the atmosphere burning after the almost instantaneous thunderclap.

After an hour, with each of us feeling we've enjoyed enough of God's splendor in this storm, the storm moves on, the winds and seas calm, and I set course for Isla Fomentera, just south of Ibeza. As dawn illuminates our approach, we don't like the anchorages at Fomentera, so we continue to Ibeza where, using the autopilot, we grab a mooring ball.

I'm not going to enter a marina without being able to steer, so I take off the compass and look into the pedestal at the helm. On the ends of the steering cables, a fifty-weight chain loops over a sprocket on the steering wheel shaft. It broke. On the end of the chain are two master links. I loosen the cables at the rudder, take off one of the master links and repair the broken chain, then re-adjust it at the rudder. I always expend anxiety on things I fix like this, but it gets us home.

Next, I inspect the damage to the sails. We aren't leaving Ibeza without repairs.

Ibeza is a place where people go to be seen by people who care. Being neither, we thought it a good place to skip, but with two hundred miles between here and the next possible place for sail repairs, we're stuck. We motor into the most expensive marina of our voyage at €130 per night. During the high season, two weeks ago, it would have been €350 (a euro costs about US$1.30).

We call a sail shop that picks up our sails and treats us as fairly as any place we've been. It takes two days for them to rush through our repairs, and by the time we finish paying for the marina and the sail repairs, the bill for the storm ends up around US$1,000. That seems the going rate for mishaps, as it cost about the same to go over the reef in Tahiti, and again for hitting the pier in Phuket.

We now set sail for Gibraltar.

After two days and 300 miles of comfortable sailing, the wind, always indecisive in these parts, decides to blow into our faces. We round Cabo de Gata and enter Almerimar Marina, near Almeria, Spain. It is the highlight of our time in the Mediterranean since Kekova Roads, Turkey, and I feel brilliant for letting Lorrie talk me into stopping here.

Almerimar is a community built around a marina, with condominiums, shops, restaurants, and chandleries. The restaurants are good, there's an onsite, full-service grocery store with prices only a little higher than the big one near town, and a public bus to anywhere.

Walking back from the store to *Faith* one day, I see an American flagged boat, *Area Rea,* with little shoes on the dock. They have a small washing machine next to the power pedestal on the quay of the marina. The skipper tells me they lashed it on deck when they first got it, but after a few near-losses, he now lashes it to something down below. *Area Rea's* lifelines are decorated with cloth diapers to justify the washer.

We also meet *Sunset Sam*, a boat-load of kids just a couple spots away from *Faith*.

We celebrate Halloween in Almerimar, and Greggii leads the pack of kids trick-or-treating through the streets of the condo development where they all make quite a haul.

After two weeks enjoying the hospitality of the marina, the hospitality of other cruisers, and the hospitality of the southern coast of Spain, we depart for the Canary Islands.

Sunset Sam and *Faith* plan direct routes, while *Area Rea* plans to stop in Morocco. Our homeward journey resumes, and their passage-making journeys begin. When we leave, we look forward to a seven- or eight-hundred mile sail.

The milestone of this passage is flying through the Straits of Gibraltar. We have forty knots out of the east from the funneling mountains of Spain, Gibraltar, and Morocco to give *Faith* a boat speed of nine knots. The tide is also favorable, giving us an additional three knots. It's not the most pleasant two hours, but we make good time.

Six days after Almerimar, we arrive at Las Palmas, Gran Canaria.

We know Gran Canaria will be crowded. It's the starting point for the Atlantic Rally for Cruisers—the ARC. Two hundred fifty boats entered the ARC to cross the Atlantic this year and are congregating here for the start in two weeks.

Part VII. Coming Home

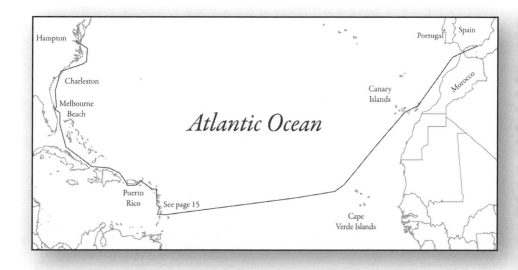

Las Palmas, Gran Canaria to Fort Pierce, Florida
4 November 2007 to 18 February 2008

We Are Circumnavigators

The time has arrived for new captains on *Faith* during our last major blue-water passage. Emily and Amanda take the helm as co-captains for our Atlantic crossing. I'm happy to take watches and will be there if they need me, but this passage is theirs.

In Las Palmas, there's everything from soup to stainless steel nuts, but because we're on our final leg, I abstain.

The anchorage isn't very good, and the marina is full because of the ARC, so we re-anchor several times. We're chastised by a French woman in possession of a volume of American vulgarities when we go stern-to to the seawall, supposedly in her path of swing should the wind change. We move because I don't want her, having freshly begun her own voyage, to die of rage before her first crossing.

On the afternoon the ARC leaves, we enter the marina for our last days here. We fill our water tanks, do some last-minute provisioning, and laze about in the nearly empty marina, a ghost-town of yesterday. The chandleries, so busy leading up to the start, are closed on Monday, taking a one-day breather from all the activity.

Three days after the ARC started in light breezes, we leave for the best weather we ever have during an ocean crossing (23, 24).

The rule-of-thumb for this passage is to head south-west out of Las Palmas, to somewhere around 200 miles from Cape Verde, making it south to fourteen degrees of latitude, then ride to St. Lucia on the fourteenth parallel.

Our new captains provide the nicest passage of our trip. We have a party to celebrate our return to the tropics and another to celebrate the halfway point. These parties are in addition to our regularly scheduled bingo game.

We also crank up the music for an hour of dance time every day. Dancing isn't easy in a moving boat, as the floor gets heavy when you try to be light, and you become weightless when you want to stomp.

The sailing is great. Thirty-five knots of wind holds us consistently between seven and ten knots of boat speed, plus a current of up to one knot. A two-meter following sea is overlaid atop a four-meter swell, also following, causing us to surf occasionally and log over ten knots.

Having not lost my optimism, I pick fifteen days in our family bet; Greggii, 16; Emily, 17; Amanda, 18; and Lorrie, 19. Right now it's between Greggii and me. It looks as if the wind will hold for the next five days, and even increase a bit, so I have a good chance.

I talk with a tanker, fourteen miles away, that I see only on radar. It's the only thing we've seen in three days, and even now, we don't make visual contact. He's bound for Brazil and says he always wanted to sail the Atlantic, but he has to stay with the tanker for now.

The fishing is great, with two mahi mahis landed on each of two consecutive days. *Faith* is intermittently showered with flying fish.

I suggest to our new captains that they keep the wind between 150° and 160°—180° is from straight behind—to prevent what is called an accidental jibe. When sailing downwind, a jibe occurs when the wind shifts (or the boat turns or rocks) to the other side of the mainsail. The main blows to the other side of the boat and pops with a fury when it fills again.

We almost made 200-mile days several times on previous passages. On this passage we make three 200-mile days.

After passing Cape Verde, but still in the first half of the passage, we take a large swell from the north; probably the result of a storm or other weather far to the north of us. It is not annoying, just odd to be riding the wind and one swell from behind and to have another swell coming from the side.

After we get past the swell from the north, the seas build. The distance a wave has to build is called fetch, and grows with our distance from the African coast.

We enjoy a fresh breeze all the way to St. Lucia, with high seas to match. High seas are fine if the distance between crests is enough, and on this passage, that distance is a quarter-mile. I try to estimate the height of the swells, and they appear about as high as *Faith* is long. That's probably impossible, but that's how they look. It's fun sailing and surfing on these massive hills.

Fishing is an unnecessary risk in these seas, so we quit near the passage's halfway mark. We cross the Atlantic Ocean in sixteen days, one hour and eight minutes; Greggii won the bet. But something big has happened in the lives of all of us.

We make landfall and drop our anchor in Rodney Bay, St. Lucia. We were here before—at 9:30 AM on January 15, 2004. We return on the morning of November 15, 2007, at 8:30. We have crossed twenty-four time zones, three hundred and sixty degrees of longitude, and after three years, nine months and twenty three hours, we return (2).

WE ARE CIRCUMNAVIGATORS!!!

Island Hopping and Near Miss

Our arrival in the Caribbean marks a return to a place where we can put the anchor down and know it will hold in the sandy bottom.

It's time to party, which is not normally a good thing to do before breakfast, but we do anyway. Lorrie bought some fluted crystal champagne glasses in Las Palmas for this purpose, and we pop the cork. Two corks as a matter of fact, and a little rum for me at least. I had the night watch and knowing that landfall was to occur, the landfall marking the finish line, I don't sleep at all. No sleep, no breakfast, excitement, champagne, and rum. When I wake up several hours later, I'm justifiably chastised for disappearing to my cabin for several hours of much needed sleep.

We spend our time in St. Lucia, relearning why we didn't like St. Lucia too much on our first trip through, with all the tourism blanketing reality.

Our last time dealing with officials was in Greece, where we turned in our cruising permit to the customs officials in Corfu. It's my understanding, again probably wrong, that Greece and Spain, by their physical locations, are the gatekeepers to Mediterranean Europe. None of the other countries care much.

We're again dealing with officials in St. Lucia. The ARC is still arriving with several boats every day, and the officials are used to boats arriving from Europe that have no clearance from previous ports. They clear us in.

When we ask for our departure clearance, we have them mark St. Maarten as our destination, freeing us from the task of clearing in and out of every island on our way there.

We go next to Saint Pierre, Martinique, to begin our island hopping to get back to the United States.

We celebrate our fifth and final Christmas abroad in Iles Des Saintes, after stopping overnight in Portsmouth, Dominica. Iles Des Saintes is a pretty island cluster administered by Guadaloupe.

In the channel between two islands in Iles des Saintes, we start our motor to safely enter the anchorage at Anse Du'Bourg, furl up the jib, and let down the main. Soon, we hear an annoying *beep-beep-beep* coming from the engine instrument panel. The temperature gauge registers *hot*, so I turn off the engine to investigate. I'm greeted in the engine room with a faceful of the sweet-sticky steam of hot engine coolant. There are two things that can cause the engine to overheat. The belt that drives the captive water pump is by far the easiest fix, but since that isn't the problem, I must replace the pump impeller that circulates sea water. I get my tools out, and find the spare impeller. In the meantime, the girls unfurl the jib to sail *Faith* in figure-eights while I change it.

Now we approach the anchorage with a properly cooled motor.

We learned to enjoy the French during our travels, if for no other reason than the bread. Two things can be said about the bread in any French territory. First, it's cheap, because the French have price controls on a few staples, including bread; and second, it's always good. Actually, it isn't only the bread; all of the French we meet, with the exception of the raging lady in Las Palmas, are delightful.

Two days later, we're at Deshaies, Guadeloupe. We leave a couple of days after arriving, trying to make Antigua, but at eight miles out we get hammered by high seas and thirty knots on the nose. We return to wait for better weather.

Once we are re-anchored, a man motors to us in a dinghy. He asks if I know anything about clearing in, as he can't find anybody at the customs office. I say no, but that I don't worry about it much because the French are reasonably laid back, at times almost bothered by such a task.

He introduces himself as Neal Petersen, and joins us for coffee. He tells us a little about himself, and how he came to be here today. He was born coloured in apartheid South Africa. If this wasn't obstacle enough, he had a birth defect that should have left him unable to walk. At five years old, he had a hip replaced in the hospital's coloured wing, where doctors train. Neal's life, with the help of key people along the way, is a testimony to what happens when you choose not to let adversity become an obstacle. Neal overcame barriers, competed in, and finished the BOC Challenge, a single-handed around-the-world sailboat race in a boat he designed and built himself.

The more he tells, the more we're struck by the challenges he overcame.

We join Neal and his wife, Darlene, on their boat, *El Gecco*, for New Year's Eve. They invite Brad and Petra, from *Freebirds*, another boat in the anchorage, and we become friends with all of them.

The next time we leave Guadeloupe, the weather cooperates; we sail to Antigua.

Emily and I walk the half mile to Nelson's Boatyard, to clear into Antigua Customs and Immigration, only to find that Antigua requires the whole crew to come in and sign the immigration forms. Returning to *Faith*, we're reminded of our previous visit. We leave. St. Maarten's Simpson Bay is easy enough to enter at night, as we recall, knowing it will be very late when we arrive.

We have been sailing for over four years in many different countries, weathers, seas, and risk levels. On our approach to St. Maarten at 1:00 AM, under sail with the trade winds, we have the closest encounter of our voyage. I see a masthead light on another yacht two miles away. When we see both the red and the green parts of the light, it means the vessel is pointed at us. He's heading south, we're heading north. I try to stay on course, because as our separation closes, he remains on the port side of our bow, where he should be, according to navigation rules. I continue to see both his red and green, and try to call him on the radio with no response. The closer we get the more nervous I get. With only a couple of hundred yards of separation, he turns to port, directly into our path. By rights, he should have turned to starboard, as should I, so that we would both be looking at the other's red, or left, or port-side light. Were I able to see his red, I would veer a little to starboard, to increase our zone of safety, but I don't know what he's doing. Everything in this situation, as far as the rules are concerned, would have me hold my course, so that he knows what I am going to do. If I think we need more separation, I am to turn to starboard.

It's a good thing I don't, because at the last minute, this forty-five-foot ketch turns to cross *Faith's* bow. We miss the ten-foot dinghy he's towing by less than the length of that dinghy. I don't know if it is equipment malfunction, sleep deprivation, or alcohol that causes his behavior, but we're glad he's behind us.

We anchor in Simpson Bay for the night, go through the drawbridge at the 9:00 AM opening, and anchor comfortably in the lagoon to prepare for friends to join us. We've been talking to Dale, Linda, and Cassidy, great friends we left in Michigan, for several months about when they're coming to visit, and while we were in St. Lucia, plans were laid for St. Maarten.

Dale, Linda, and Cassidy

It's hard to express what their visit means.

We meet them at the airport and go to *Faith* to enjoy every inch of our week together. We leave through the morning drawbridge to go to the airport beach. Dale researched St. Maarten, and the airport beach is on top of his list.

Most planes take off and land going east, into the trade winds. Thirty feet separates the runway of the St. Maarten-Juliana Airport from the fence. Outside of the fence is a two-lane road, divided by a high curb. Next is seventy-five feet of beautiful, sugar-sand beach.

The attraction is to lie on your back, on the beach, in the middle of the flight path of the approaching planes and jets, the biggest being the Air France 747 that arrives and departs every afternoon.

Lorrie stays on *Faith* to prepare lunch. I'm to pick her up in an hour. The rest of us go, and lay our blanket in the middle of where the runway would extend to. We watch a couple private jets land. Somebody suggests our blanket might not be in the best place during takeoff. Then a jet, I don't know one jet from the other but I think it's a 737, prepares to take off.

Dale, Emily, Greggii, and I do the only natural thing to do when not-too-bright people face the back side of jet engines at close-range. We cross the road to grab onto the fence, to see what it's like. The next thing I know, my glasses blow off my face. We can't let go of the fence without risking injury. Once the plane takes off, we turn around and see Linda hugging Cassidy, who was blown over like tumbleweed by the wash, and is in fear-generated tears. I tell everybody about my glasses, and they are found near the water, a hundred feet away. We then heed the advice about our blanket not being in a good place. Linda shakes out the sand, and we move.

I go to *Faith* to pick up Lorrie and the chicken fajitas she prepared. We arrive and Lorrie puts out our picnic lunch in time for the 747 to approach. We wait until it lands to say grace. It goes over low and slow and loud, and it's beautiful to see the sand rolling in horizontal whirling waves away from its path.

While I'm busy watching the aftermath of this machine, Lorrie tries to protect the product of her last hour's labor from the sandstorm. I'm not sure, but I think she serves me the fajita made with the food most exposed.

Dale, Greggii, and I can't help but wonder why girls and boys react so differently when exposed to the same stimuli.

After lunch, Emily, Amanda, Greggii, and Cassidy swim, play, and watch jets, mostly private, come in and take-off again.

Lorrie and Linda begin to talk about returning to *Faith* to move to a different anchorage, but Dale and I know a secret. We know that 747s don't make airlines money sitting on the ground, and that the 747 that ruined our lunch is going to take off again.

Sometime.

We encourage the kids to keep swimming, or sunning in the case of Emily and Amanda, and let's just all relax. This is a nice beach.

Our procrastination is rewarded when we see that 747 pull away from the gate and begin taxiing in our direction. This is going to be great.

I ask around, "Emily, are you going to hold on to the fence?"

"I don't know."

"Amanda, are you going to hold on to the fence?"

"I don't think so, but I'll take pictures for you."

"Dale?"

"Gee, I'm not so sure about that."

Then, "No, Greggii, you're not going to hold on to the fence."

Personally, I'm pumped, and can't understand why everybody else is so apprehensive.

Darwin hit on it briefly with natural selection. Forrest Gump's mamma summed it up with, *stupid is as stupid does.* I'm glad that some genetic traits in me skip a generation; like the *gee, I've never stood behind a 747 when it took off* curiosity gene. My kids are a safe distance from my heroic act of stupidity.

The only guys that wait with me have just polished off a couple bottles of rum in celebration of their own stupidity. The 747 gets into position and I run across the road to grab the fence. I look to my left, nobody, then to my right, and again, nobody; I perform solo. When you are holding onto the fence you are standing in the road, and the curb in the center means no vehicles can go around you. Everybody on the island, who's been here long enough to drive, knows you don't want to be on the road at the end of the runway when a 747 is taking off. Everybody, that is, except the guy driving the pickup truck delivering a new refrigerator who's honking his horn at me while the 747 runs up its engines. I have my glasses in my pocket.

When it's over, I go, somewhat shaken and high on adrenaline, to where Emily, Amanda, and Dale are standing and we watch the jumbo jet fly out of sight and the pickup truck drive the rest of the way past the runway with the refrigerator tipped over in the bed. They comment on a leak I sprung on my outer ear, probably from a piece of flying sand.

We go back to *Faith* to find an anchorage for the night.

We sail and we fish just long enough to let Cassidy reel in a barracuda and to let everybody feel enough seasick to decide not to sail again.

We go to Marigot, on the French side, and taxi to Ocean Beach where afterwards Linda spends as much time deleting pictures on Dale's phone as Dale spent taking them. Apparently, he's researching the European method of minimizing tan lines.

It's during their visit that I, after snorkeling for a long time, learn I can't be in the water as long as I could before. I blame malaria, and bundle myself up in blankets until morning.

We're all sad when we take Dale, Linda and Cassidy to the airport for their return flight.

Coming Home

After visiting with Dale and Linda and Cassidy for the week, and after being away for over four years, the time has come for us to go home.

We go to the fuel dock for a routine fueling, but after dumping twenty gallons of gasoline into our diesel tank from the hose the woman at the station hands me, we sit for most of the day waiting for a truck to come pump our tank dry and start over. The station pays the cost, and we figure out a fair value for the fuel in our tank before the mishap. I pay only for the fuel we would have taken to begin with.

Then, we leave St. Maarten. Leaving late in the afternoon, we find ourselves at the Baths on Virgin Gorda in the morning. In the afternoon, we're in Roadtown at the Village Cay Marina—the same marina that served as the Tortola terminus of the Caribbean 1500 four years ago.

Then we leave the world behind. Our next port of call is in the United States of America.

We drop anchor at Isla de Culebra, Puerto Rico.

On arrival, I telephone customs, as instructed when I received our customs decal on the internet in St. Maarten. The official is busy and asks if he can call me back. When he does, I read the decal information to him, tell him of our crew, and of *Faith*, and in a matter of minutes, *Faith* and her occupants legally arrive in the United States of America.

We make our way around the south shore of Puerto Rico, stopping at Punta Salinas, Ponce, and Boqueron. On our last leg, sailing from Ponce to Boqueron, we're accompanied by a school of dolphins.

We enjoy the lovely Boqueron while preparing for the 1,000-mile passage to Florida. We want to be as close as possible to Dad and Mom's condominium in Melbourne Beach. Fort Pierce inlet is our destination.

Greggii and Lorrie want to celebrate their birthdays in Florida with Dad and Mom.

We pass between Great Inagua Cay and Haiti with 600 miles to go. Eight little, pink-bellied dolphins weave in and out of the bow wave and jump just in front of us for a time.

This passage, between Hispaniola, Cuba, and the Bahamas, in the Old Bahama Channel, offers the best fishing of our entire voyage: three small tunas and one four-foot wahoo.

Waters are calm and a violet-orange sunset closes our passage and our voyage.

Tides are caused by the gravitational pull of the moon, and to a lesser extent, the sun. A lunar eclipse accompanied by *super* tides marks our arrival.

Mom and Dad meet us at the marina and we secure *Faith* to join them at the condo.

> *I feel happy to be here, and still a little sad to be here too.*
> *Sometimes it's a little better to travel than to arrive.*
> Robert Persig, *Zen and the Art of Motorcycle Maintenance*

Afterword

And here am I, in the twenty-first century, still having to contend with having been woven into a culture that is always a mixture of gift and fracture, truth and lies, nourishment and pollution, creation and sin.

David I. Smith, *Learning from the Stranger,* Eerdmans, (2009)

In four years and a half of traveling the globe, we found no strangers. We found people everywhere engaged in life, in love, in vocation, and in worship.

Curiosities abounded, but rather than focus on the curiosities of others, we gained a perspective allowing us to see our own cultural curiosities. In residential architecture, homes are designed to isolate parents from children—an American curiosity. As a nation, we have determined that corporations, as legal entities, possess the human right to free speech—an American curiosity. We consume far more than this planet is capable of supporting; we are quick to sue each other; we profess love for our freedoms while we allow the erosion of those freedoms in the name of security—American curiosities all. We embrace the notion of rugged individuals, and flee from social responsibilities aimed at assisting those not sufficiently rugged.

Another American curiosity was brought to our attention from people in every

244

place we visited where it became a topic of discussion. "The Constitution of the United States of America is the greatest document ever written" (sometimes qualified by "except the Bible," or "except the Koran"). People everywhere aspire to the ideals held forth in that document, and surprisingly, people everywhere seem to have a better understanding of that document than we do.

Just as a first date provides only so much knowledge to want or not want to learn more, so too it is in our travels. America, my motherland by birth, can never be a first date, and the depth of that relationship holds insights into wonderful characteristics and flaws gained only in a familial relationship. I cannot undo the knowledge of here any more than I can gain a similar knowledge of any of the other places we visited.

It would be pleasant to say we went in search of the world and we found it, but it would be an exaggeration.

It is impossible, as outsiders and as amateurs, to gain a solid understanding of the cultures we experienced. Perhaps this account attributes a higher degree of goodness to people of other cultures than is warranted. I make no apology for that, as interests far more powerful than I work endlessly to vilify these same people.

If my small voice can cause only a flicker of doubt of the reams of misinformation of the black deeds and darkness surrounding those unfortunates born outside our borders, I will call it success.

Certainly, the creation we experienced has been stained by evil, in the same sense that my own heart has.

We hit the ground running, more of necessity than desire. From the Canary Islands, and pinpointing our future position only to be somewhere on the East Coast, we scheduled Emily to take the SAT College Entrance Exam in Annapolis.

Amanda was invited to the Thornapple-Kellogg High School prom, so after moving up the coast from mom and dad's condo, to Charlestown, and then to Hampton, we rented a car for me to take Lorrie, Amanda and Greggii home. Emily stayed on *Faith* to study.

The acorns and webs and six-legged carcasses gave evidence that our house was occupied during our absence. We spent a good portion of our first days home cleaning up the mess these squatters left.

I returned to Emily and *Faith* to make the run to Annapolis. In the paperwork for the test, Emily requested the results to be sent to four Michigan institutions: the University of Michigan (her first choice), Michigan State University, and Calvin and Hope Colleges. Since it was already May, we didn't think she would be able to begin anywhere in the coming fall.

Within a week of receiving her test score in early June, Emily received a phone call from the admissions office at Calvin. They wanted to know if she would apply, and if they could expect her in the fall. She is currently there majoring in International Development and Sociology.

Amanda, who on arrival had doubts about her level of education compared to her peers, wanted to complete her senior year of high school at Thornapple-Kellogg with the same students she grew up with.

I gained a respect I didn't previously have for public education—either the district had done many things right while we were gone, or I changed—after working with the high school to place Amanda in the most important classes. Her high-school diploma, like Emily's, is a home-school diploma, signed by me.

Amanda is currently majoring in International Relations at Calvin College.

Both girls live on campus, only forty-five minutes away, but our home has witnessed change.

Greggii has been experimenting with organized American sports: football, basketball, and baseball, none of which he had played before, as well as participating on a swim team. He is currently in the seventh grade at Thornapple-Kellogg Middle School, serving on the student council.

Either in spite of or because of the lives we lived over the course of our voyage, Lorrie and I share a relationship with each other and with our children that I cannot imagine having otherwise. God gave us the opportunity to witness, as a family, His created goodness, and for that I am truly grateful.

John and Linda, who helped us so much in the beginning of our journey, are now living in England. They sold *Magic Dragon*. They came to Michigan to visit us for several days this past year, and we remain close friends.

Davina, from Toau, got married and moved to New Caledonia.

Thomas and Helén, moved to Australia soon after they visited us in Sydney. Both engage in grueling workouts to compete in triathlon events in Australia and New Zealand. Nicole has discovered a passion for travel; she now studies at university. Lucas has graduated from high school, and works now to discover his own direction. Nadine maintains her passion for horses, which has expanded to the ownership and care of her own horse. *Smilla* remains docked nearby.

David and Virginia set sail out of Sydney on their own boat; their last report has them returning home from their own journey through Indonesia. They are currently somewhere near Papua, New Guinea.

Following his return to Saumlaki, Nelis found the right girl and is now married.

Ardi calls us on our birthdays, as well as staying in touch through email and Facebook. He continues to work on *Chilli* and to take care of Sara.

Joe continues raising his family and running his pharmacy in Langkawi.

Hashim has recently married, and Halim's wife has given him two more children since our stay there.

While composing a research paper, Emily contacted Dr. Ahmad Shono, who has returned to Jordan following his administration of the UN Hospital in Eritrea. We remain in contact via email.

Maggie Gobran called this past year when she visited Michigan. Emad continues his ministry with Stephen's Children.

I received an email from Werner and Cathy on *Legend II*. Their own voyage led them to a marina in Deltaville, Virginia, where they noticed *Faith* sitting lonely in storage. We visited with them for a week. Emily, Amanda, and Greggii joined them aboard *Legend II* as they sailed up the Potomac and into Washington, D.C. They are currently in the Pacific Ocean, eventually bound for home in New Zealand.

Faith awaits her next journey.

This story holds an occupational hazard. After Emily told me of her disgust with her unshaven legs during our longest passage, and after I explained to her how that disgust, that self-loathing, was fabricated and maintained by entities whose foundation for existence would crumble should people ever collectively become not disgusted with themselves, she said, "You think funny, Dad."

It seems we all think funny now.

You will never be completely at home again because part of your heart will always be elsewhere. That is the price you pay for the richness of loving and knowing people in more than one place.

Miriam Adeney

The reader is invited to visit http://www.faithofholland.com for more information and photographs from the Granger family's journey on *Faith*.

Sailing Faith: The Long Way Home seeks to demonstrate that the world and people everywhere are wonderful gifts from our Creator, to be explored and marvelled at. Gregg A. Granger is available for speaking engagements with a parallel message.

Please feel free to contact Gregg with comments, suggestions, and enquiries at gregg@faithofholland.com, or connect with other readers on the Facebook page, Sailing Faith: The Long Way Home.

Above all, Thank You for helping make this book a success.